'Is strategic silence simply strategic inaction, hiding something from someone, not telling the truth, overall bad thing? Or it is a more complex concept and central to the PR theory and PR practice as Rumen Dimitrov argues in his ground-breaking publication *Strategic Silence: Public Relations and indirect communication?* After reading the book, one is left definitely with a new understanding and vision on the enormous power of silence in communication – silence of public relations about its silences, the relation between strategy and silence, silence and indirect communication and strategic silences in plural.'

Irina Bokova, Director-General, UNESCO

'This book shows that much remains to be done in the field of strategic communication, since for the first time silence as indirect communication and its fitting in the strategical dimension are analysed in detail. Dimitrov's work is not only pioneering; it is the most innovative and critical essay published in recent years. From a broader perspective, it is already an indispensable book for communication theory.'

Jordi Xifra, Professor, Pompeu Fabra University, Barcelona, Spain

Strategic Silence

Mainstream public relations overvalues noise, sound and voice in public communication. But how can we explain that, while practitioners use silence on a daily basis, academics have widely remained quiet on the subject? Why is silence habitually framed as inherently bad and unethical?

Silence is neither separate from nor the opposite of communication. The inclusion of silence on a par with speech and non-verbal means is a vital element of any communication strategy; it opens it up for a new, complex and more reflective understanding of strategic silence as indirect communication.

Drawing on a number of disciplines that see in silence what public relations academics have not yet, this book reveals forms of silence to inform public relations solutions in practice and theory. How do we manage silence? How can strategic silence increase the capacity of public relations as a change agent?

Using a format of multiple short chapters and practice examples, this is the first book that discusses the concept of strategic silence and its consequences for PR theory and practice. Applying silence to communication cases and issues in global societies, it will be of interest to scholars and researchers in public relations, strategic communication and communication studies.

Roumen Dimitrov is Senior Lecturer of Public Relations and Advertising at the School of the Arts and Media, University of New South Wales, Sydney, Australia. Roumen has conducted various international research projects for the European Commission, United States Agency for International Development and UNESCO.

Routledge New Directions in Public Relations & Communication Research

Edited by Kevin Moloney

Current academic thinking about public relations (PR) and related communication is a lively, expanding marketplace of ideas and many scholars believe that it's time for its radical approach to be deepened. *Routledge New Directions in PR & Communication Research* is the forum of choice for this new thinking. Its key strength is its remit, publishing critical and challenging responses to continuities and fractures in contemporary PR thinking and practice, tracking its spread into new geographies and political economies. It questions its contested role in market-orientated, capitalist, liberal democracies around the world, and examines its invasion of all media spaces, old, new, and as yet unenvisaged. We actively invite new contributions and offer academics a welcoming place for the publication of their analyses of a universal, persuasive mind-set that lives comfortably in old and new media around the world.

Books in this series will be of interest to academics and researchers involved in these expanding fields of study, as well as students undertaking advanced studies in this area.

Strategic Silence
Public Relations and Indirect
Communication

Roumen Dimitrov

Routledge
Taylor & Francis Group

LONDON AND NEW YORK

First published 2018 by Routledge

2 Park Square, Milton Park, Abingdon, Oxfordshire OX14 4RN
52 Vanderbilt Avenue, New York, NY 10017

Routledge is an imprint of the Taylor & Francis Group, an informa business

First issued in paperback 2019

British Library Cataloguing in Publication Data
A catalogue record for this book is available from the British Library

Library of Congress Cataloging in Publication Data
Names: Dimitrov, Roumen, 1956– author.
Title: Strategic silence : public relations and indirect communication /
Roumen Dimitrov.
Description: Abingdon, Oxon ; New York, NY : Routledge, 2018. |
Includes bibliographical references and index.
Identifiers: LCCN 2017020372 (print) | LCCN 2017034082 (ebook) |
ISBN 9781315657851 (eBook) | ISBN 9781138100039 (hardback : alk. paper)
Subjects: LCSH: Public relations. | Communication.
Classification: LCC HM1221 (ebook) | LCC HM1221 .D56 2018 (print) |
DDC 659.2–dc23
LC record available at https://lccn.loc.gov/2017020372

ISBN: 978-1-138-10003-9 (hbk)
ISBN: 978-0-367-87466-7 (pbk)

Typeset in Times New Roman
by Wearset Ltd, Boldon, Tyne and Wear

For Ivelina, Ruja and Yavor,
my fellow sailors
in the high seas of silence.

The greatest events – they are not our loudest but our stillest hours. Not around the inventors of new noise, but around the inventors of new values does the world revolve; it revolves inaudibly....

The dew falls on the grass when the night is most silent.... It is the stillest words that bring on the storm. Thoughts that come on doves' feet guide the world.

Friedrich Nietzsche, *Thus Spake Zarathustra*

A wheel is useful,
because of the hole at the centre of the hub.
A clay pot is useful,
because it contains empty space.
Doors and windows are useful,
Because they are gaps in the walls.
The value of what is there,
Lies in what is not there!

Lao Tzu, *Tao Te Ching*

Contents

PART VI
Silence beyond strategy 203

19 Silence as system 205

20 Silence as skillset 214

PART VII
Conclusions 227

Conclusions 229

Foreword

Silence itself – the things one declines to say, or is forbidden to name, the discretion that is required between different speakers – is less the absolute limit of discourse, the other side from which it is separated by a strict boundary, than an element that functions alongside the things said, with them and in relation to them within over-all strategies. There is no binary division to be made between what one says and what one does not say; we must try to determine the different ways of not saying such things, how those who can and those who cannot speak of them are distributed, which type of discourse is authorised, or which form of discretion is required in either case. There is not one but many silences; and they are an integral part of strategies that underline and permeate discourses.

Michel Foucault, *The Will to Knowledge: The History of Sexuality, Vol. 1*

Acknowledgements

This book was made possible by an Australian Learning and Teaching Council award in 2010, which set the start of my empirical research about strategic silence. Subsequent research grants from the School of the Arts and Media, University of New South Wales and a Long Service Leave in 2016 gave me the means and time to work on the book. I'd like to thank Dr Nick Richardson, who conducted most of the interviews with PR practitioners on this topic. Professors Jacquie L'Etang, Jordi Xifra, Chuck Marsh, Tom Watson, Judy Motion, Lee Edwards, Theo van Leeuwen, Ronan McDonald, Bill Ashcroft, Andrew Murpyhy, Jim Macnamara and Ramaswami Harindranath helped me with encouragement and suggestions. The editor of the series, Dr Kevin Moloney, supported me in such a professional and friendly manner, and everyone else at Routledge, that I never felt any doubt about the publisher – only about myself. Last but not least, I'd like to thank my wife, Ivelina, who believed in this book way before I began to believe in it. Without her support I would not have started, let alone finished it. Only she knows my silences that this book tries to break and keep.

Part I
Introduction

Introduction

Theoretical significance

Silence is one of the most undervalued problems and concepts in public relations. The discipline has kept silent on its silences. This has partly been because others have defined silence for it from outside – and mostly negatively. Silence as hiding something from someone. Silence as not telling the truth. Spin doctoring. There is a widespread bias against silence. Either it is considered the opposite of communication or the bad side of it. Breaking silence is good. Silencing is bad.

This book takes a different position. Silence is neither the opposite of communication nor of any of its modes such as language. Silence is neither bad nor good. It could be both. But so non-silence, speech for example, too. Communicative silence is a carrier of meaning. Structurally, it makes communication possible. Strategically, it makes indirect communication efficient. Strategic silence is the extreme form of indirect communication.

There are mounting and compelling reasons for public relations to face silence as an important professional issue, articulate it as a concept, and put it openly where it belongs in theory and practice. Because its place is not in the periphery. It is actually right in the centre of PR theory. Silence has always been there, although tacitly, in PR practice. Understanding silence is essential for our grasp of strategic communication.

Scott Cutlip named his history of public relations in the US, *The Unseen Power*. With that title, he wanted to uncover the hidden roots of the 'influential role of public relations in our society' (Cutlip, 1994, p. xi). In *Public Relations Democracy*, Aeron Davis discusses evidence from the UK: 'Within the industry, public relations is considered to be most effective, when acting invisibly'. He cites a Director of Corporate Affairs: 'Over the year, it is 50:50. [Fifty] percent of the job is keeping stuff out of the press. I had ten years in Whitehall, and 70 percent of press relations there was keeping stuff out of the papers' (Davis, 2002, p. 13).

We need a PR theory, which informs the practitioner and public about the enormous power of silence. We need controlled knowledge, which harnesses that power – which provides guidance about how to recognise and use it strategically and, at the same time, deal with its social, political and moral implications.

There are theoretical and practical reasons to start the discussion today. The theoretical reasons are old and new. The older one is that nearly all public relations approaches do not adequately reflect its silent practices, including its silent tactics and strategies. Do not try to find 'strategic silence' or 'silence' in the index of any PR book. On this topic, PR theory has not caught up with a relatively recent but intense development in other disciplines – such as ethnography, anthropology, functional linguistics, political geography, critical discourse analysis, pragmatics, semiotics, feminist and education studies – which have redeemed and elevated silence as a fundamental issue of human being and interaction (Dimitrov, 2015).

But the main theoretical reason relates to the profession. PR has always been more strategic than other professional communications, including marketing and advertising. This is so because its true domain is indirect communication. Strategic is when we instrumentalise one thing for another – when we are silent about the means for our goals or the goals of our means or both. Either way, it is the elephant in the room – the unsaid that is meant.

The advantage of PR in the promotional mix has always been strategic – of grand design to retail, of telling to selling. But the disadvantage of strategic work is that it is ideal, intangible and immeasurable. PR practitioners are at the strategic heart of the communication process, where there is nothing else but imaginary in flux. They are only indirectly related to financial information, customer numbers, retail figures and other empirical data, which marketers, for example, can demonstrate and impute to themselves (Dimitrov, 2008).

Silence only doubles that ethereal and ghostly shape of PR strategy. But a main argument in this book is that there is no understanding of strategy without understanding silence. And vice versa. The legitimacy and reputation of PR hinge on an informed conversation with stakeholders about the silence in PR strategy and strategy in PR silence.

Practical significance

Although silence is the most radical form of indirect communication, this does not mean that its practices are extremist and at the fringes of society. Far from this, some of the most silent, multilayered and entangled processes of communication take place right at its centre.

The book argues that this is not just a fact but also a *trend*. In the current and future society, the centrality of indirect, including strategic and silent communication, is on the rise.

Communication campaigns are increasingly fought not on what is said but on what is not said.
If this is true, then the role of public relations as the most indirect, including most strategic and silent of all communications will become even more critical. But then we have to learn how to deal with the implications of that trend.

Let us stop by two examples. The first is from the media industry. Content creation, which includes content marketing, native advertising and marketing journalism, is a new intermediary that has emerged between business, media and the public relations people (Hallahan, 2014). It is a response to the increasing inefficiency of advertising interruptions, paid by business. New content marketing must look like editorial content, paid by the audience.

Utilising forms of editorial policy for promotional content is strategic. That move *from hard sell to soft sell* is basically a move from direct to indirect communication. It is 'stealth marketing' (Goodman, 2006), advertising which 'does not speak its name' (Bednarski, 2014). The more indirect and strategic marketing becomes – utilising storytelling for pitching – the more invisible and silent, but also more irresistible and efficient, its message becomes (see Chapter 12).

This poses a double challenge to public relations. Marketing and advertising encroach on what it used to do best (publicity, telling rather that selling). And they also pull it out of its comfort and push it to compete with them in direct production and retail of content (where PR has never performed best). It is important that in their response, public relations people do not trade off their strengths for their weaknesses.

The other example is from politics. In France, the leader of the far-right National Front, Marine Le Pen, has rebranded the National Front. She has been at pains not to be seen as the political heir of her father, Jean-Marie Le Pen. Strategic silences, *politics of unsaying* have helped her to secure continuation of the ideology without the continuation of its ideologue. The logo of the National Front and even her family name are conspicuously absent from the documents of the party. A main field of reframing her image has been anti-Semitism. Her father was notorious with his direct assaults on Jews. He once referred to the Nazi gas chambers as a 'detail of history' in a country that deported about 76,000 Jews during the Second World War. Marine Le Pen, in contrast, publically condemned anti-Semitism. When a party official recently denied Holocaust on camera, she instantly sacked him (Willsher, 2017).

Yet anti-Semitism is still constitutive for the National Front – as it is for any nationalist right-wing movement. But it has become more indirect. Its strategy has shifted from the said to the unsaid. In her 2017 Presidential campaign, Marine Le Pen used the silent strategy of dog-whistle anti-Semitism. She used, for example, hints and insinuations she did not have to explicitly define. She frequently evoked, for example, a Franco-Israeli telecommunications magnate, alluding to international financial conspiracies (of you know who). She also kept reminding the voters that her principle opponent, Emmanuel Macron, was a former investor banker at Rothschild, founded by the famous Jewish family. The new strategy was to attack not what Macron used to do but where he used to do it[1] (McAuley, 2017). The more mainstream the National Front has grown, the more indirect – silent that is – its communication strategies have become. More frequently it frames its messages not as outright denials but as implicit assertions.

I have conducted over 20 semi-standardised interviews with professional communicators about their use of strategic silence. I discuss most of the findings from those interviews in Parts V and VI. A striking outcome has been the importance of silence as *communicative capacity* – as both strategy and skillset. The career pathway of a PR practitioner starts from the entry level of learning how to talk. It only completes, gets crowned (if at all) at the advanced level of knowing how to shut up. It takes lots of professional experience and practical wisdom to evolve one's communication skills from 'making your voice heard' to 'noise curation' and 'not giving a story a leg'. Only few communicators reach that highest level of professionalism.

This is not only a problem of biography, of personal learning as climbing the ladder of indirect communication up to the mastery of silence. It is a historical, generational problem too. The professional cohorts have changed. The interviewees shared that 20 years ago their main concern was to teach their clients how to talk. And most of those clients proved to be quick learners. Today, the problem is rather the opposite one. Communicators are now trying to educate their clients about when to stop and how not to talk.

In the PR industry *the ability to do nothing and credibility to say 'No' to bosses and clients has become the most valuable – and highest renumerated – professional asset.*

Strategy is proactive, not reactive. Strategy ponders many steps in advance, not only the next move. *Strategy influences the questions, not the answers* in the public consciousness. Influencing the answers is a noisy battle. Influencing the questions is fought in silence.

Overview of the book

The book is divided into five distinctive parts, separated from the Introduction (*Part I*) and Conclusions (*Part VII*).

Part II (Chapters 1–3) critically examines the silence of public relations about its silences. How does the European and American culture influence professional choices in PR? Why is silence banned in the positivist tradition? How do new media developments relate to silence? Why is silence not a product that PR can easily pitch and sell? And who is silent and who is not in the collaboration and conflict between journalists and communicators? What happens when we include the public in this equation? It concludes with an analysis of the media-source relations in story-telling, where the PR silences are only a small fragment of a bigger picture of silence and invisibility within the communications professions. PR practitioners and journalists, for example, are more visible to each other than to their publics.

Part III (Chapters 4 and 5) explores elements of a theory of strategy and silence in the works of the scholars whose ideas have mostly influenced this book. They are Michel Foucault, Jean Baudrillard, Pierre Bourdieu, Stuart Hall, Norman Fairclough and, to a lesser extent, Jürgen Habermas. None of them has formulated an explicit theory of silence, let alone strategic silence. But all of them have detected and, to a degree, conceptualised the intrinsic – if not identical – relation between strategy and silence.

Part IV (Chapters 6–10) builds a model of indirect communication, which, like a ladder, moves from lower to higher steps of complexity. The ladder of indirectness does not put any universal claim. It only suits the particular goals of this book. Yet it conceptually prepares the discussion of selected strategic silences in *Part V.* The ladder of indirectness visualises, among others, two critical ideas. The first is that any degree of indirectness is mediated by silence, although of a different type. And the second idea is that the higher the degree of indirectness, the more silent – but also richer and polyvalent – communication becomes. The paradox of silence here is that more talkative and eloquent it appears at the top of the ladder, the more difficult it becomes to identify it as such. But exactly this makes silence most efficient and strategic.

Part V (Chapters 11–18) defines strategic silences in plural, not in singular. There is no single silence or taxonomy of silences. Silences are relational categories, which we can only define relative to non-silences. As strategies, silences are highly situational and contextual. They usually work in package with other, more or less complex strategies. There are many strategic silences such as discursive and non-discursive, engaging and disengaging, explicit and implicit, complicit and defiant, and normalising and transforming. From my initial picks, I have selected only those, which – at various rungs on the ladder of indirectness – are trending and perhaps indicative of future developments in PR strategy.

Part VI (Chapters 19 and 20) interrogates silence beyond strategy – as communicative capacity. Strategies, of course, are also part of that capacity. But other, equally important elements are the inter-organisational system of knowledge and professional skillset. In the new communication environment, which is crowded with agents clambering for public attention, not shouting louder but noise curation is increasingly the way of making it possible to be heard. In the digital 24/7 media cycle, PR as choreography of public attention involves not only attracting and keeping but also deflecting and diverting the attention of publics, an increasing number of which potentially target us not less actively than we target them. In such noisy environment, the art of influencing the questions, not the answers, requires not only deft strategic silences but daily, systematic and proactive work on 'being boring' and preventing tangential issues from taking hold over our agenda.

Part II introduces silence by critiquing the silence of public relations about silence. *Part III* and *IV* are the theoretical ones. The first though is eclectic, fragmented, joggling with deeper concepts, which often resist my attempts to use them for my very specific purpose. The second, with the ladder of indirectness in the middle, is more systematic. It offers a model, a progression of logical steps, which develop strategic silence as the highest degree and ultimate realisation of indirect communication. *Part V* is the central one – the PR kitchen where the ingredients for strategic silence are stored, mixed and cooked. But read *Part VI* as well, because it continues the narrative of building silence as communicative capacity – not only as strategic resource but also inter-organisational system and professional-personal skillset.

Note

1 The old habits, however, die slowly. When, in 2017, Marine Le Pen let slip that France was not to blame for rounding up and depositing 13,000 Jews from accords Paris in the 'Vel d'Hiv' Olympic Stadium before deporting them to the Nazi Konzlagers, the vast majority of them to Auschwitz, this was just a mishap (although she then doubled-down to defend her statement) on the slippery slope of her steep learning curve.

References

Bednarski, P. J. (2014). Native advertising: The marketing trend that dare not speak Its name (unless required). *MediaPost.com*. Retrieved 12 June 2017, from www.media post.com/publications/article/217622/native-advertising-the-marketing-trend-that-dare. html.

Cutlip, S. (1994). *The unseen power: Public relations, a history*. Hillsdale, NJ: Lawrence Erlbaum Associates.

Davis, A. (2002). *Public relations democracy. Public relations, politics and the mass media in Britain*. Manchester: Manchester University Press.

Dimitrov, R. (2008). Promoting eco manufacturing: An Australian case. *Journal of Public Affairs, 8*, 233–247.

Dimitrov, R. (2015). Silence and invisibility in public relations. *Public Relations Review, 41*, 636–651.

Goodman, E. P. (2006). Stealth marketing and editorial integrity. *Texas Law Review, 85*, 83–152.

Hallahan, K. (2014). *Publicity under siege: A critique of content marketing, brand journalism, native advertising and promoted user endorsements as challenges to professional practice and transparency*. Paper presented at the 17th International public relations research conference, Holiday Inn, University of Miami Coral Gables, Florida.

McAuley, J. (2017). Marine Le Pen says 'France' is not to blame for handing French Jews to Nazis during Holocaust. *The Canberra Times*. Retrieved 12 June 2017, from www.canberratimes.com.au/world/marine-le-pen-says-france-is-not-to-blame-for-handing-french-jews-to-nazis-during-holocaust-20170410-gvi65q.html.

Willsher, K. (2017). France's Front National suspends party official over Holocaust denial. *Guardian*. Retrieved 12 June 2017, from www.theguardian.com/world/2017/mar/15/benoit-loeuillet-france-front-national-holocaust-denial.

Part II

Why is PR silent about silence?

1   The Western bias against silence

Logocentrism in the European tradition

But where does that silence about silence come from? Some sources point at the *Eurocentrism* of many communication theories. And what they also say with that, is *logocentrism* (for many, Bruneau, 1973; Glenn, 2004; Jaworski, 1993; Kalamaras, 1994; Kurzon, 1998; Tannen & Saville-Troike, 1985). The West is talkative. It sees civility as being on speaking terms. It values silence less than the East. After Nietzsche proclaimed that God was dead, the West found a new refuge of humanity in language. Language became the hallmark of Western civilisation, its quintessential distinction from Eastern cultures.

The Good News begins with the word of God. The spark of the Enlightenment is the discourse. Thomas Mann eminently ruled, 'Speech is civilization itself. The word, even the most contradictious word, preserves contact – it is silence which isolates' (Mann, 1927, p. 518). Where speech is everything, silence is nothing. And Ludwig Wittgenstein finishes his *Tractatus Logico-Philosophicus* with the (mistaken by many) stance, 'What we cannot speak about we must consign to silence' (Wittgenstein, 1961, p. 151).[1]

The Western cultural bias against silence informs a host of logocentrist approaches in social and communication science – from Saussure's theory of the linguistic sign to Habermas' concept of communicative action. Communicators achieve understanding and rationality through talking – through 'language games' or 'ideal speech situation', for example. Yet when silence is *defined by language and as the opposite of language*, then it also falls off communication as *non-communication*. Because there is no rationality outside speech communication, silence is *irrational* per definition.

Binomial separation of silence

Some communicators do not need to read Wittgenstein or Habermas to rather subconsciously convey the notion of silence as non-communication. Relying on practical experience and common sense, they reaffirm the Eurocentrist bias against silence as an unfortunate state of not doing properly your job as communicator.[2] Scott Crebbin, Public Relations Consultant, assigns silence to spin:

> The days of remaining silent are not gone but they're becoming far less an opinion. Quite simply, if you do not engage and communicate in a transparent and proactive way, others over whom you have no control are going to do it on our behalf. If you spin, you are dead. No one wants to be spun. They want an authentic, transparent conversation, and out of that comes respect.
>
> (Personal interview, 24 February 2012)

Silence as 'spin'? As the opposite of 'pro-activity', 'transparency', 'authenticity'? In PR folklore, there is little or no chance for silence, because there is an historical *trend* against silence. Leading that development is the event of the Internet and new digital news cycle. You have to fill the 24/7 news vacuum. Silence is a *spacious metaphor*. In that incessant news cycle, 'there is no room for silence', 'no place to hide'. Silence is the void, the negative of news and information.

Silence and news make up two units in a linear, one-dimensional and quantitative relation. They are like the binary digits of 'zero' and 'one'. Silence is 'zero', no information. News is 'one', information. Grant Butler, Managing Director of *Editor Group*, reflects:

> I think, it's about the 24-hour news cycle – there is nowhere to hide. You used to be able to hide after a paper is gone to bed. You can't do that anymore really. I think due to the iPhones and [new media] technology there is more chatter. If you were to analyse journalism, you would find more words saying less.
>
> (Personal interview, 9 April 2013)

More words say less. But is that less or more silence? When do more words say more and when less? What makes information more prominent – noise or silence?

Problematising and naturalising

The historical and sociocultural system of *capitalism* produces *negative* silences – including the silence of public relations on its silences – as necessary condition of its reproduction. Today – and, I will later argue, as never before – public relations has become a central, strategic and, in Cutlip's words, 'invisible power' in the symbolic order of the late, multinational and financial capitalism. It has changed its functions with the change of order. PR was educating and persuading in the national state. Now it is rather branding and promoting in the global order (Lash, 2002).

PR uses silence to shape that order both from its margins and from its core. From the *margins*, silent strategies help *problematise* that order by various transformative means such as absence, disbelief, denial, dissimilation, camouflage, resistance, disruption and so on. Here public relations functions as an agent of social innovation – as practical critique of global capitalism. Removed from its corporate cradle, citizen groups, advocacy organisations and social movements use PR to change the society from the margins – even when the PR activists are usually middle-class professional women,[3] no outsiders by any means (Dimitrov, 2008).

From the *core*, strategic silence *naturalises* the capitalist order by tacit mechanisms such as automaticity, routine, obviousness, implicitness and other discursive and non-discursive means. As a result, we take that order for granted and without question. Here, PR assists in the performative reproduction of the society. Dominant powers, vested interests, accidental conventions and artificial norms appear as 'nature'. When people *take the normal for natural*, they do not see the world as their product and themselves as collective agent. Fatalism and fetishism stabilise by naturalising. We can no longer recognise the world as our creation. We lose the relation to ourselves. We do not act as moral subjects. We abdicate from our responsibility.

Silence is neither good nor bad. It can be both. Ontologically, strategies of silence effect naturalisation and problematisation, stabilisation and change of the status quo. Thus, the Western bias against silence can come both from the 'Right' – as the silence of subversion – and from the 'Left' – as the silence of suppression. Silence remains suspicious whatever colour of the political spectrum it takes.

Socialised in public relations

The bias in public relations against silence is a Western, perhaps an Americanised bias. I have written to the authors from a recent collection about public relations in Asia (Watson, 2014). I asked them about their take on the traditions of silence in their countries. As a practicing meditator (not a good one), I am anecdotally familiar with the value Hinduism and Buddhism place on silence as a way of cleaning and emptying the mind from wasteful thoughts. In those traditions, silence also opens the senses for the fullness of the world and 'reality as it is' (Gunaratana, 1991; Mahatera, 1962; Suzuki, 1970).

I asked colleagues from India, China, Thailand and Japan about their experience with the rich traditions of silence in their homelands and its possible application in public relations. I was in for a surprise! They all replied – and as one. They told me they did not know. They were modern, Westernised academics. My generation, the older one, came to public relations from other disciplines. We paid a biographical price as outsiders but also reaped some intellectual benefits (Dimitrov, 2009). Their generation, the younger one, is *socialised* in public relations. They are practicing what they have studied – mostly from American textbooks.

How do we measure silence?

The culture of measurement is the culture of quantifying. Even the so-called qualitative analysis is such only at the beginning – when we establish empirical types, which we then transform into quantities and measure (George & Bennett, 2005; Weber, 1990). Even when measurement of communication includes external factors and effects such as the 'cash value' in the 'return on investment' method (Watson, 2005), the logic of measurement reproduces the logic of the ledger. The qualitative and non-linear differences between use values are flattened to the quantitative and linear sum of the exchange value.

Measurement effectively deletes both the semiotics of communication and material conditions of its production and dissemination. Positivism is the way capitalism is commensurate with itself. Quantitative measurement legitimises unseen power in markets, including the relatively privileged position of the professional communicator. The only difference between PR practice and theory here is that the theory is more aware of the positivist (operational, functional) nature of practice. This gain of critical consciousness, however, has changed the theory rather than the practice (Edwards, 2014; L'Etang, 2005; Moloney, 2002).

The cultural logic of computation has only reinforced a narrow view of *rationality*, which dates back to the Enlightenment,[4] that the human mind is all calculation and one can thoroughly quantify the social (Golumbia, 2009). Various thinkers in humanities – notably Immanuel Kant (Kant, 1998), Hans-Georg Gadamer (Gadamer, Weinsheimer & Marshall, 2004) and Jacque Derrida (Derrida, 2003) – have sought not to deny the importance of measurement in society but rather to differentiate between rationality (Verstehen) and reason (Vernunft). They were in the quest for an idea of the *reasonable* as a broader (holistic, qualitative, semiotic) category and a base for critique of the quantification of reality.

The ideal for a *critical Enlightenment* has remained so – an ideal. The Internet has introduced instant measurement as self-promotion of the measurement, not the measurer. Calculating web traffic has become a matter of survival for online publishing. Social media tools such as *Klout* (for influence) or *Facebook Insights* (for engagement) sell without much explanation ready products that are epistemologically problematic. *Facebook Insights*, for example, defines engagement as the sum of all 'Likes', 'Shares' and 'Comments' and, separately, as the sum of all 'Post Clicks'. It presupposes the contents of all those metrics equivalent – that is indifferent from one another. But what is engagement? Is it a means or an end? And are the 'Likes' really as engaging as the 'Shares' or 'Comments'? As with other social media, the self-promotional strategy of *Facebook* is to convince its users that its analytics would think for them and instead of them. *Facebook* knows better than the users what they need and offers it to them already processed, digested and headache-free – as slick charts and simple numbers. *What it sells is what, not how.* What is hidden in the black box is how diverse qualities transform into equivalent quantities and the ramifications from that.

The question of how to measure (public) silence is even more vexing than the question of how to measure (public) relations (Chia, 2006). Preoccupied with the second question – which is critical for the legitimacy and authority of the profession – PR is not even asking the first one. If we measure relations like things, then immaterial phenomena like silence cease to exist. If silence does not allow measurement, it draws unnecessary attention to the limits of the profession. Quantifying is the Esperanto between sellers and buyers in the market. Not being able to be measured betrays lack of transparency, accountability and responsibility. If silence makes PR look unprofessional, then only silence about its silence saves its face.

The management by objectives (MBO) approach (Nager & Allen, 1984) requires visibly verifiable goals. The screen-modified, image-realistic model of MBO encourages PR practitioners to evaluate performativity through visualisation. Visual and verbal knowledge, however, are irreducible to one another. Their nexus is problematic. Visualising is still not grounding in knowledge. Visualisation usually works with spatial metaphors. Relationships as processes and silence as temporality defy such visualisation (Grunig & Hon, 1999).

The visible is tangible, measurable. Measurement is recognition (Luke, Barraket & Eversole, 2013) But how do you measure silence, asks Michelle Schofield:

> One of the things that frustrated me in corporate PR was when they were telling me, 'You must be able to measure everything'. And I'd say, 'Okay, you tell me how to measure me keeping a story from page one of the [*Australian*] *Financial Review* to down the back of the paper and to page twenty-two and two paragraphs? That's invaluable'. And you know what? None of them could tell me [...] because you were trying to place a value on an intangible thing. And how do you show it to your bosses? If they don't see the value of what you do, it's a very hard thing to convince them.
>
> (Personal interview, 7 March 2012)

The difficulty to measure silence is one of the practical reasons PR is silent on its silences. Most stakeholders do recognise evidence-based arguments only (Watson, 2005). Silence, of which conditions and effects may well be material, eludes such direct measurement.[5] In other words, silence does not provide the evidence that supports the legitimacy and credibility of the profession.

In reality, one can and must research silence. It may be difficult or impossible to quantify it with the old positivist methods. But the semiosis of silence is equally material and motivated as that of words. In the next chapters, I will discuss new approaches and methods of working with silence. Measuring silence is politically problematic rather than technically impossible. Silence only appears to be ideal and immeasurable in methods that delete the sociocultural and historical condition of its production and distribution. There is nothing in silence that PR should be scared of. But the education of clients in that regard should start with the self-education of PR.

Notes

1 This quotation is often misinterpreted. Wittgenstein does not mean that one has to remain silent when one does not have anything to say. On the contrary, he warns against the use of speech when it may obscure the meaning of silence. If silence is nothing, that would contradict his own basic premise that both elements of any comparison must be defined (Bruneau, 1973, p. 20). One cannot interpret an unknown quality by itself (Ansehn, 1957, p. 10).
2 Common sense is a paradox state of the everyday mind. It is a fragmented unity. You may use silence and reject silence and find no contradiction between both acts.
3 Interestingly, the social structure of activists in Western societies, especially when we consider three of their statuses: gender, education and profession, is almost identical with the structure of public relations employees (and to double it up, of public relations students at my university, for example) who are predominantly middle-class women (men do business, production, maths; women, society, reproduction, arts) with tertiary education (but not necessarily a communication degree in PR) (de Bussy & Wolf, 2009; Demetrious, 2000; Edwards & Pieczka, 2013; Fawkes, 2014; Holtzhausen, 2014). Both structures of citizen activists and professional communicators curiously mirror each other. I leave it to the reader to decide if this is more than a coincidence.
4 Compare, for example, Leibniz' reduction of 'rationality' to mathematical formulae and logical syllogisms with Voltaire's 'critical rationalism' that recognises reason outside calculation (Simanowski & Golumbia, 2014).
5 As I will later show in the case of *Kentucky Fried Rabbits* it is hard for a consultant to invoice a CEO about being silent and not doing anything for a number of days.

References

Ansehn, R. N. (1957). Language as idea. In R. N. Ansehn (Ed.), *Language: An inquiry into its meaning and function* (Vol. 8, pp. 3–17). New York: Harper & Row.

Bruneau, T. J. (1973). Communicative silences: Forms and functions. *Journal of Communication, 23*(1), 17–46.

Chia, J. (2006). Measuring the immeasurable? *PRism Online PR Journal, 4,* 1–16.

de Bussy, N. M., & Wolf, K. (2009). The state of Australian public relations: Professionalisation and paradox. *Public Relations Review, 35*(4), 376–381.

Demetrious, K. (2000). Public relations in the third sector. In J. Johnston & C. Zawawi (Eds.), *Public relations theory and practice* (pp. 428–454). Cross Nest, NSW: Allen & Unwin.

Derrida, J. (2003). The 'world' of the Enlightenment to come (exception, calculation, sovereignty). *Research in Phenomenology, 33*(1), 9–52.

Dimitrov, R. (2008). ChilOut: Strategic communication by small advocacy groups. *Australian Journal of Communication, 34*(3), 129–143.

Dimitrov, R. (2009). Public relations: Critical debates and contemporary practices (Jacquie L'Etang & Magda Pieczka, Eds; Book review). *Canadian Journal of Communication, 34,* 315–327.

Edwards, L. (2014). *Power, diversity and public relations*: New York: Routledge.

Edwards, L., & Pieczka, M. (2013). Public relations and 'its' media: Exploring the role of trade media in the enactment of public relations' professional project. *Public Relations Inquiry, 2*(1), 5–25.

Fawkes, J. (2014). *Public relations ethics and professionalism: the shadow of excellence.* New York: Routledge.

Gadamer, H.-G., Weinsheimer, J. & Marshall, D. G. (2004). *EPZ truth and method*. New York: Bloomsbury Publishing.

George, A. L., & Bennett, A. (2005). *Case studies and theory development in the social sciences*. Cambridge, MA: MIT Press.

Glenn, C. (2004). *Unspoken: A rhetoric of silence*. Carbondale: South Illinois University Press.

Golumbia, D. (2009). *The cultural logic of computation*. Cambridge, MA: Harvard University Press.

Grunig, J. E., & Hon, L. (1999). How to measure relationship? *PR Reporter, 42*(40).

Gunaratana, H. (1991). *Mindfulness in plain English*. Taipei: Corporate Body of the Buddha Educational Foundation.

Holtzhausen, D. R. (2014). *Public relations as activism: Postmodern approaches to theory and practice*. New York: Routledge.

Jaworski, A. (1993). *The power of silence: Social and pragmatic perspectives*. Newbury Park, CA: Sage.

Kalamaras, G. (1994). *Reclaiming the tacit dimension: Symbolic form in the rhetoric of silence*: New York: SUNY Press.

Kant, I. (1998). *Critique of pure reason* (Paul Guyer & Allen W. Wood, Eds., Trans.). Cambridge, UK: Cambridge University Press.

Kurzon, D. (1998). *Discourse of silence* (Vol. 49). Amsterdam: John Benjamins Publishing.

Lash, S. (2002). *Critique of information*. London: Sage.

L'Etang, J. (2005). Critical public relations: Some reflections. *Public Relations Review, 31*, 521–526.

Luke, B., Barraket, J., & Eversole, R. (2013). Measurement as legitimacy versus legitimacy of measures: Performance evaluation of social enterprise. *Qualitative Research in Accounting & Management, 10*(3/4), 234–258.

Mahatera, P. V. (1962). *Buddhist meditation in theory and practice*. Colombo: M.D. Gunasena & Co.

Mann, T. (1927). *The magic mountain*. New York: The Modern Library.

Moloney, K. (2002). *Rethinking public relations: The spin and the substance*: New York: Routledge.

Nager, N. R., & Allen, T. H. (1984). *Public relations management by objectives*. Lanham, MD: University Press of America.

Simanowski, R., & Golumbia, D. (2014). Computerization is always going to promote centralization even as it promotes decentralization. Interview with David Golumbia. *Dichtung Digital, 44*.

Suzuki, S. (1970). *Zen mind, beginner's mind*. New York: Weatherhill.

Tannen, D., & Saville-Troike, M. (Eds.). (1985). *Perspectives on silence*. Norwood, NJ: Ablex Publishing.

Watson, T. (2005). ROI or evidence-based PR: The language of public relations evaluation. *PRism, 3(1)*. Retrieved 12 June 2017, from www.prismjournal.org/fileadmin/Praxis/Files/Journal_Files/Issue3/Watson.pdf.

Watson, T. (Ed.) (2014). *Asian perspectives on the development of public relations: Other voices*. New York: Palgrave Macmillan.

Weber, R. P. (1990). *Basic content analysis* (2nd edn). Newbury Park, CA: Sage.

Wittgenstein, L. (1961). *Tractatus logico-philosophicus*. London: Routledge & Kegan Paul.

2 Silence does not sell

Seller's market of labour, buyer's market of product

In Sydney, Australia, where all big international PR companies have their branches, the market for public relations labour is still a sellers' market (Public Relations Professionals, 2012). This has not been the case with other communication professions. The university admission stats at the University of New South Wales, where I teach, speak for themselves. I started the PR and Advertising Bachelor degree in 2011 with 52 students. Today, the yearly enrolment in that popular degree has increased and stabilised at about 270 students. The larger number of undergraduate PR students also compensates for the decline in other media disciplines, particularly journalism.[1]

How do we explain that unsaturated appetite, in a cosmopolitan city like Sydney, for communications professionals? And how is it relevant to the topic of silence?

PR practitioners are *intellectuals*. As experts, they sell their knowledge-intense labour on the market. To legitimise their knowledge, they tout it as *trans-contextual*. What they sell must appear publically relevant – something that almost everyone can make use of. Yet, their professional interest – and instinct – is to keep their knowledge as a scarce resource. To protect the profession (and its value) also means to make it exclusive one way or another. Open claim of general relevance of the product and covert interest to limit the access to the tools of production constitutes the ideology of the profession (Konrad & Szelenyi, 1979). Every professional ideology is silent about the particular interests it protects – silent about keeping the value of knowledge high by obstructing the access of the general public to it. Saying that, PR practitioners, like journalists, could not emanate the old 'real professions' such as medicine and law. They have never managed to build the necessary walls – economic, educational, self-regulatory, biographical and so on – to privilege and shield their occupation from the others. Specialists from all walks of life have always had easy access to professional communication. That is why public relations, like journalism, has been a rather 'weak profession' (Dimitrov, 2014).

The labour-power of the PR experts consists of their communicative skills and strategies. The distinction of that power, however, is that it is not only labour but also *capital*. It is *symbolic* or *cultural* capital in Bourdieu's work (1977, 1986, 1997). And it is also *media* capital (as a form of cultural capital), if we follow Aeron Davis' borrowing from Bourdieu (Davis, 2002, pp. 173–177). As intellectuals, the communicators are owners of both *labour* and *capital*. That is why they are both *bourgeois* and *proletarians* at the same time. Therefore, they neatly fall into Marx' definition of intellectuals in capitalism as a *stratum* and not as a class (Konrad & Szelenyi, 1979, p. 68).

That dual economic status results in internal personal conflicts. It often splits the consciousness of the intellectual into a *quasi-schizophrenic* mode. Gilles Deleuze and Félix Guattari (1983) – but also Frederic Jameson (1988) – took the psychoanalytical concept of schizophrenia from Sigmund Freud and Jacques Lacan and elevated it to a central metaphor of the intellectual reproduction of the capitalist order. 'Schizophrenic disjunction' (Jameson, 1988), for example, may partly explain the ostensibly ideology-neutral concept of *excellence* in public relations (Grunig, 1992) but also in the neo-liberal model of 'best practice' and 'quality teaching' university (Readings, 1996). Today, excellence stands for the promotional capacity of the expert to communicate over the labour–capital divide through calculated euphoria and fragmented intensities without revealing the professional dilemmas, moral costs and personal burnouts that a 'divided unification' entails.

The new technologies have freed the intellectual labour as *variable* capital – the knowledge that the practitioner owns – from the shackles of the *fixed* capital – the physical, infrastructural and financial means of production that the capitalist owns. In the transition from manufacturing to servicing and knowledge economy, *ideal work* – work not obstructed by physical control and proximity of production site – expanded in all sectors, and especially in the communications. Its material costs such as investment in computers and software have also gone so low that they no longer present an insurmountable barrier to the intellectuals and a reason for them to sell their work to someone else who has the material means. Ideal work has made the communicators creatively more independent. Still, it did not freed them from the schizophrenia of their role.

Today, they have the real choice not to work for salary but to self-employ themselves – to sell not their labour, but its products on the open market. In a networked economy, even more of them become *intellectual entrepreneurs*. They establish small businesses, work from home and multi-task on external projects. Notably, they often offer a more flexible and cost-effective alternative to the big full-service houses.

I have started with the similarities between the intellectual professions. In one important aspect, however, the ideal work of the communicator is different from that of the journalist, writer or artist, although perhaps not unlike the work of the composer, architect and actor. In capitalism, intellectuals no longer labour for feudal patrons but for anonymous buyers on the market. In other words, they are no longer personally dependent but economically free (at least secure). In capitalism, the opposite is true. They are personally (politically) free but dependent on the market.

The buyers of *authors* (the first group) – book writers, for example – are their publics. If one does not have a public they do not have a publisher. They can self-publish. But this is all they can do. This alone cannot buy a public. A public must buy their book. For authors, publics and buyers are essentially the same. Authors create first; then they sell. The product comes first; then comes the buyer. The public sanctions an author as an intellectual by buying the product. If the public is the buyer, the relation between intellectual and public is very open. The author is forthright with the public because the author's motive to write the book is not different from the interest of the public to read it and the author appeals to a buyer *as public* (value for money) rather than to the public *as buyer* (economic benefit).

It is possible that authors do not find buyers for their product. The risk is entirely theirs. Markets do not tolerate intellectual minorities. They repress them through polite indifference. If the public is the buyer, there is no niche to hide. Values shift quickly. What is important to the writer may not be relevant to the public. The writer may be behind or ahead of the reader, perhaps misreading the reader. If the intellectual product does not sell, that means the market-based society does not recognise its author as intellectual. The author's reaction then could be to turn to their professional tribe for support. See, for example, the self-promotional character of the ceremonial awards of a guild. Or the author may just stop creating and shut up for good.

There are many such artistic silences: silence as suicide (Kleist, Lautréamont); silence as (self-)punishment (Hölderlin, Artaud); silence as disavowal of own work, which does not negate it but rather validates it anew (Rimbaud, Valéry); silence as renouncing the audience (Nietzsche); silence as rejecting the market (Becket: 'too proud for the farce of giving and receiving'); and silence as critique of the language as a medium (Mallarmé, Stein, Burroughs) (Sontag, 1982).

In contrast to that group of intellectuals, which the author exemplifies, the second one, to which I include PR practitioners, has the reverse relation to markets. Composers, for example, belong to that group. They still depend on their modern patrons. Commissioning their work is often a prerequisite for its creation. Professional communicators see a huge difference between nameless publics and distinguished sponsors – like the composers see the Maecenas. The public is not the buyer; it is the buyer's public. The buyer comes first, then the product. The communication product is custom-tailored to the particular needs of a buyer. No buyer – no product. Their work depends on proactive buyers who hire or contract them. In other words, they work *first for* organisations and clients, and only *then with* publics. Sponsors purchase communication expertise to *work* their publics. Public relations is an instrument of communication between buyers and publics. It is not the buyer who mediates between PR and publics. PR mediates between buyers and publics. The loyalty of the practitioner is first to the buyer and then to the public. Buyers are courted. Publics are targeted and thus, publics and buyers are equally stakeholders. (Just some stakeholders are more equal than others.)

The discourse of public relations is first the discourse of markets and, second, the discourse of publics. The market of public relations labour is a seller's market. The market of public relations products, however, is a buyer's market. Public relations is open to publics based on its seller's interest, but it is closed to publics based on the buyer's interest. Those contradictions partly explain why public relations is silent about its silences.

Silence does not violate the senses

Paul Virilio was among the first who drew attention to the increasing speed of the global world (Virilio, 1986). And speed is noisy. Virilio's verdict: Reacting to the moment instead of reflecting about the time, people give up their interpretative freedom and, with that, their conscious relation (responsibility) to conditions of their existence. 'The future is certain', according to a Soviet joke, 'it is only the past that is unpredictable' (Lukes, 1985, p. 146). In Western society, suspended temporality makes the future unpredictable as well. For Virilio, 'a society which rashly privileges the present – real time – to the detriment of both the past and the future, also privileges the *accident* [my italics]' (Virilio, 2006).

Silence supplies space and time for making sense – for putting something in context, in relation. Speed cuts silence. Accidents are events that do not make sense. The media speed them up and blow them out to promote them as calamity. We are even shorter of the resource of silence – of the ability to stop or divert the deluge of events to fill context in them and connect their dots. Even more events, of which we cannot make sense, emerge as accidents.

Immediacy and ubiquity bring catastrophes in our home. Accelerated, history becomes 'accidental' through the rapid pile-up of facts. Events, which were once successive, now look simultaneous. Virilio speaks of the sudden 'synchronisation of emotions'. In the fast-track media, horror and death have replaced sex[2] and even action as the dominant scoop. The result is a *censorship by illumination* – a 'fateful blinding by the light'. The accident violently accentuates the instant and – as in an overexposed negative – blinds and empties the time between two instances. Similarly, Baudrillard speaks about the 'instantaneousness of communication' that 'miniaturizes our exchanges into a series of instants' (Baudrillard, 2012, p. 24).

The accident rises as the chief instant. It embodies the instantaneousness of communication. It dominates, it rules over the less noticeable instants. The media industry 'exposes the accident not to be exposed to it' (Wilson, 1994). It no longer reflects – it only reproduces and amplifies the disasters. The 'effect of exemplarity' leads to involuntary hatred and victimisation of arbitrarily fixed perpetrators.[3] It is no longer the ecology of risks in the face of environment pollution. Virilio calls for 'an *ethology of threats* [my italics] in terms of the mystification of public opinion, of a pollution of public emotion' (Virilio, 2006).

Jean Baudrillard calls it 'double obscenity' (2012, p. 28). Obscenity, because we are no longer alienated as spectators. Guy Debord uses the metaphor of the spectacle to stress the *alienation* of the majority of people from the means of symbolic production. We watch the world as a spectacle and from a distance. We participate in it only symbolically. We are captured in its mystery because we are excluded from the secrets of its production (Debord, 1994). For Baudrillard, our problem now is not alienation but *identity*. The screen corners us by the over-proximity, unnecessary full visibility and brutality of 'everything you want'. This is 'pornography' – an all-encompassing term, which, for example, describes not the Internet of pornography, but the pornography of the Internet.

Obscenity is double because both public and private spheres are disappearing. The stage, the public space – the stage of the body, landscape and time – is vanishing. Capital is now expanding not away from the individual (alienation) but inside it (obscenity) as the omnipresent visibility of corporations, brands and products. The private sphere is also disappearing because privacy – the minimal distance, which individuals need for securing enclosure and as imaginary protector – yields to the unnecessary (pornographic) revelation of the world in its proximity and immediacy. It is not the world revealed as full of secrets but the secrets of the world fully revealed. We are fed with every secret we do or do not want to know. We learn about them only when they are no longer secrets.

Obscenity imposes the world on us in real time, 'as it is'. (The obscenity of Trump 'telling it as it is'.) We cannot escape from it because it is in us. Not the reality is external to us but we are external to the reality. It turns out that real-time experience of the world is more violent and more unimaginative than the symbolic escapades of alienation.

> Obscenity begins when there is no more spectacle, no more stage, no more theatre, no more illusion, when everything becomes immediately transparent, visible, exposed in the raw and inexorable light of information and communication.... *We no longer partake in a drama of alienation, but are in the ecstasy of communication* [italics by J.B.]. And this ecstasy is obscene. Obscene is that which eliminates the gaze, the image and every representation.
>
> (Baudrillard, 2012, p. 26)

The ecstasy of communication, essential in promotional cultures, does lead not to satisfaction but to daydreaming (according to John Berger, see Chapter 6) or to numbness – according to Baudrillard. It is imbued by the violence of tell-it-all real-time that demobilises rather than motivates. It is the numbness of the deafening signal – not of the silent void.

It seems like only yesterday when Fredric Jameson was analysing Jon de Bont's 1994 flick *Speed* as the epitome of action movies such as *Die Hard*, *Lethal Weapon* and *Cliffhanger*. They all use the plot merely as pretext 'for a succession of explosive and self-sufficient present moments of violence' (Jameson, 2003, p. 714). What makes *Speed* stand out is that its title does not signify change or acceleration of time, not some instances of action itself, but the 'absence of temporality altogether'. In an almost full absence of plot, a bomb on a bus is set to explode if it should slacken its speed below 50 miles per hour. The speed-control mechanism becomes an 'allegory for the new form, which must never slow down at its generic peril' (p. 715).

Jameson refers to what the Russian Formalists called 'motivation of the device'. That form introduces motivation not by the subject (protagonist of the story) but by the object (intricate mechanism of a bomb). It is the beginning of the end of the action hero (who is still needed to deactivate the bomb) and the end of the beginning of catastrophe movies where reality is no longer constructed by human action ('faschistoid' nature represses liberal culture). It is a way to escape discourse and narrative (where subjects suppose reason and are 'motivated') and stick to the indexical mechanisms of disasters (nature) and madmen because both are non-rational and incomprehensible (see Chapter 8). It plucks whatever gaps and holes in the plot with absolute closure of the space, which is virtually impossible to escape. Jameson concludes:

> The closure now becomes allegorical of the human body itself and reduction to the vehicle of closure in these films represents the reduction to the body that is a fundamental dimension of the end of temporality or the reduction to the present.
>
> (2003, pp. 715–716)

But this is of course impossible because the historical tendency of 'late capitalism', this reduction to the present and reduction to the body, 'is in any case unrealizable; human beings cannot revert to the immediacy of the animal kingdom' (Jameson, 2003, p. 717).

This devise is different from the *objective correlative* that T. S. Eliot developed. Eliot's method uses an object – for an instance a thing, a circumstance or an event – for a symbolic purpose, to imply a meaning larger than what is actually there.[4] Objective correlatives naturally *show* rather than *tell*. They are silent strategies of word economy, which help the reader to relate a recurrent object to the story and put the picture together on their own (Gingerich, 2012).

What Jameson refers to is rather the opposite of the method of objective correlative. Self-explanatory devises do not symbolise but dehumanise. For example, we do not try to understand the terrorists and their motivation. On the contrary, what we see are possessed madmen and blind tools of evil forces – not political activists and freedom fighters. The Islamic State took that Western format and turned it against the West. It pushed it further from fiction to documentary, from propaganda to promotion. The same motivation by the devise of the imminent apocalypse. The same real-time ecstasy of the close-up slaughter. The same numbness of indifference between victim and perpetrator. The same video camera that now turns from obscene profit maker into a PR weapon.

In *The literature of silence*, Ihab Hassan speculates – rightly, it turns out – that the transition from the visual culture of the printed word to the 'total' culture of electronic media may resemble a reversal to oral, tribal culture. He reminds us of what McLuhan says in *The Guttenberg Galaxy*: 'Terror is the normal state of any oral society, for in it everything affects everything all the time' (Hassan, 1968, p. 28). Since Virilio, Baudrillard and Jameson wrote about the automated violence of simulated terror, Hollywood movies have become even darker, louder and more apocalyptical. *The Lord of the Rings, Game of Thrones, The Hunger Games* and other not funny games profess disaster and desolation. Telling is also the transformation of *Star Wars* over time. The first episodes brimmed with fun, humour, self-parody and Yoda's wisdom of silence. Luke had to go through the apprenticeship of Eastern meditation, becoming at peace with himself to start 'feeling the force' – to yielding to it in order to become one with it. Compare this with the last episodes, in which the corporate tent plays safe by overdoing it. A new space station and annihilation power dwarf the previous ones. Deafening explosions replace thoughtful action; shooting replaces saying, which is less – not more, silence. The universe spirals down in hellish fire, which, in Virilio's words, 'censures our imagination by illumination'.

Accidents do sell, but they exhaust the energy for action. PR is most efficient – it influences and mobilises most – when it communicates in quiet, when it takes the spectator's – or choreographer's – seat and offers the stage to the public it wants to activate. Silence is not talking about silence. Catastrophes horrify communicators for two reasons. First, they imply something irrational and out of control – a shadow of culpability even in the best possible response. And, second, those who peddle disasters are prone to reducing them to 'PR disasters'. This is one of the most over-exploited clichés in journalism, because it is easy to confuse *what is* with what *appears to be*. Indeed, PR work is appearance management. In this respect, rightly or not, PR is at the receiving end of any negative publicity. Even if it is responsible (guilty) *last*, it may appear responsible (guilty) *only*.

And the censorship by illumination reveals one more reason PR is silent on its silences. In the machine metaphor of the 'fully functional' Western society (Heath, 2006), silence is nothing but malfunction (see Chapter 1). In the aesthetics of lurking accident and unmotivated terror, silence appears as the ultimate disaster – when the machine of information and communication grinds to a full halt.

Silence does not click-bait

The Internet and social media have only obfuscated the *externality of PR* to what we used to call *publicity* – the traditional and offline, mostly print and broadcast, media cycle. Today, *media management* seems to engulf public relations. Everything has become media management – as a means, not an end. Managing supposes separation. Someone handles something. Media use, however, has become instant and immediate. It has become *unmediated*, in a paradox sense.

Today, PR seems to manage not the media but *through* the media. It looks like it mediates management rather than manages media. It is a process full of simulation, smoke and mirrors. Public relations strategy, for example, has never been media strategy only, let alone social media strategy. The digital media, however, offer their own instant analytics and promote themselves as *the* strategy of communication. This is the veiled essence of their selling pitch of tools such as *Google Analytics* or *Facebook Insights*. As if we no longer need to think strategically because those media already do it for us.

This assumed fusion of agency and communication in social networking (Castells, 1996); this apparent – but not proven – loss of externality to the media, is happening is at a cost. PR practitioners feel forced to act even more often as 'social media strategists' in crowded blogosphere[5] markets (Dimitrov, 2008). Here, they collaborate with or compete against 'trust agents' (Brogan & Smith, 2009) who zealously guard their authority and influence as online opinion leaders. Being at pains *to be in conversation* with their publics, online agents – including professional communicators in their role as bloggers – produce an excessive amount of noise, which they hope would be decoded as voice.

In the blogosphere, sounds overlap and cancel one another out as noise. Noise is deafening silence, literally (see Chapter 20). If voices do not allow one another to be heard, just being silent seems absurd, self-defeating. If it is hard to be heard – not even trying to speak? What nonsense! What sells is the quickest soundbite that dents silence and repels it by resonating. Silence is no option. Silence does not sell.

The payment structure of blogging reflects speed and quantity, not accuracy and quality. Higher *traffic* begets higher *earning*. Web traffic is indifferent to content. Measured as the number of posts (*Gawker*), page visitors (*Forbes*) or page views (*Business Insider*) traffic is the ultimate norm for paying staff and freelancers (Holiday, 2012, p. 43f.). Web traffic is also what brings advertising money to a blog.

When the culture of communication flows, what pays off is traffic. Labour and content that create traffic are exchangeable, equivalent. What produces web traffic is the click of the user. *Clickability* has become an end in itself. There are many strategies of increasing the number of clicks, and none of them involves silence. For example, which titles are most click-friendly? The most read titles in the online edition of the *New York Times* are: 'Is sugar poisonous?'; 'Do cell phones cause cancer?' They are framed as questions. What else? They are lies (Holiday, 2012). As Michelle Schofield, Manager Corporate Communications, *Communities NSW* puts it, 'Why don't they want' to ask the obvious question? Because that will kill the story' (Personal interview, 7 March 2012).

One clicks, reads, gets distracted, moves on, gets curious, clicks again. There is no loyalty left on either site of the interface in this impulsive, repetitive and distracted present (Rushkoff, 2013). Only unmotivated curiosity lives on. One compulsively chases the next moment with no memory left from previous moments.

Silence does not sell if it does not sell quickly. Speed pierces pauses for reflection and contemplation. Speed is shallow, clever and light-minded. The attention span of Internet users is very short. Speed is the formula of the new attention economy. Attracting and prolonging the attention no longer works. Distracting and 'stealing' the attention, is how click-baits generate traffic. The difference between silence and noise is between lingering on a text and fumbling between pages. Silence slows the traffic. Noise accelerates it.

Long stories – whole narratives and discourses –no longer sell on the Internet. There is no space and time for that. But *indexes* such as images, slogans and soundbites fill the flow. They flash like dots so close to one another, that one does not see the need to connect them. In online story-telling, *dialogue* and *engagement*[6] are the means – not the ends. They do not let the user off the hook.

Blog stories are short and sweet. But they are more than that. They are the genre of distracted presence. One has to follow the commandments of creating online content. For example, do not lose the reader at the beginning (famous slogans, idioms, anger), in the middle (teasing, gradual dissolving of the suspense) and at the end (call for action, promotion as solution). A good ending answers all questions from the beginning, but a *great* blog ending provides for the traffic. It opens the door for discussion, tempts readers to make a comment and asks more questions (Hemani, 2014).

In sum, traffic-conscious bloggers should avoid *closure* – that is falling silent due to a reasonable solution and return to clarity. Silence does not sell online – silence as practical utility and cognitive clarity, as stepping back and stopping the time, as deeper immersion and internal dialogue, as getting out of the routine and learning again, as personal introspection and self-interrogation. Silence does not sell because there is no 'silent pitch', no 'silent competition', no 'silent conversation' and no 'silent traffic'. If we are looking for a collocation, 'silent killer' is what it is more likely to find first.

Even when PR and journalism meet and overlap in the area of online content, a difference remains. As important as web traffic is for PR practitioners, it remains a means rather than an end. In contrast to bloggers, online entrepreneurs, content creators and freelancers, traffic is not what earns the bread of the PR profession. It is not what makes or breaks it. I suspect that, in a way, this is valid for all communication professions. The day web traffic becomes its ultimate goal, this will push journalism to its final destination. For better or worse, journalism will then cease to exist as a profession (Dimitrov, 2014).

There are many ways to be heard. One is to be louder than others. Another way is higher *valence* – the degree of positive or negative emotion. In his book *Trust me, I'm lying: The confessions of a media manipulator*, Ryan Holiday professes about his transgressions. He helped his friend Tucker Max to promote his movie, 'I hope they serve beer in hell', which targets a certain type of young adult male. For such a B-rated movie, Holiday decided that any publicity would work – especially a negative one. His strategy was not to skirt the people who do not like such offensive and politically incorrect movie, but to provoke them and make them denounce it and spread the word about it so that it makes young adult men want to go and see what they should not see.[7] For almost no money, the promotion was a glaring success. Holiday explains the rationale behind the strategy:

> *The most powerful predictor of what spreads online is anger* [italics by R. H.].... While sadness is an extreme emotion, it is a wholly unviral one.... Sadness depresses our impulse for social sharing. It's what nobody wanted to share the Magnum photos but gladly shared the ones of the *Huffington Post*. The HuffPo photos were *awe*-some; they made us angry, or they surprised us. Such emotions trigger a desire to act – they are arousing – and

that is exactly the reaction a publisher hopes to exploit.... Regardless of topic, the more an article makes you feel good *or* bad [italics by R. H.], the more likely it is to make the Most E-mailed list....

(2012, pp. 63–64)

Communication is affectual work. As media manipulator, Holiday knows that high valence, especially negative feelings such as anger and indignity, motivate to action. Yet he is also aware that emotions, which are too strong such as help-lessness and despair, do rather paralyse – they make people speechless if not helpless. In contrast, pithy and empathy drive us to do something, get us up from our computers to act. Feelings, which are too weak such as sadness and content do not mobilise – do not make people move. But anger, fear, excitement and laughter drive us to like, share and comment.

There is a lesson for communicators here, because in relation to valence, PR and journalism start to differ. What creates web traffic is not necessarily what pushes for action. Extremely high negative valence may still be able to increase traffic but at the same time, its potential to affect action diminishes. Conversely, extremely low valence may kill traffic, but despite – or because – of that, it can do an excellent PR job. In the first case, communication silences; in the second, silence communicates (see Chapter 7).

Negative valence campaigns, based on anger, fear and hatred neither wield unlimited power (no determinacy between the urge to click and urge to act) nor are effective in most situations (notoriety as substitute for publicity). Promoting strong negative feelings is a legitimate strategy not only in selling B-rated movies but also in social movements and political campaigns. In the 2016 US President race, Donald Trump used his skills as showman to arouse fury against the estab-lishment among white male workers in order to mobilise their vote politically. Paradoxically, he used the silence of others as a proof that he was telling the truth. Speaking louder than other candidates was his proof that he was representing the 'silent majority' of voters. One cannot be silent and 'tell it like it is'.

Testing the limits of the highest negative valence – from open pro-gun, anti-immigrant and anti-Muslim tenors to covert sexist, anti-disabled and racist undertones – Trump was also testing the hypothesis of the *advertising equiva-lency between earning free media and political campaign spending*. At the time I write this, it looks like Trump's media strategy succeeded as election campaign but failed as government communication (Ingram, 2017).

Trump was, early in his campaign, warned to 'turn the volume down' by the then South Carolina Governor and Republican, Nikki Haley.[8] The following passage from a Haley speech in 2016 is worth placing in a PR textbook:

Some people think you have to be the loudest voice in the world to make a difference. That's not true. Often the best thing we can do is turn down the volume. When the sound is quieter, you can actually hear what someone is saying. And that can make a world of difference.

(Johnson, 2016)

Thriving on the anger of the populace puts a leader behind and not ahead of it. In 'Dealing with an angry public', Lawrence Susskind and Patrick Field suggest a 'principled leadership' approach, in which leaders tap into the energy of fury to negotiate 'mutual gains' instead of just riding its wave and eventually falling behind (Susskind & Field, 1996).

Silence kills traffic. The quantitative and linear logic of traffic measurement (i.e. of exposure, engagement and influence) does not recognise silence as communication. Even Holiday goes not beyond the observation that above and below a certain point, high valence does no longer mobilise. Yet a qualitative and non-linear understanding of communication will see silence as the more adequate medium for both overly high and relatively low valence. At the upper end, 'The deepest fears and most intense joys are wordless – or undifferentiated, repetitive sounds. In short: Silence is the language of all strong passions: love, anger, surprise, fear' (Bruneau, 1973, p. 34). And at the lower end, a major PR function is to 'turn the volume down' – to curate the noise of excessive negative and positive feelings and to restore a less conflicting, uneventful, even dull image of a person or organisation.

Silence is the unmatched medium of intense or subtle feelings when people find no words and look for other ways of expression. Those ways are equally symbolic or indexical but more open and polysemic than language. They are often closer to doing and showing rather than to declaring and shouting.

We see in silent communication a reverse order. To use the terms of Gestalt psychology: Not words are the 'background' and silence the 'figure'. The opposite takes place. *Words become the figure and silence the background.* We understand words in the context of silence – not silence in the context of words (see Chapter 8). Silence can be the strategy and tactic to mobilise in situations of either extreme or delicate feelings, when words either understate or overdrive. Important is that in silence, the PR logic of getting outcome is not the same as the media logic of getting output. Understanding silence as communication can help delineate the boundaries where PR and media no longer overlap – where the media is external to PR and where PR is external to the media (see Chapter 19).

Silence does not sell. But it could pay off.

Notes

1 In the Open and Information Days of my university, instructive is the attitude not of the prospective students (still uniformed) but rather of their parents (uninformed, but reflecting public opinion). Both parents and students ponder the pluses and minuses of the media disciplines, including public relations and journalism. On balance, they decide that journalism lends more prestige and allows more creativity and independence (with the presumption that all journalism is modelled after the genre of investigative journalism), whereas public relations offers more job opportunities and a higher salary (not unimportant for the repayment of the student debt). Indeed, the industry has not picked yet, at least not in Sydney. As Richard Lazar, the Managing Director and CEO of *Professional Public Relations Asia-Pacific*, the largest Australian public relations agency, told me, 'There are hundreds of job places in the industry we cannot fill

due to the lack of skilled practitioners' (Personal interview, 16 May 2013). Perhaps the most frequent question parents ask is whether the undergraduate degree in Public Relations and Advertising is not too theoretical. Their major concern is with the vocational, not academic value of public relations education. The students themselves show a slightly different anxiety. Is there much writing involved? They love texting but hate writing. If they could write, they would rather choose journalism.

2 Virilio cites a French film festival official, 'At last death will replace sex and the serial killer the Latin lover' (Virilio, 2006).

3 It took the tragedy of September 11 to put an end to the master-plot of Hollywood flicks with surprisingly young (but with heavy accent) Nazi-Germans or fluent in their English North Korean terrorists. It has also put an end to the proliferation of movies with infiltrating suicide bombers of Middle-Eastern appearance, whose evil intentions the FBI manages to thwart.

4 Although Eliot has not invented the objective correlative, he widely used and developed its concept. In *Hamlet and his problem* he says,

> The only way of expressing emotion in the form of art is by finding an 'objective correlative', in other words, a set of objects, a situation, a chain of events which shall be the formula of that *particular* [italics by T. S. E.] emotion; such that when the external facts, which must terminate is sensory experience, are given, the emotion is immediately evoked'
>
> (Eliot, 1919, p. 941)

5 I use *blogging* as the generic term in online journalism that includes all web logs such as websites, Facebook and Twitter.

6 Michael Schudson argues about why conversation and dialogue are not the souls of democracy: 'Conversation that serves democracy is distinguished not by egalitarianism but by norm-governedness and public-ness, not by spontaneity but by civility, and not by its priority or superiority to print and broadcast media but by its necessary dependence on them'. Schudson suggests 'that institutions and norms of democracy give rise to democratic conversations rather than that the inherent democracy of conversation gives rise to politically democratic norms and institutions (1997, p. 297).

7 Ryan Holiday ordered billboards with belligerent messages such as 'Sexism isn't the same as misogyny, you stupid bitch' and 'Blind girls don't see you coming'. He then defaced some of them and sent their photos to blogs. He issued bogus complaints about the movie from fake e-mail addresses. He alerted LGBT and women's rights groups about local screening of the movie and baited them to go to the theatre and openly protest, knowing that there will be media coverage for that. 'Trading up the chain' from billboards and local sites to the legacy and national media, he got the movie banned by the city of Chicago and also damning editorials by the *Washington Post* and *Chicago Tribune*.

8 Nimrata 'Nikki' Haley is an Indian-American politician. She served as Governor of South Carolina from 2011 to 2017. Surprisingly, and despite her previous critique of Trump, the new US President appointed her as the new US Ambassador to the United Nations in January 2017.

References

Baudrillard, J. (2012). *The ecstasy of communication.* Los Angeles, CA: Semiotext(e).

Bourdieu, P. (1977). *Outline of a theory of practice* (Vol. 16). Cambridge: Cambridge University Press.

Bourdieu, P. (1986). Forms of capital. In J. E. Richardson (Ed.), *Handbook of theory of research for the sociology of education* (pp. 241–258). New York: Greenwood Press.

Bourdieu, P. (1997). The forms of social capital. In H. Lauder, P. Brown, A. S. Wells, & A. H. Hasley (Eds.), *Education, economy culture and society* (pp. 35–58). New York: Oxford University Press.

Brogan, C., & Smith, J. (2009). *Trust agents: Using the web to build influence, improve reputation, and earn trust*. Hoboken, NJ: Wiley.

Bruneau, T. J. (1973). Communicative silences: Forms and functions. *Journal of Communication, 23*(1), 17–46.

Castells, M. (1996). *The rise of the network society*. Oxford: Blackwell.

Davis, A. (2002). *Public relations democracy. Public relations, politics and the mass media in Britain*. Manchester: Manchester University Press.

Debord, G. (1994). *The society of the spectacle*. New York: Zone Books.

Deleuze, G., & Guattari, P. F. (1983). *Anti-Oedipus: capitalism and schizophrenia.* Minneapolis, MN: University of Minnesota.

Dimitrov, R. (2008). The strategic response: An introduction to nonprofit communications. *Third Sector Review. Special Issue: Third Sector and Communication, 14*(2), 9–50.

Dimitrov, R. (2014). Do social media spell the end of journalism as a profession? *Global Media Journal: Australian Edition, 8*(1).

Eliot, T. S. (1919). Hamlet and his problems. *The Athenaeum, 26 September*, 940–941.

Gingerich, J. (2012). Understanding the objective correlative. *LitReactor*. Retrieved 12 June 2017, from https://litreactor.com/columns/understanding-the-objective-correlative.

Grunig, J. E. (1992). *Excellence in public relations and communication management*. Hillsdale, NJ: Lawrence Erlbaum.

Hassan, I. H. (1968). *The literature of silence: Henry Miller and Samuel Beckett*. New York: Alfred A. Knopf.

Heath, R. L. (2006). Onward into more fog: Thoughts on public relations' research directions. *Journal of Public Relations Research, 18*(2), 93–114.

Hemani, K. (2014, 22 January 2014). *How storytelling can do wonders in blogging*. Retrieved 12 June 2017, from www.kumailhemani.com/storytelling-blogging/.

Holiday, R. (2012). *Trust me, I'm lying: the tactics and confessions of a media manipulator*. London: Penguin.

Ingram, M. (2017). Trump's media strategy is a trap, and we're all taking the bait. *Fortune*. Retrieved 12 June 2017, from http://fortune.com/2017/01/27/trump-media-trap/.

Jameson, F. (1988). *The ideologies of theory: Situations of theory.* (Vol. 2). Minneapolis, MN: University of Minnesota Press.

Jameson, F. (2003). The end of temporality. *Critical Inquiry, 29*(4), 695–711.

Johnson, B. (2016). Haley's State of the Union response: 'Turn down the volume' for a 'world of difference'. *PJ Media*. Retrieved 12 June 2017, from https://pjmedia.com/news-and-politics/2016/1/13/haleys-state-of-the-union-response-turn-down-the-volume-for-a-world-of-difference/.

Konrad, G., & Szelenyi, I. (1979). *The intellectuals on the road to class power*. New York: Harcourt Brace Jovanovich.

Lukes, S. (1985). *Marxism and morality (Marxist introductions)*. Oxford: Oxford University Press.

Public Relations Professionals. (2012). Job prospects. *Job outlook: An Australian Government Initiative*. Retrieved 12 June 2017, from http://joboutlook.gov.au/occupation.aspx?code=2253&search=&Tab=prospects.

Readings, B. (1996). *The university in ruins*. Cambridge, MA: Harvard University Press.

Rushkoff, D. (2013). *Present shock: When everything happens now*. New York: Penguin.

Schudson, M. (1997). Why conversation is not the soul of democracy. *Critical Studies in Mass Communication, 14*, 297–309.

Sontag, S. (1982). The aesthetics of silence. In S. Sontag (Ed.), *A Susan Sontag Reader* (pp. 181–204). New York: Farrar/Straus/Giroux.

Susskind, L., & Field, P. (1996). *Dealing with an angry public: The mutual gains approach to resolving disputes.* New York: Simon and Schuster.

Virilio, P. (1986). *Speed and politics: An essay on dromology.* New York: Semiotext(e).

Virilio, P. (2006). The museum of accidents. *International Journal of Baudrillard Studies, 3*(2).

Wilson, L. (1994, 1 December). Cyberwar, God and television. Interview with Paul Virilio. *Ctheory* Retrieved 12 June 2017, from http://ctheory.net/ctheory_wp/cyberwar-god-and-television-interview-with-paul-virilio/.

3   Silent symbiosis

Getting attention or directing attention?

In the previous chapter, I argued that both PR and journalism are intellectual professions, which legitimise their relatively privileged positions by doing two things: by being vocal about serving the public interest (claiming to represent trans-contextual, transcendental knowledge) and also being silent about their particular self-interests (including professional self-interest). Both 'weak professions' belong to the stratum – not class – of intellectuals, who have their own hidden agendas while selling their expertise on the open market. Journalists sell it direct, as *retailers*, to their audiences. PR practitioners do it indirectly, as *wholesalers*, to organisations, clients and media, who target their own publics (see Chapter 12). PR expertise does not have a direct, home-grown or ultimate public. It all depends on who hires or contracts PR practitioners. It looks like PR is the mediator who communicates between sponsors and publics. In fact, PR is the mediated. The mediators – organisations, movements or individuals – determine the status of PR, including its publics, objectives and strategies.

As communication professions, PR and journalism owe their privileged positions to their relative monopoly over the scarce resource of the public sphere. The scarce resource in markets is money. In the public sphere, it is attention. Both systems of material and symbolic exchange are interconnected. Programme rating and online measuring systems gouge attention and transform it into money. Money buys communication expertise. Communication expertise begets money.

The new global economy is increasingly becoming attention economy (Davenport & Beck, 2001; Goldhaber, 1997). In the new media environment, 'everyone has become a publisher' (Shirky, 2008), but not everyone has been a user of all new producers. The proliferation of online speakers has not found its match in an equal amount of digital listeners. Thus, the attention economy is a buyer's market rather than a seller's market.

As long as we equate PR and journalism and emphasise the common for both, we would be satisfied with the description of their scarce resource as *attracting and keeping the public attention*. Yet I would argue, that this is not all, and perhaps not the most important aspect in the monopoly of special knowledge that PR possesses. (I doubt that this is true even for journalism.)

And here silence enters the stage.

The opposite of public attention, i.e. the lack of such, is not necessarily (but it could be) an entropic state of silence. Silence is not a black hole, which eats out the web of communication and puffs out the flame of attention. Silence as *the most indirect form of communication*, can also draw and preserve attention (see Chapter 7). And noise can lull someone's vigilance more than anything else. Then, getting attention is only a PR means. It is not its final product.[1] And it is only one of its means. Evading, deflecting and arranging attention are equally important and legitimate means.

As I will later argue, PR as indirect communication is both internal *and* external to the media sphere and cycle (see Chapters 19, 20). Playing the media game is only part of the PR game. Choosing when and how not to be present in the media is a vital part of its professional judgement. Therefore, PR skills and strategies are about the *management* or *choreography of attention.* Its communicative capacity is, of course, about attracting and keeping attention. But it is also about *diverting* and *avoiding* attention. Management of attention means *directing rather than drawing attention.*

The differences between PR and journalism are more or less subtle. One of them is the dual character of PR publics. The publics of PR usually split into two kinds – media audiences and target publics. In a perfect world, they are one and the same. There, PR can easily identify target publics as media audiences. Then media and message strategies look like two sides of the same coin. But in reality, target groups and media audiences are never the same. Influencing the audiences (output) does not guarantee changing the publics (outcome). The sponsors of PR – representatives of the target publics or not – also keep outside the media cycle. Their interest is not to be the target of PR, although part of the interest of PR is exactly that (Berger, 2005; Holtzhausen & Voto, 2002). Both interests (sponsors) and results (targets) often rest outside the public sphere.

Intellectuals are *re-distributors* of resources – from one class to another, and a little bit for themselves as a helping hand (Schelsky, 1975). PR practitioners *distribute* and *re-distribute* attention. It could go either way and end with more or less attention. Often seeking and avoiding attention do coincide. We speak to remain silent, and our silence speaks. We talk about something and mean something else. We talk about anything not to talk about something. We draw the attention of some to divert the attention of others. The re-distribution of attention symbolically reproduces the hierarchies of power in the society.

The dominance of journalist silences over PR silences

Journalism *represents* the silences of its publics. It also *presents* the publics with its silences. The Western bias against silence finds its match in the *professional ideology* of journalism. My analysis of Google Alerts updates in English showed that Western journalists frame silence almost entirely in negative terms (Dimitrov, 2015). The most commonly employed cliché is 'break silence'. From it there are derivatives such as 'silencing' (suggesting coercion) and 'silent on' (implying culpability). Often, modifiers such as 'bought', 'shameful' and 'deafening' only trivialise the meaning of bad silence.

The self-interest of journalism in the overuse of 'breaking silence' is double. On the one side, it is superior to other words or phrases – 'silent/silent on' for example – because it carries higher news value. It sells better because it is at least a promise for breaking news. It is self-advertised news in contrast to the news that has not happened. On the other side, the negative cliché is a *code word* (Fish, 1994) – a barely veiled insinuation – against everyone who hides information from the public eye. On the surface, journalism promotes its democratic function as a watchdog of the public interest. The rally against silence, however, is also a dog whistle against the resistance of information sources, including PR.

Sources and media are differently self-interested. That is why they are in constant cooperation and struggle with each other. Sources open up and shut up depending on the interests of their sponsors. The self-interest of the journalists is to keep their sources as open as possible, as well as to retain their exclusive right either to name or protect their sources. Ideologically, the media promote a perfect imbalance in the power relations between them and their sources. The media should decide when, where and to whom the sources should speak or remain silent. In other words, negative silence as a journalist ideologeme indirectly targets sources by conditioning the public against the attempts of the sources to fight back their independence and speak or remain silent on their own terms. In that regard, there has been a professional-ideological and discursive dominance of the media silences over the silences of the sources – including PR silences. That imbalance of symbolic power, however, is gradually lessening with the current transformation of sources into media (everyone becoming a publisher) and media into sources (no journalist protection for the new media).[2]

Core and periphery

Along those lines of conflict and cooperation, PR and journalism live in a state of symbiosis (Anderson, 1993; Davis, 2009). PR sources vie for the attention of journalists and editors only when they have not accumulated 'media capital' (Davis, 2002). Once the media start perceiving them as reliable, credible and regular sources, the direction of dependency also starts to reverse. No longer has the source chased the media; the media chases the source (Gandy, 1982; Turk, 1985). Subsidised information starts capitalising. Not only the source works for the information; the information starts working for the source.[3] This reverse 'asymmetry' has eluded the excellence model in PR.

In closeness, there is more silence. In closeness, more is presupposed. People do not spell out to one another the context they are familiar with. More context allows less text. At the core of mutual relations, there is *knowing silence*. People communicate with half a word. Silence is double: we do not say what we know and we know what we do not say (see Chapter 18). Contrary to the dominating discourse, PR practitioners and journalists equally share silence and invisibility. For example, the differences between the professions of PR and journalism are smaller than the differences between the institutional domains and issues where PR and journalism work together. The more invested representatives of both professions are in an area of expertise – e.g. in sport, including publics and fans – the more visible they are to each other and the less visible to publics, journalists and communicators in other, peripheral to sport, domains.

At the core of thematic networks there is full visibility. People of different professions are close and fully visible to one another. Close relations means foremost *being equally invested* in the issue around which the network is built. It is equivalency of knowledge, but also of emotion and belonging. It is epistemological and ontological closeness that may take shape in affinity, trust and other interpersonal qualities.

The invested, however, are invisible to the periphery of the non-invested, including to those from their own profession – agents to agents, journalists to journalists and communicators to communicators. Thematic-spatial closeness is greater than the professional one – even more so in the weak professions. The gravity of the topical core is stronger than the gravity of the profession. In other words, the inter-professional relations here are closer and more transparent than the intra-professional relations to and from the margins.

The core is more silent; the periphery is more verbose. From outside, people feel obliged to record and report whatever they think and discover – and what may be obvious from inside. They talk to fill in the missing context. The filters of silence – heuristics, habit and judgement – would kick off later. From the margins, one is restless and suspicious. At the centre, one is confident and reassuring. From the periphery, timing is punctuating the silence by speech. At the core, timing is structuring, organising by silence.

In the US, 'bullpens' refers to the collection of reporters assigned to cover a government department. They are closer with the communicators of that department than with bullpens who observe other departments. The effect is 'stovepiping': journalists who cover one section of government remain uninformed about what goes on in other departments. In 2015, President Barak Obama's officials experienced that first hand when they failed to promote the strategy of his administration on ISIL in Iraq and Syria. Their 'whole of government campaign' fell on deaf ears partly because of the fragmentation between department-based clusters. Communicators and journalists were very close to each other in each cluster, but had almost no contact with representatives of their own profession who were serving or covering other departments.

The White House tried to respond to the inefficiency of stovepiping by a new 'whole of government' approach. One and the same speaker started briefing many bullpens, many times. Yet, as the Treasury Department's acting undersecretary for terrorism and financial crimes, Adam Szubin, attested, 'there is a real knowledge gap.... We feel like we repeat things all the time, but it's not penetrating' (DeYoung, 2015).

Another example: In the *Australian Football League* (AFL), a three-year scandal about an alleged illegal use (never entirely proved) of experimental drugs in the Melbourne club *Essendon* (known as *the Bombers*) finished with the conviction of 34 players of the club by the *World Anti-Doping Agency* (Holmes, 2016). No one from the club's administrators was found guilty. I will save the reader the complexity of the case, in which things were not as they looked.[4] An informal PR industry watchdog announced the Bombers' supplements scandal the 'PR Disaster of the Decade'. It had generated about 90,000 negative media mentions –double the amount of negative publicity for any other scandal in Australia (McCusker, 2016).

The sheer amount of that publicity came from the scandalised periphery in the football industry. In the Melbourne milieu, those were the *tertiary prevention* professions such as the police, lawyers and councillors who favour civil and criminal sanctions 'after the fact' rather than primary prevention through cultural and educational programmes (Dimitrov, 2008). The core – including PR practitioners, journalists, coaches, players and doctors – remained circumspect and mostly silent. Familiar with the vagaries of the football code, both communicators and journalists who were personally and professionally invested in the code, kept closer to the players and also to each other. They tried – unsuccessfully – to tone down the external critics who were finding a scapegoat in the footballers used as guinea pigs instead of going after those who were in charge of the illegal supplements programme.

Communicators and journalists interact according to their agenda. Journalists are as strategic as communicators. If they seem less strategic, this is only because they are perhaps better strategists. In difference (particular professional interests) and unity (common ideology as intellectuals), they target not only each other as professionals, but also their respective publics. Doing that, they (more the journalists than the communicators) exaggerate the differences between their professions and (more the communicators than the journalists) play down the differences between their professions and the public.

The message is the story

Story-telling is the Kingsway of managing public attention. A good story helps people to make sense of their experience in the most 'natural' way – through everyday pondering rather than scientific analysis. PR practitioners get their message across mostly through news stories – indirectly through subsidising news media and directly through the use of their own media (Heugens, 2002; Somerville, 2011).

PR practitioners and journalists are strategic in sharing a story. Depending on their strategy, they may cooperate or clash. If there are no conflicts of interest, the story that the communicator offers is the story that the journalist needs. In that case, the *message is the story*. It works well for both. Scott Crebbin, a PR consultant, says:

> I don't think many people talk about it. Maybe it's the elephant in the room. Who are we [the PR practitioners] invisible to? Especially when you look at sports stars, the agents get a lot of coverage now, and they are the ones who

control the messaging now for the player. It's the media that go through the agency; they very rarely talk to the player. Now, is that invisible? It might be invisible to the public but not to the journalist.

(Personal interview, 24 February 2012)

At the core, the communicator is fully visible to the journalist. The journalist, however, does not pass his visibility to the public. Why this silence? The PR practitioner has not asked him not to. Although, it is what the communicator wants because he expects the journalist as a more credible speaker to take ownership of the story and, as a consequence, of the message. He is strategic. A message directly imprints on the mind of the reader when it is indirectly communicated. The journalist remains silent about the source because his interest coincides with that of the practitioner. Both want to uphold the credibility of the journalists, although for different reasons. The interest of the journalist is to maintain his authority as independent investigator and public advocate. It makes a difference whether he suggests a story to the public or someone has suggested that story to him.

The guild-paternalism hidden behind the claims of 'quality journalism' is something that PR practitioners learn to appreciate and use for their own ends. But it is a posture – 'we better know what the reader needs' – that they cannot indulge. On the contrary, what communicators constantly do is reassure the clients that they best know what they want – especially when they have rightly chosen their own service.

If the agendas clash, PR practitioners can refuse information without necessarily affecting their relations with the media. Steve Riethoff, Managing Director of *Reservoir Network*, states:

People say communications are the gift of the gab, but it is the knowing when to shut up. There's silence but not over an ethical issue. It's over aspects of the business we don't want to promote. I am not stopping journalists from writing the story, and I am not going to help them. We do not try to get them on the news, and we don't try to get them out.

(Personal interview, 30 April 2012)

The strategies range from refusing to comment to being verbosely silent (see Chapter 7). Michelle Schofield says:

I would never say, 'Let's be invisible on this one' or 'Let's remain silent'. I may use the term, 'Let's not comment and withdraw from the story', 'don't give the story oxygen', 'let's run dead on this' and 'let's not give the story legs'. Somebody being silent also tells a story as well for the journalist, so they don't totally come away empty handed. It's worse for broadcast journalists than it is for print journalists because print journalists can nuance and, you know, they have more words to play with to tell the story.

(Personal interview, 7 March 2012)

This may not be satisfying for the media, however. Not getting the desired story may have a withdrawal effect that could lead to compulsive escalation.

The messenger is the story

If that is the case, the default strategy – tactic rather – a journalist always has in store is to make a story from the fact that the messenger is not giving a story. The journalist decides to confront his source in public. The focus then shifts from the story of the hidden messenger to the hidden story of the messenger. *The messenger is the story.*

This manoeuvre – half-blame and half-bluff – is risky. The PR practitioners I have interviewed insist that they have seldom experienced such retaliation. Why on earth would a journalist sacrifice their established relations with their source for a flash of uncontrolled discontent and short-lived satisfaction? Why should they give up their cool for a bout? Why should they trade a strategy for a tactic? When the messenger becomes the story, the *process of messaging*, along with the messenger, also becomes visible. Then both the PR practitioner and the journalist, who have been equally involved in the process, get exposed. Scott Crebbin:

> You are trying to give them [the journalists] the right story and there are strategies around why you do certain things. You piss them off but that's par for the course. So, it's very rare that they will attack you for not giving them something. To me that's just shooting the messenger. It's fine when, say, a journalist wants to out a publicist and make that a story. But there are reputations built around. So, you know, the next time the journalist wants to get something – that could play against them. I think the notion of being invisible is starting to diminish somewhat. I think the *mechanics* [my italics] of it are probably invisible but so is everything in terms of what people do and the mechanics of everything.
>
> (Personal interview, 24 February 2012)

'Mechanics' alludes to 'machination'. Yet it is more likely that a journalist makes a story only of those with whom they do not have an established relationship of collaboration. The core and periphery effect is valid here as well. Ironically, they mostly identify as 'spin doctors' (whatever that means) those who remain silent, remote and unknown to them – the communicators who manipulate them least.

The media is the story

The process of the message is the ultimate no-go zone for both professions. Michael Wolff, the *Vanity Fair* media reporter, witnessed that first hand in the Obama years:

Even though I've been invited to the White House for a talk with [the then Press Secretary Robert] Gibbs, there's an abrupt cancellation when, after some chitchat with [the then Deputy Press Secretary Bill] Burton, it becomes clear that my interest is in *process* [italics by M. W.] rather than, per se, message. And then kind of sudden vaporisation – no Gibbs, according to Marissa Hopkins, his assistant, 'for the foreseeable future'. 'The process aspect of the media, the insider stuff, is not – is not our thing', says Burton, whose entire career in the press offices of Dick Gephardt, Tom Harkin, John Kerry, and Obama during his Senate term has been nothing but media process. 'We won't miss you if you don't do the story'.

(2009)

Strategy is indirect communication. Strategy is invisible. Visible are the tactics. Strategy is an honest trick. The communicator is a full-time trickster. He is a diversion wizard. As the pickpocket showmen, Apollo Robins, points out, physical visibility is only a tool:

If I come at you head-on … I am going to run into that bubble of your personal space very quickly, and that's going to make you uncomfortable. So, what I do is I give you a point of focus, say a coin. Then I break eye contact by looking down, and I pivot around the point of focus, stepping forward in an arc, or semicircle, till I am in your space.… See how I was able to close the gap? I flew in under your radar and I have access to all your pockets. It's all about the choreography of people's attention. Attention is like water. It flows. It's liquid. You create channels to divert it, and you hope that it flows the right way … I was using the old sales technique called 'Feel, Felt, Found', where you empathize with the customer. Also the improved technique of never using a negative – agree and add on instead.

(Green, 2013)[5]

'*Choreography of people's attention*': this is another good definition of professional communication. If a publicist spells out the genesis of the message, they will kill the message. In the communication industry this would be considered self-defeating, possibly mad. Is it not the silence over the process the background that gives the message its meaning? How visible should the novelist be in her book? Does the photo of a columnist published beside his name render him more visible? How visible is an artist in his self-portrait? Would he become more visible if he laid bare the process of this painting and what exactly he wanted to achieve? Would Michael Wolff himself disclose the genesis of his purposefully naïve pissed-offness that frames his article? Wolff would not do it; no one would do it.

If they disclosed their process, *the media would become the story*. This is what the media fear most. For the reasons above, this rarely happens. Such occurrence was the recent phone and e-mail hacking of scandal in Britain involving the now defunct *News of the World* and other newspapers published by

Rupert Murdoch's *News International*. It resulted in a special parliamentary commission, media law changes, arrests and sentencing of journalists (Smith, 2012). PR practitioners, curb your glee! Even you do not want the media to become the story. One can hear the message in a story only if the message is silent over its story.

There are many reasons – hidden in the contradictive positions and interests of the intellectuals in the capitalist society – that compel both communicators and journalists to remain silent about their silences. But there is a plain one, where nakedness is no reason for closing our eyes. They are silent about their silences because without the first the second would not work.

Notes

1 Neither for journalism. Any professional form of public communication produces both sound and silence as well as presence and absence. Any form is about directing attention rather than producing it.

2 Even with third-generation laws such as those in some US states, New Zealand and Australia, which partly protect journalists sources in the social media, the idea to protect not the journalist – then who is a journalist in the social media and who is not? – but the *act* of journalism is still on the drawing board (Dimitrov, 2014).

3 In 2001–2005 refugee advocacy groups in Australia visited 'boatpeople' refugees who were locked in remote detention centres. The government at this time had banned journalists from entering the centres. As a result, visiting activists who then informed the journalists accumulated media capital not only due to their commitment to inform the public but also because they, along with staff from inside risking their jobs and even freedom, were the *only* sources of information about the situation. What also added value to that activist media capital was 'the public relations bonus of non-instrumental integrity' (Dimitrov, 2007). The bearer was a carer. You cannot bear an issue (communication) if you do not care for those affected by it. Today, the Australian government has learned from its errors and moved the detention centres offshore to Nauru and Manus Island in Papua New Guinea. It has deliberately placed them outside the country's jurisdiction and Human Rights obligations. (There is a bipartisan consensus on this policy.) The tyranny of the distance effectively denied the refugee advocates access to those offshore centres and devalued their media capital.

4 For more on that topic, see Mazanov (2016).

5 As Apollo Robbins attests, he has learned his craft from sources as disparate as aikido, sales and salsa dancing, as well as from books such as Robert B. Cialdini's 'Influence: The psychology of persuasion' (1993) and David W. Maurer's 'Whiz mob: A correlation of the technical argot of pickpockets with their behavior pattern' (Maurer, 2003). Pickpocketing as the magic of attention diversion is more than a metaphor. It is the art and science of strategic communication. Recently, the US Department of Defense approached Robbins to consult him in matters of behavioral influence, con games and political-military counter-deception (Whaley, 2007). The D.O.D. has also invited Robbins as adjunct professor to its new research and training facility at Yale University (Green, 2013). It all is about the artful diversion of the attention from the process of the message.

References

Anderson, A. (1993). Source-media relations: The production of the environmental agenda. In A. Hansen (Ed.), *The mass media and environmental issues* (pp. 51–68). Leicester: Leicester University Press.

Berger, B. K. (2005). Power over, power with, and power to relations: Critical reflections on public relations, the dominant coalition, and activism. *Journal of Public Relations Research, 17*(1), 5–28.

Cialdini, R. B. (1993). *Influence: The psychology of persuasion.* New York: Morrow.

Davenport, T. H., & Beck, J. C. (2001). *The attention economy: Understanding the new currency of business.* Cambridge, MA: Harvard Business School Press.

Davis, A. (2002). *Public relations democracy. Public relations, politics and the mass media in Britain.* Manchester: Manchester University Press.

Davis, A. (2009). Journalist–source relations, mediated reflexivity and the politics of politics. *Journalism Studies, 10*(2), 204–219.

DeYoung, K. (2015, 31 December). Obama thinks his Syria strategy is right – and folks just don't get it. *Washington Post.*

Dimitrov, R. (2007). ChilOut: Strategic communication by small advocacy groups. *Australian Journal of Communication, 34*(3), 129–143.

Dimitrov, R. (2008). Gender violence, fan activism and public relations in sport: The case of 'Footy fans against sexual assault'. *Public Relations Review, 34*(2), 90–98.

Dimitrov, R. (2014). Do social media spell the end of journalism as a profession? *Global Media Journal: Australian Edition, 8*(1).

Dimitrov, R. (2015). Silence and invisibility in public relations. *Public Relations Review, 41*, 636–651.

Fish, S. (1994). *There's no such thing as free speech and it's a good thing, too.* New York: Oxford University Press.

Gandy, O. H. (1982). *Beyond agenda setting: Information subsidies and public policy.* Norwood, NJ: Ablex Publishing.

Goldhaber, M. H. (1997). The attention economy and the net. *First Monday, 2*(4). Retrieved 12 June 2017, from www.uic.edu/htbin/cgiwrap/bin/ojs/index.php/fm/article/view/519/440.

Green, A. (2013). A pickpocket's tale: The spectacular thefts of Apollo Robbins. *The New Yorker.* Retrieved 12 June 2017, from www.newyorker.com/reporting/2013/01/07/130107fa_fact_green?printable=true.

Heugens, P. P. (2002). Managing public affairs through storytelling. *Journal of Public Affairs, 2*(2), 57–70.

Holmes, T. (2016). Guilty: A devastating verdict for Essendon and its players. *ABC: The Drum.* Retrieved 12 June 2017, from www.abc.net.au/news/2016-01-12/holmes-a-devastating-verdict-for-essendon-and-its-players/7082930.

Holtzhausen, D. R., & Voto, R. (2002). Resistance from the margins: The postmodern public relations practitioner as organisational activist. *Journal of Public Relations Research, 14*(1), 57–84.

Maurer, D. W. (2003). *Whiz mob: A correlation of the technical argot of pickpockets with their behavior pattern.* Lanham, MD: Rowman & Littlefield.

Mazanov, J. (2016). After the Essendon saga, any reform to anti-doping regimes must give athletes a greater say. *The Conversation.* Retrieved 12 June 2017, from http://theconversation.com/after-the-essendon-saga-any-reform-to-anti-doping-regimes-must-give-athletes-a-greater-say-53212.

McCusker, G. (2016, 5 January). Bombers doping scandal is PR disaster of the decade! *PRdisasters.com* Retrieved 12 June 2017, from https://prdisasters.com/2015/12/18/ bombers-doping-scandal-is-pr-disaster-of-the-decade/.

Schelsky, H. (1975). *Die Arbeit tun die anderen: Klassenkampf and Priesterschaft der Intellektuellen.* Opladen: Westdeutscher Verlag.

Shirky, C. (2008). *Here comes everyone: The power of organising without organisations.* New York: Penguin.

Smith, S. (2012). UK Journalists Union question anonymous source protection in News Corp investigation. *iMediaEthics.* Retrieved 12 June 2017, from www.imediaethics. org/index.php?option=com_news&task=detail&id=2678.

Somerville, I. (2011). Managing public affairs and lobbying: persuasive communication in the policy sphere. In D. Moss & B. DeSanto (Eds.), *Public relations: A managerial perspective* (pp. 167–192). London: Sage.

Turk, J. V. (1985). Information subsidy and influence. *Public Relations Review, 11*, 10–25.

Whaley, B. (2007). *Textbook of political-military counterdeception: basic principles & methods.* Washington, DC: Foreign Denial & Deception Committee, National Defense Intelligence College.

Wolff, M. (2009). The power and the story. *Vanity Fair, July 2009.* Retrieved 12 June 2017, from www.vanityfair.com/politics/features/2009/07/wolff200907.

Part III

Strategy and silence

Michel Foucault, Jean Baudrillard,
Pierre Bourdieu, Stuart Hall,
Norman Fairclough and Jürgen Habermas

4 Strategy as discursive practice

Discursive practice

Silence, including strategic silence, is not abstract. The practice of signification – including talking and writing – produces silence not in isolation but in dialectics with what is not silence. Silence and non-silence mutually determine one another, and their concrete play constitutes unique variations in strategic communication. Should we try to pin down a singular silence – like a butterfly in a herbarium? – it will fall apart and disappear without a trace. This is another reason why PR is silent on its silences. It is actually not, but every attempt to speak about it in an abstract, isolated and individualist way leaves its theory empty-handed as the empirical silences slip through its fingers.

We have to start from the basics. Silence is strategic, when we use it as a means – along and in concert with other means – to achieve a goal. Objective is the measurable 'what' to achieve. Strategy is the conceptual 'how' for the 'what'. Tactic is each single 'what' for the 'how'. All tactics of a strategy are the package of 'what' for the 'how'. But strategy is more than the sum of tactics. It is the qualitative conversion of their quantitative accumulation. Strategy is the global, holist and integral image of the multitude of tactics (Wodak, 1996, pp. 112–113).

Tactics do not converge into strategy. It is the other way around. Strategy converges into tactics. This is a common mistake communications students and novices in the profession alike, make. Tactics seem easy. Everyone knows what media alerts, press conferences and Facebook pages are. Tactics seem obvious: literal and tangible. Strategies are more elusive: vague and intangible. It is safe to start from what one knows best. Let us first put together some possible tactics. But how many of them would be enough? Where is the red line? How many tactics does the budget allow? Should we stop yet? Oh, they are already too many? Then let us make a U-turn. We will take some off. What does the budget say, again? Are they just right? Is that it? Then we have the strategy. Or do we? It seems natural to move from the easy bit to the more complicated part – bit it is not. We have to approach strategy not from the direction of tactics.

A way of thinking of strategy is as *discursive practice*. This goes beyond 'what' and 'how', beyond ends and means. Foucault ascribes to discursive practices *strategic intelligibility*. In discourse, language is strategic and intelligible because it articulates differences beyond cognition and representation – differences in action and power. Even theory no longer represents it. It 'does not express, translate or serve to apply practice: it is practice' (Foucault, 1980, p. 208). 'Discourse is what necessarily extends beyond language' (unpublished lecture cited in Davidson, 2003).

There is struggle fuelled by intentions, needs and circumstances. But it is fought and decided on at a different level – that of *discursive practices*. This is also the battleground of strategic silence. Strategies as discursive practices reflect relations of power. *Discourses are strategic because they also have non-discursive effects.* As such, they are naturalised in knowledge, festered in relations, embedded in identities. In other words, they are difficult to change (Lakoff, 2010).

PR has to start from here: What are the strategic dimensions of discursive practices, which we are limited to use (tactically), and even more limited to change (strategically)? What can we do in relation to the actually existing and dominant strategies, which are out as practices in the society before and irrespective to our strategic intent? 'Discourse', says Foucault, 'is not simply that which translates struggles or systems of domination, but is the thing for which and by which there is struggle, discourse is the power which is to be seized' (1981, pp. 52–53).

Professional communications – including public relations – are much smaller and less significant players in the discursive filed than they are ready to admit. They modulate some conditions and contexts of struggle, in which discourses emerge, rise, fall and re-emerge again. Discursive practices are repetitive and essentially collective patterns, through which everyone represents and constructs the society, although often in an unreflected and routine – 'doxic', in Bourdieu's terminology – fashion. Strategies in that sense are bigger than people and organisations. They defy any voluntaristic claim of origin and authorship by any single agent – however specialised or powerful they are. Their laboratory is the *discursive practice*, of which PR practice is a constitutive but rather modest part.

Strategy in silence, silence in strategy

What we say and do not say has a function in the order of discourse. Foucault insists that silence, like power, is productive. One may use its force not only to prohibit and repress but also to enable and resist.

> Silence itself – the things one declines to say, or is forbidden to name, the discretion that is required between different speakers – is less the absolute limit of discourse, the other side from which it is separated by a strict boundary, than an element that functions alongside the things said, with them and in relation to them within over-all strategies. There is no binary division to be made between what one says and what one does not say; we must try to determine the different ways of not saying such things, how

those who can and those who cannot speak of them are distributed, which type of discourse is authorized, or which form of discretion is required in either case. There is not one but many silences; and they are an integral part of strategies that underline and permeate discourses.

(Foucault, 1990, p. 27)

Whether a silence is strategic or tactical depends on the empirical context of its functions within a discourse. It is also possible that a silence has multiple strategic roles depending on the discourse from which we interpret it. And, in the same vein, silence can work as strategy in one sense and as tactic in another. There is neither a single and 'correct' interpretation of strategic silence nor a fixed transition between silent strategy and tactic.

There is not only strategy in silence. There is also silence in strategy.

Foucault analyses discourses both at strategic and tactical levels. The *tactical productivity* of discourses reflects practices as realisations of choices between *polyvalent* (i.e. silence as admission of guilt or discrete accusation) and *equivalent tactics* (i.e. addressing a rumour or remaining silent about it). Silence, like discourse, can be both an instrument and effect of power. It can reinforce but also undermine power, 'loosen its holds and provide for relatively obscure areas of tolerance' (Foucault, 1990, p. 101).

Discourses also provide for the *strategic integration* of tactics. Yet, there is a major problem here. When we apply tactics, we deal with appearances. We align them easily with our aims and objectives. As I argued above, tactics seem easily quantifiable. Their logic is clear. Their functions make sense. We can count them separately and as a sum. We can compare them directly. In contrast, we imply and infer the existence of overarching strategies, which invisibly bind them not only to one another but also as a never entirely fathomable entity:

The logic is perfectly clear, the aims decipherable, and yet it is often the case that no one is there to have invented them, and few who can be said to have formulated them: an implicit characteristic of the *great anonymous, almost unspoken strategies* which coordinate the loquacious tactics whose *inventors and decision-makers are without hypocrisy* [my italics].

(Foucault, 1990, p. 95)

PR is born in the flow of the modern discursive practices. It is designed as technology – 'excellence' as universal means – to achieve outcomes by both *influencing through discourse and 'seizing the discourse'*. This is not a tautology. It is not only that PR *has* strategy – PR *is* strategy. It is a strategic response to an environment increasingly shaped by indirect discourse. PR is strategy. PR strategies are only tactics in the big picture of discursive practices. What PR practitioners believe to invent and coordinate 'without hypocrisy'; what they measure and report in all clarity to themselves, stakeholders and their bosses; and what they present as evidence for communication effects they use to legitimises their profession and build their personal authority, are all tactics at the impersonal level of 'great anonymous, almost unspoken strategies'. We will find integrating strategies at the level of collective, anonymous and silent discursive practices but not at the level of individual, intentional and planned action, even when the agent is a group, institution or super-organisation.

Jean Baudrillard defines strategy as *full emptiness* using the metaphor of martial arts:

> Strategy of absence, of evasion, of metamorphosis. An unlimited possibility of substitution, of concentration without reference. To divert, to set up decoys, which disperse evidence, which disperse the order of things and the order of the real, which disperse the order of desire, to slightly displace appearances in order to hit the empty and strategic heart or things. This is the strategy of oriental martial arts: never aim straight at your adversary or his weapon, never look at him, look to the side, to the empty point from when he rushes and hits there, at the empty centre of the act, at the empty centre of the weapon.
>
> (2012, pp. 58–59)

Strategy is what is not in relation to what is. It is present through its absence. It is the blind spot that binds visible things in unity of relevance.[1] It is most powerful when silent and invisible. Its success is proportional to the ability to hide its mechanisms (Foucault, 1990, p. 86). Tactics are effective the opposite way. Only when they are visible from all sides and unambiguously understood, only when they appear in full, they help strategy entirely disappear. This is the mystery of strategic communication. Many cannot define it because strategy is indefinable.

Here there is a dramatic, critical difference between tactic and strategy. Tactically, knowledge is knowledge, conversation is conversation, and truth is truth. Tactically, they are self-explanatory, for the sake of themselves. Tactics are the way they are. That is why PR students and novices do not think they have a problem with tactics. But with strategy, nothing is the same. Strategically, knowledge, conversation and truth are not obvious, not taken for a given. They are silent forces. In discursive struggle knowledge functions as power, conversation as promotion and truth as 'regime of truth' (a particular perspective that displaces other particular perspective as the universal, the 'consensual' one).

Messages are statements. But, contrary to the PR collocation 'message strategy', they are short of being strategies. Single message statements are rather tactics at the level of discourse. In *Power and Sex*, Foucault cautions that statement is one thing and discourse another. 'They share common tactics even though they have conflicting strategies' (Foucault, 1988, p. 114). For example, the message of 'always more sex' and 'more truth in sex' may serve the strategy of sexual liberation by removing normative prohibitions on sexual desire. Or it may aid the strategy of commodification by creating heuristic equivalences between whatever is promoted and sexual references (Pratkanis & Aronson, 1991), which actually leads to the opposite political effect. The 'liberation' of the consumer protects and expands markets that are threatened by the liberation of sex as non-commodity. PR textbooks are full with taxonomies of 'universal' and 'ready-to-go' tactics. As if tactics have inherent qualities. As if they are identical with themselves. Yet the same books remain vague and indecisive about strategies. They point laconically and committedly – and rightly – at their intermittent, hide-and-seek and non-linear logic.

Silence and secret

Pierre Bourdieu shares Foucault's anti-structuralist thrust but at the same he tries to salvage the notion of human agency, which Foucault discards in his anti-humanist critique of subjectivism (Paden, 1987). For both, strategy is *not a free choice*. It is not an individual, conscious and rational choice that opposes collective norms, rigid rules and objective constraints. They both reject the existence of an isolated and rational subject. Unlike Sigmund Freud, however, Foucault and Bourdieu do not locate strategy – as inexplicable as it is – in the *unconscious*.

This is important when we reconstruct their interpretations of strategic silence. It is anything but things we do not do because we do not say because we are not aware of them. For Freud, we are silent on contents, which we have 'repressed', pushing them deeper to the level of the unconscious. They can stay there for long, resurfacing sometimes as dreams, slips and forgetfulness. The unconscious is mute per definition (Akhtar & O'Neil, 2011). In contrast, both Foucault and Bourdieu are not interested in the unsocialised, abstract-individual, psychological qualities of silence.

For Foucault, 'the discourse of struggle is not opposed to the unconscious, but to the secretive' (1980, p. 214). As the pioneer who has discovered power where no one has expected and seen before, he is interested not in 'cheap psychoanalysis' of the implicit and unsaid about sex – which is the central point in his *History of Sexuality* – but rather in the explicit, manifest forms of silence as secret. Power works best when it is hidden. And power hides to work best. It is harder to identify who has power but easier to see who does not. Secrets emerge as an issue at the moment when some cannot 'freely' hide their power and start masking it by force. Taboos, censorship, bureaucratic language and double-speak work that way. There is no secret in being clueless; the secret *is* the clue. Being 'secretive' is already curious if not suspicious. It means the holder of power cannot any longer hide it without extra effort.

Baudrillard also links the secret with the promotional culture of seduction as appearance for the sake of appearance:

> Yet there is nothing seductive about truth. Only the secret is seductive: the secret which circulates the rule of the game, as an initiatory form, as a symbolic pact, which no code can resolve, no clue interpret. There is, for that matter, nothing hidden and nothing to be revealed.

> (2012, p. 56)

Foucault limits the discursive to the linguistic. But he does not follow the tradition of discarding silence as the 'mystical', as the spiritual that is beyond comprehension – a lasting assumption in logocentrism (Bindeman, 1981). He also steers away from silence as the 'ineffable' – as the experience we cannot translate into words.[2] Foucault believes that statements – in the strategic use of language – are never hidden and never hide. They are rather silences disguised in words. And words disguise silences. Secrets provide for the circular motivation and 'will to knowledge', as Foucault sees it in the *transformation of sex into discourse.*

> Under the authority of a language that had been carefully expurgated so that it was no longer directly named, sex was taken charge of, tracked down as it were, by a discourse that aimed to allow it no obscurity, no respite.... What is peculiar to modern societies, in fact, is not that they consigned sex to a shadow existence, but that they dedicated themselves to speaking of it *ad infinitum*, while explaining it as *the* secret.
>
> (Foucault, 1990, pp. 20, 35)

He is certain that we can better understand texts and their statements when we rise to the conditions of their historical formations. And this is what he always does. His theory *is* practice. We can know everything that each age says if we are familiar with the conditions laid down for its statements. Of course, this is possible only partially, in approximation. 'Un-hiding' is an infinite movement towards full disclosure, a direction rather than a destination. 'We need only to know how to read, however difficult that may prove to be. The secret exists only in order to be betrayed, or to betray itself' (Deleuze, 2006, p. 46).

Foucault's concern is with secrecy as explicit, manifest silence (see Chapter 10). Like the public secret, manifest silence is a paradox. It is silence that one can hear. It is where the cracks in power are its only visible feature. It is where a statement hints at its conditions of expression, which are still to be discovered. Secret and silence are not identical, though. As demonstrated in *History of Sexuality*, silence can be used strategically as *exhaustive representation* – that is, to preserve something as a secret by infinitely and relentlessly revealing and explaining it.

Strategy and practice

When it comes to silence, both Foucault and Bourdieu do believe in the power of knowledge and reflection as tools of 'un-hiding' power. The more visible power is, the less power it is. The knowledge gained is power too, more power. In that regard, Foucault borrows from Kant. For him, knowledge can expand and beat muteness within a 'historical a priori' – an impossible category in Kant's terms (Deleuze, 2006). Yet the point Foucault makes is a Kantian one. He believes that with a 'toolbox' anchored in language[3] and history, one gains power over language and discourse, which are practices. So one can affect and change all other practices.

Bourdieu is also tempted to measure 'progress' by how far discursive practices spread over 'non-linguistic' practices – by how far society has overcome
muteness (1977). And his notion of discourse is also logocentrist, language-
based rather than multimodal, semiotic. He defers from Foucault, however, in
some key aspects. Bourdieu is more circumspect about theory as immediate
practical action. Foucault claims that theory unearths and validates 'local',
'authentic' knowledge. For him as a post-structuralist, the ethical and political
function of theory is to debunk and resist 'totalising', dominant knowledge.
Intellectuals are externally and internally split. They are both agents of the
system, ideologues and saboteurs, 'enlighteners'. Either way, they have the
means to see things others do not see and say things others do not (cannot/should
not) say.

Yet Bourdieu is sceptical about the messianic, heroic or activist role of the
intellectual. Unlike Foucault – and perhaps like Habermas – he believes that
representation, including a scientific one, is good even when few represent many.
He does not pit 'local knowledge' against the general and dominant one. As a
sociologist, he is concerned with reflection and self-knowledge as the partial,
imperfect but only humanly 'objective' way of overcoming the limits of prac-
tical knowledge. Here, Bourdieu is in a group with Louis Althusser and Stuart
Hall. He is also closer than Foucault to Marx' notion of practice. He agrees with
Foucault that both theoretical and practical knowledge have strategic properties.
But, whereas Foucault is mainly concerned with how theory changes practice,
Bourdieu favours the opposite way of how practice changes theory. Bearing with
Marx, he distinguishes between the 'things of logic and logic of things'
(Bourdieu, 1990, p. 61). In his work, strategic silence emerges from the *logic of
things* – as *practical mastery*.

Bourdieu's concept of *practice* aims to avoid both structuralist objectivism
(Claude Lévi-Straus) and subjectivism (Jean-Paul Sartre). He finds the gist of
strategy in the inner necessity, feeling of the game. Strategy is the practical
mastery acquired from the experience of the game. A seasoned player reinforces
its rules but, at the same time, enjoys the freedom of interpretation. Bourdieu
locates the practical mastery in the *habitus* – an internal system of corporal dispositions and cognitive templates (1988). He believes that habitus links agency
with practice and facilitates the interaction between individual bodies. Habitus
and doxa are internalised automatisms, which escape conscious control and are
outside discoursing. This is important, because Bourdieu ties discourse with
consciousness.

Non-discursive practice includes silent strategies: automated routines, self-
evidences and repetitive technics of body and mind. They are silent as long as
they are successful and successful as long as they are silent. When people
recourse to discursive tools – and for Bourdieu that is to verbalisation and ration-
alisation – their habit is disturbed and condition arise for an 'epistemological
break'. It must not be tragedy or failure that stops automated action and triggers
reflection: 'What went wrong?' 'What went right?' is an equally important
prompt, which ensues from a humanly positive event. It could be a lull (children

relaxing) or celebration or happening, where people step back and look at what they used to do in order to make sense of it. And there is a neutral and more controlled starter of reflection – the scientific method. Learning is reflective; acting is discursive.

Bourdieu defines agency is a *double game strategy*. It consists of 'playing in conformity with the rules, making sure right is on your side, acting in accordance with your interest while all the time seeming to obey the rules'. The habitus 'as the feel for the game is the social game embodied and turned into a second nature' (Bourdieu, 1990, p. 63). Silently, the imminent necessity of the game *imposes itself* on the free player. I see parallels here to Baudrillard's strategy of Eastern martial arts. And I recollect Herrigel's *Zen and the Art of Archery* (1953) as well as how Bindeman interprets it in *Heidegger and Wittgenstein: The Poetics of Silence*:

> He was taught Zen Buddhism, not by direct philosophical instruction but through his learning the technique of Zen archery. But he was not taught how to shoot an arrow with a bow at a target; he was shown how to breathe, how to hold and loose the bowstring, and finally how to shoot in such a way that the bow and arrow used him as an instrument. He learned how to let go of his conscious self, and to let it happen on its own a skill that his body has acquired by habit.
>
> (1981, p. 12)

Bourdieu makes an important point. Yes, strategic communication is purposeful. And, yes, intentions, goals and plans play a role. But this is secondary. In practice, strategies are primarily habitual, routine-like, and *automatic*. 'The necessity of the game', 'the logic of things' 'impose themselves' on the individual behaviour as practical mastery. They require and enable obeying to rules and flouting them at the same time. Kellermann, for example, claims that that *all* communication is strategic. Communication is already structured and materialised in flows that do not necessarily relate to the consciousness of those involved or affected. Strategies are learned and articulated tacitly – pre-consciously, post-consciously or 'reflectively' – rather than 'reflexively' (Kellermann, 1992).

This appreciation of collective and habitual practice of discourse is the line that connects the oeuvres of Foucault and Bourdieu and finds a succession in the works of critical discourse theorists, notably Norman Fairclough. For him, strategic discourses, whether consumerist or bureaucratic, instrumentalise scientific outcomes for non-scientific purposes. Communicators *simulate* particular subject positions, identities and relations to construct brands, organisations and institutions as *synthetic personalities* – from the sneakers that are part of our personality to the fatherland we are ready to die for (Fairclough, 2001, pp. 176–180). Simulation syntheses alienated and fragmented relations *as if* they are personal and integral, vertical inequality *as if* it is horizontal equality, and virtual cycles *as if* reality comes to itself. And, in its consequences, simulation is indeed real. Practice permits, 'as if' will become 'as it is'. Simulation fakes *and* makes.

But exactly in this 'as if' we see silence as strategic discourse. Fairclough, in this grand tradition, is adamant that, once skilled and trained in strategic discourses, people reproduce them collectively and routinely rather than individually and consciously (1992). This is not a statement of fact, but an explanation how discourses do work. A strategic discourse type such as an advertisement, interview or official record utilises science and uses it for other purposes. But it is not science. It is strategic because it is indirect and instrumental. Silence helps synthesise and make sense of this improbable coexistence of 'what is' and 'what is not' in such kinds of mediation.

Habitual behaviour is not incidental. It is not the opposite of the purposive action, which is determined in advance with a particular outcome in mind. Automatic behaviour is *structured in practice, not necessarily in mind.*[4] Strategic patterns are practices rather than principles. Any complex task requires the acquisition of tacit knowledge – of implicit skills and strategies that circulate freely in the flux without the clumsy and often violent intervention of thought and language. Automatism articulates practice in time.[5] Habitual behaviour is not illogical or involuntary. Automatisms are often intentional but – as long as they are successful – outside conscious monitoring and control. Unaware is not mindless. 'Communication is not primarily mindless because it was never primarily mindful; rather, communication is primarily implicit while being inherently strategic' (Kellermann, 1992, p. 295).

Bourdieu's 'sense of the game' refers not to some abstract and inherent logic of rules but to the negotiated 'social agreement' between players – that is to the negotiated relations with other participants and what they regard tolerable. This includes, for example, market transactions as 'honest cheating'. Strategic silence, however, becomes critical in Bourdieu's theory of practice especially when he shifts his gaze from habitus to the *symbolic exchanges* between people in 'virtuosic' interaction, nested in a constantly negotiated network of relations (King, 2000).

This is worth analysing because Bourdieu's emphasis on symbolic exchanges comes close to what we in PR call 'communicative competence'. There is something ethereal in the practical mastery. One freely juggles with interpretative schemata and props them up with indicative and non-verbal gestures. And one does it with a 'good feel' – seemingly oblivious of explicit rules, correct representations and abstract 'maps'.

Notes

1 Philippe Sollers contemplates the waters between three points of land in Venice and calls the architect Andrea Palladio who has created two of its most beautiful churches, *San Giorgio Maggiore* and *Il Redentore,* a strategist:

> The sturdy thrust of his Redentore was deliberate, so, seen from the waters, in the future, boats would look as if drifting past the temple of time regained. A strategist, he established an impregnable triangle: San Giorgio, the Redentore, the Dogana [the former custom house, now museum, which Sollers pronounces 'the centre of the world']. On one side, Byzantium and the flamboyant Gothic of the past; on the

other, ancient Greece, revived forever with the Renaissance and Counter-Reformation. Monstration, demonstration. An infernal wound for the backward-looking and modernists alike'.

(Sollers, 2014, p. 178)

2 As in Michael Polanyi's (1966) concept of 'tacit knowing', for example.
3 For Foucault, the language, the said and unsaid, is the discursive. The light, the spatial and visible, is the non-discursive. He considers both dimensions qualitatively different and irreducible to each other. The discursive has priority to the non-discursive. Otherwise, there is no casual or other relation of determinacy between both. A third, binding tool emerges between them – the diagram. But it is the tool of the theorist to keep their indirect interplay together (Deleuze, 2006).
4 I follow here Hall's critical interpretation of Althusser that the articulation of difference and unity should avoid too simple, linear or dual models of determination such as basis and superstructure. Or economy and culture for that matter. Or sexism and racism. Hall gives his personal record about his experiences as a black person in Jamaica and the UK. For him, they are not only and not predominantly determined by the capitalist mode and production. Hall counters the 'necessary no correspondence' relativism of postmodernism with the 'no necessary correspondence' principle of possible co-determinism. For example, the ideology of a class may be or may be not determined by its position in the economic relations of capitalism. There is always a complex of co-determinants in place. Empirical knowledge of the concrete historical context is imperative. Hall's 'no guarantee' breaks with teleology – there is *no necessary correspondence* and also no necessary non-correspondence (Hall, 1985, p. 94). In January 2016, the outgoing ambassador of Australia in the US, Kim Beasley, commented on the then running for President Republican candidate Donald Trump:

> The Republican Party now represents the white working class, attitudinally. Be it on guns. Be it on same sex issues. Be it on migration. Be it on religious matters. You represent the attitudes of the white American working class. Your problem is you don't represent their interests.

Trump's appeal? 'That somehow … out of his apparent business success, everyone will be winners. It's a magic man concept. It's not a program' (O'Malley, 2016).
5 This idea is central for the concept of strategic silence, which rests on practical articulations and automatisms such as Raymond Williams' *structures of feeling* (Williams, 1977) and Bourdieu's *habits* and *doxa* (Eagleton & Bourdieu, 1992).

References

Akhtar, S., & O'Neil, M. K. (2011). *On Freud's 'negation'*. London: Karnac Books.
Baudrillard, J. (2012). *The ecstasy of communication*. Los Angeles, CA: Semiotext(e).
Bindeman, S. L. (1981). *Heidegger and Wittgenstein: The poetics of silence*. Washington, DC: University Press of America.
Bourdieu, P. (1977). *Outline of a theory of practice* (Vol. 16). Cambridge: Cambridge University Press.
Bourdieu, P. (1988). Vive la crise! *Theory and Society, 17*(5), 773–787.
Bourdieu, P. (1990). From rules to strategies (interview with P. Lamaison). In P. Bourdieu (Ed.), *In other words: Essays towards a reflexive sociology* (pp. 59–75). Stanford, CA: Stanford University Press.
Davidson, A. I. (2003). Introduction. In M. Foucault (Ed.), *Society must be defended: Lectures at the College de France 1975–76* (pp. XV–XXiii). London: Penguin.
Deleuze, G. (2006). *Foucault*. London: Bloomsbury.

Eagleton, T., & Bourdieu, P. (1992). Doxa and common life. *New Left Review, 191*, 111–121.

Fairclough, N. (1992). *Discourse and social change*. Cambridge: Polity Press.

Fairclough, N. (2001). *Language and power* (2nd edn). London: Pearson Education.

Foucault, M. (1980). Intellectuals and power: A conversation between Michel Foucault and Gill Deleuze. In M. Foucault (Ed.), *Language, counter-memory, practice: Selected essays and interviews* (pp. 205–217). Ithaca, NY: Cornell University Press.

Foucault, M. (1981). The order of discourse. In R. Young (Ed.), *Uniting the text: A post-structuralist reader* (pp. 51–78). Boston: Routledge & Kegan Paul.

Foucault, M. (1988). *Politics, philosophy, culture: Interviews and other writings, 1977–1984*. London: Routledge.

Foucault, M. (1990). *The will to knowledge: The history of sexuality*, Vol. 1. London: Penguin.

Hall, S. (1985). Signification, representation, ideology: Althusser and the post-structuralist debates. *Critical Studies in Media Communication, 2*(2), 91–114.

Herrigel, E. (1953). *Zen in the art of archery*. New York: Random House.

Kellermann, K. (1992). Communication: Inherently strategic and primarily automatic. *Communications Monographs, 59*(3), 288–300.

King, A. (2000). Thinking with Bourdieu against Bourdieu: A 'practical' critique of the habitus. *Sociological Theory, 18*(3), 417–433.

Lakoff, G. (2010). Why it matters how we frame the environment. *Environmental Communication, 4*(1), 70–81.

O'Malley, N. (2016, 23–24 January 2016). Beazley bids a fond farewell to Washington. *The Sydney Morning Herald*.

Paden, R. (1987). Foucault's anti-humanism. *Human Studies, 10*(1), 123–141.

Polanyi, M. (1966). *The tacit dimension*. London: Routledge & Kegan Paul.

Pratkanis, A. R., & Aronson, E. (1991). *Age of propaganda: The everyday use and abuse of persuasion* (pp. 115–123). New York: W. H. Freeman and Co.

Sollers, P. (2014). *Venice: An illustrated miscellany*. Paris: Plon & Flammarion.

Williams, R. (1977). *Structures of feeling in Marxism and literature* (pp. 128–135). Oxford: Oxford University Press.

Wodak, R. (1996). *Disorders of discourse*. London: Longman.

5 Instrumental and communicative action

Action and practice

Bourdieu's theory of *symbolic exchange* opens opportunities of exploring silence as *strategic communication*. In my opinion, symbolic exchange overcomes the artificial opposition between *strategic* and *communicative action*. In the Jürgen Habermas' opposition, strategic action is teleological. It is instrumental with things and strategic with people as objects. Communicative action, in contrast, validates normative and consent-oriented claims (Habermas, 1985, 1987). Strategic action uses communication as a means for another ends. Communicative action is not only a means but also an end itself. As 'discursive redemption of validity claims', it becomes, so to speak, the common denominator for other actions.

Habermas' dualist concept of action has a normative intent. He presupposes that totalitarian societies are based on the first type of strategic, instrumental and manipulative technology, whereas democratic societies establish procedures of consensus-building communicative action. Critically minded PR academics are also not immune to the appeal of this model due to its tempting contrast between organisations (system, strategic action, communication as a means) and publics (lifeworld, movements, communication as an end) (Bentele & Wehmeier, 2007; Burkart, 2007; Leitch & Neilson, 2001; Roper, 2005).[1]

Habermas' dualist concept constructs a fundamental chasm between strategy and communication. As a consequence, he follows it up with other divisions along the way of theoretical modelling. For example, the split between strategic and communicative action gets its pragmatic translation in the separation between instrumental-performative and value-normative and between perlocutionary (effect-oriented) and illocutionary (understanding-oriented) speech acts. Even in the old-fashioned and 'pure' grammatical terms, he sees the reproduction of the same rift in the division between imperative (direct commands and requests) and indicative mood (factual statements and validity claims) (Habermas, 1985; Tugendhat, 1985). In his rationalist and polarised model, silence is always strategic, but this is bad news, not good news for silence. Reduced to instrumental rationality and affectual commands, silence is on the non-communicative, mute and irrational side.

Habermas' assault on strategic communication as instrumental, manipulative and deceptive – in lieu with his long-term vision of PR as a new, anti-democratic tool of the systemic colonisation of the public sphere by private corporate interests (Habermas, 1970, 1974, and more recently 2009) – confuse PR academics, especially those who share progressive views. Is it possible to 'purify' strategic communication, to distil it as communicative action? Could it be both communicative and strategic? Is it really possible to simulate 'an ideal speech situation' and 'put in brackets' social and political differences? Nancy Fraser's critique of Habermas' model rejects such assumptions. Even if in a sterile, simulated situation of communication, when the practitioners skilfully pretend that they are equal, the consent they reach would only reinforce the differences in symbolic power (Fraser, 1985, 1990).

Perhaps a more productive approach would be the opposite of 'ideal speech situation' – a 'real speech situation', in which the participants first address (deconstruct) their own differences instead of hanging them in the closet (Mickey, 2003)? Perhaps appreciating the multitude of agonist positions and irreconcilable opinions is more democratic than seeking consent that validates *one* claim (Mouffe, 1999)?

Bourdieu's symbolic exchange is practice. It governs the bodies and forms of life. It is a collective thrust of history. It is made by people and thus worth changing by people, but not in the transactional (marketing) way of intellectual and individual author rights. Symbolic exchange is politics, at the centre of communal and associative practices. In contrast, Habermas' communicative action remains somehow distant, aloof and hovering in the academic terms of 'law and order' society. 'Action' emphasises the performative quality of language – words as the coordinate system of deeds. Lash comments on those differences between 'practice' and 'action':

> To define culture as symbolic practice is to emphasise *practice* in contradiction to *action*. Action is individualistic, it is a question of the 'I', or at best a collection of atomised 'Is'. Practice is communal; it is of the 'We'. Action takes place at the level of consciousness, practice foregrounds the unconscious and preconscious. Action is of the mind; practice is bodily. Action wields clear and distinctive ideas, practice works in regard to symbols. Action deals with preference schedules and choice of the marketplace, practice with background assumptions, horizons and habitus. Action takes on the assumption of positivism, practice of hermeneutics. Action speaks of political decision-making, practice of political culture. Action has to do with individual choices in the context of decided-upon procedural rules; practice is inseparable from the very real concerns of good life.
>
> (2002, p. 32)

In my opinion, Bourdieu's notion of the social world as symbolic exchange is more productive. Habermas is concerned with *relations of communication,* Bourdieu with relations of *symbolic power.* Communicative action is about the *meaning of speech* – utterances, statements and ides that the interlocutors validate and legitimise through a better argument. Symbolic exchange is about the *value* and *power of speech* – accessibility, acceptability and authority of the participants. Habermas appeals for unbiased, self-aware and attitudinal *linguistic competence* that would deliver deliberative consent. Bourdieu counters such 'abstract' and 'idealist' notion through his concept of *symbolic capital* to under-line that competence is not something that can be simulated in laboratory but is inseparable from the speaker's positions in the society.

Traditional, positivist PR is not concerned with the conditions for the forma-tion of a situation of communication. It takes them for granted. They are transpar-ent to it. We communicate when we communicate, period. As idealism, positivism is satisfied with an abstract situation of communication between iso-lated individuals. Habermas and Bourdieu are not – although for different reasons. Habermas scrutinises the democratic quality of ordinary communication in the lifeworld. Too much distorted – strategic, in his understanding – communication hampers the pursuit of genuine communication. His solution is the creation of epistemologically privileged situations of communication by isolating and culti-vating them as 'ideal speech situations' from intersections of the society where the 'system' particularly 'skews' the 'lifeworld'. Bourdieu, however, approaches the significance of a situation of communication from the opposite end. He neither takes such a situation for granted nor tries artificially to improve it.

For him, language is mostly practice. It is made for saying and un-saying. Strategies as practices are communicative (within and outside language) and non-communicative (again, within and outside language). But they are never uprooted from practice. Communicative strategies, for example, may have as a means or effect, order or disorder, understanding or misunderstanding, agree-ment or disagreement. (One can also replace 'or' with 'and' to underline the unity and coincidence of such events.)

Bourdieu, like Foucault, asks the essential question about the *conditions for the establishment of communication*. What puts some people 'on speaking terms' and others not? How are distributed the roles of those who speak and those who do not? Which laws of discourse establish de facto and *de jure* who speaks to whom, how, where and when? How does it come that 'those who speak regard those who listen worthy to listen and those who listen regard those who speak as worthy to speak' (Bourdieu, 1977, p. 648)? PR practitioners ask themselves the same question before drafting strategies for the best possible use of the putative situations of communication. Establishing or changing those situations is often beyond their terms of reference and, frankly, power. It often goes beyond strategy and requires long-term work on transforming not only discourses but also systems such as institutions, cycles, norms, rules and procedures (see Chapter 19).

Serious and authentic

Communication versus silence? A sign of how Habermas misses the productive functions of silence is his intolerance toward every form of communication that uses indirect and ambiguous strategies. For him, only *honest* and *serious* communication is communicative action. Lying is not (Habermas, 1985, p. 153).

The black-white binary of lie – honesty is not new in communication studies. Critics of PR as spin doctoring often miss the point not because there is no problem with honesty and ethics in PR but because they indiscriminately put various forms of indirect communication, including silence, in the lie basket (Burton, 2007; Hobbs, 2016; Lamme & Russell, 2010; Munshi & Kurian, 2005; Sumpter & Tankard Jr, 1994; Tiffen, 2004).

Habermas criticises Ervin Goffman (1959) and, yes, even Pierre Bourdieu, in that regard. He insists that only a *serious* intent constitutes communicative action. He accuses Goffman (2005) of coming up with an ambiguous concept of communicative action, which includes the whole spectrum of 'impression management' – from authenticity to cynicism. He remarks that Goffman fails to recognise strategic intention disguised as performance toward consent. Instead, Goffman includes deceptive presentations of self, which are off the mark of honest communication. That way, his symbolic interaction falls into one group with Bourdieu's forms of symbolic-expressive exertion of power, which, Habermas argues, is a special form of success-oriented (strategic), but not of consent-oriented (communicative) action (Habermas, 1985, p. 177).

For Habermas, a speaker can pursue perlocutionary aims (those which affect the listener such as persuading, inspiring, scaring or incensing) only when he conceals them from the hearer (1985, p. 157). Is there an honest performative action? An honest promotional culture? Foucault asserts, power may be positive. Can manipulation (effecting without disclosing the aim) be positive too? Because this is what indirect communication is about. Truth and validity against influence and power? The force of the argument against the argument of the force? Again: Communication against strategy?

But how do we tell, for example, 'dissimulation' from 'performance'? In *dissimulation* silence has various functions. But which of them is lying? In *Simulacra and Simulation*, Baudrillard writes:

> To dissimulate is to feign not to have what one has. To simulate is to feign to have what one hasn't. One implies a presence, the other an absence. But the matter is more complicated, since to simulate is not simply to feign: 'Someone who feigns an illness can simply go to bed and pretend he is ill. Someone who simulates an illness produces in himself some of the symptoms' (Littre). Thus, feigning or dissimulating leaves the reality principle intact: the difference is always clear, it is only masked; whereas simulation threatens the difference between 'true' and 'false', between 'real' and 'imaginary'. Since the simulator produces 'true' symptoms, is he or she ill or not? The simulator cannot be treated objectively either as ill, or as not ill.
>
> (2001, pp. 170–171)

There are several major objections against the split between strategic and communicative action. The first and most basic one is that this separation may be analytical, but not a practical one. The strategic communication and communicative action essentially overlap in the flow of communication. They are not two diachronic phases but rather synchronic occurrences in the communicative cycle. There are strategies of consent, and there are consensual strategies. Communication as an end may be a means for another end. And so on.

The second objection is central for this book. PR practice has actually got it right. It distinguishes between successful (strategic) and unsuccessful action. But if action is less effective, it does not mean that it is more communicative. Practice also tells ethical from unethical action – with the political significance of 'responsibility'. But it does not discriminate between serious and insincere communication. Marketing and advertising also use entertainment even more than the newsroom for promoting content (see Chapter 12).

Similar to the Habermas paradigm of 'seriousness' as precondition of communicativeness, other – especially social media conscious – communicators also stress on the 'authenticity' of the speaker, as an identity-bound, feelings-based, and presence-building asset. When during the US presidential primaries in 2016, President Obama surprised a group of private Democratic donors and, for the first time, candidly intervened on behalf of the then presidential candidate Hilary Clinton, he attacked the common view among supporters that she was less 'authentic' than the other contender, Bernie Sanders. He played down the importance of authenticity, reminding that President George W. Bush was once praised for his authenticity (Haberman, 2016).

It turned out, Obama was wrong – at least in this case. Later on, in the TV debates, Trump's media-savvy, 'telling-it-as-it-is' and take-no-prisoners attacks, drew more Twitter acclaim and ultimately voters than Clinton's 'fake' – 'creepy', 'scary' and even 'evil' – smile (Smith, 2016). The legitimate question why no one was paying attention to how Trump smiled and whether sexism does leave any room for an 'authentic' smile of a woman in politics and especially in debates with such highly abusive man is beyond the point.

But Obama was right in principle. Baudrillard explains the 'authenticity' vogue in the mastery of self-promotion with the shift of the problem the postmodern individual faces from 'alienation' (the age of the spectacle for an disengaged public) to 'identity' (the age of Internet disembodiment and fractal subjects). One is alienated not from the others but from oneself. The narcissist escapades in the social media, Facebook for example, constitute an attempt to simulate identity by self-promotion.

> Resemblance is no longer concerned with other, but rather with the individual on his vague resemblance to himself; resemblance born of the individual's reduction to his simple elements. As a result, difference takes on another meaning. It is no longer the difference between one subject and another, but an internal, infinite differentiating of the same.
>
> (Baudrillard, 2012, p. 39)

'Authenticity' plays an important role. But it does it in promotional cultures rather than deliberative democracy. Peddling 'authenticity' may become a trap – personally and politically. There is no coincidence that the same man who is 'serous' and 'authentic' for some has reinvented 'bullshit'[2] and 'fake news' for others (Zakaria, 2016).

Habermas' seriousness tends to be literal, conscious and attitudinal – a deliberative approximation to truth by its earnest co-construction. On the way to it, any difference between what is said and what is meant has to be removed. Silence in that sense is not serious. Lack of authenticity is not serious. No productive relations can come from such strategically constructed, unserious knowledge and identities.

But this is not how global capitalist societies function. In professional communication, which is based on a multitude of promotional cultures, one can be never sure whether the other person means what he says (Tugendhat, 1985). Entertainment, showmanship and speech virtuosity use indirectness to sell serious stuff in a light-hearted way and trivial stuff in a thoughtful way. Indirectness oils the symbolic exchange in various markets. In pluralist societies, indirect discourse makes differences tolerable rather than removing them through consent (Mouffe, 1999). This often makes the difference between war and peace. In that sense, Foucault inverts Clausewitz's famous sentence, stating that politics 'is the continuation of war by other means' (Foucault, 2003, p. 15).

Practical mastery

Habermas requires a forthright and stern *attitude* toward consent to recognise and justify communicative action. As attitude strategic action is not serious (enough). That is why silence is (degrees of) lying. In that respect, there is a crass difference between Habermas' communicative action and Bourdieu's practical mastery. For Habermas linguistic competence requires formalisation and strictness. It is attitudinal: a serious attempt to achieve consent by putting strategy (that is success and power-oriented action) 'in brackets'. For Bourdieu, pure 'grammarian' competence does not exist. The symbolic power relations largely define what appears as structures of competence.

The contrast cannot be starker. Bourdieu, for an instance, investigates 'strict correctness' as a strategy of the dominated class, which is at pains to emulate the language of the dominating class. A valet who speaks like a gentleman, a footballer who speaks like the club manager and a 'tradie' (the Australian word for tradesman) who speaks like a boss, are very serious. And this is attitudinal too. They are serious because they invest *value* in the way they speak publically. They are serious because their life and career depend on the demonstration that they are inside and not outside a discourse, from which they can retrieve legitimacy for higher social positions. They are serious because they are tense, self-conscious and giving all of them to utilise a language for a purpose, which is not the language itself. The upper class, on the other side, often displays its dominance in public by *strategic under-correctness*. The strategy is 'to be oneself'. Which means to be anything but serious. The style of speaking is deliberately or accidentally lax. The show of 'common touch' and the nonchalant appearance of someone who does not give a damn about practical mastery (which is an essential part of that mastery) display that what speaks is not the formal language (seriousness, consent, competence) but the *social person* (social positions, success, power) (Bourdieu, 1977, p. 653).

If we follow Bourdieu and Fairclough, who do not exclude the argument of power, we can see that communicative action, including understanding and consent, can serve as a discursive tool, which stabilises and naturalises power relations. In that regard, Fairclough notes that what *empowerment* needs is exactly the opposite – strategic communication. For example, training of unemployed, improving their 'job-seeking skills' presupposes that if more people were trained in getting jobs, there will be more jobs. Consequently, if an unemployed person, nevertheless, does not get a job, it is his personal failure (lack of skills) – not of the system (lack of vacancies).

> It may also be that the reduction of social practice and discourse to 'skills' is itself bound to have a debilitating effect on communicative discourse, in the sense of discourse which has no underlying *instrumental goals* for any participant, but is genuinely undertaken in a cooperative spirit in order to arrive at *understanding* and *common ground* [my italics].
>
> (Fairclough, 2001, p. 180)

Strategies of empowerment must at least 'disarticulate' (silence, displace) the personal skills discourse in favour of another existing discourse that, for example, explores the full range of possibilities within the given order of discourse, without necessarily changing it. Another discursive strategy may directly attack the inter-discursive relations, the order of discourse itself – that of neoliberalism in Fairclough's example of the 'skills acquisition' sub-discourse. But this is only possible when personal and political goals can align – when an articulation is possible, an establishment of equivalency between a change of the social position (unemployed) and political change (of the order of discourse). To sum up, if for Habermas communicative action is the rational and democratic alternative to strategic action, for Foucault, Bourdieu and Fairclough – despite significant differences between their approaches – the alternative to a strategic discourse is another strategic discourse.

Instrumentality and finality

In one aspect, Habermas' concept of communicative action seems especially unproblematic. Even his critics pass it without a comment. There is a silent agreement that there may exist rare cases of 'pure' communication as an end in itself. An example is when someone seeks a discussion with somebody for the sake of discussion. He discusses, for example house building for the love of conversation (Baurmann, 1985). But how serious is that? Is such conversation not playful? How about formulaic conversation, when we talk about the weather. Are we purely interested in the weather? Or are we actually not interested in it at all, solving other problems by keeping the conversation afloat? And how about phatic communication, when PR practitioners maintain the channel of communication with clients for the sake of the relations with them – for example by courtesy calls, personal letters and custom-tailored newsletters? Is the very definition of public relations not phatic?

Habermas dichotomy of strategic and communicative action follows a long tradition in philosophy, which has its origin in Immanuel Kant's *The Critique of Judgement* (1952). Kant distinguishes between *instrumentality* and *finality*. Instrumentality is based on 'determinate judgement' – a judgement that comes from a pre-given rule. We know how to judge in advance. We do not even have to 'know', because our reaction is automatic, pre-determined. Finality, on the contrary, does not rest on a predetermined rule. We have to find it through reflection. The object, medium or piece of art is indeterminate. Through us, it still has to find its rule. As such, it becomes an end in itself. It stops us. We cannot use it to go further. It is finality, not instrumentality: purposefulness without a purpose ('Zweckmäßigkeit ohne Zweck') (Lash, 2002, pp. 67–68). I am tempted to link it to an opposition from discourse analysis: finality it is *opaque* (what the object or medium is about) and not *transparent* (what is said that the thing is about) (Jalbert, 1994).

Now Habermas is not alone in that tradition, which attempts to overcome the transience and shallows of instrumentality (strategic action) to reach the last frontier and ultimate depths of finality (communicative action). He is one of the many in its rich legacy.[3] In the contemporary information and communication society, however, the difference between instrumentality and finality is increasingly problematic. It disappears, explodes together with other differences, which were taken for granted. Post-structuralists such as Baudrillard, Derrida and Deleuze argue that the previous transcendence explodes into a more general plain of immanence, an *indifference* of the information and communication flows (Baudrillard, 2012; Deleuze, 1995; Derrida, 2004). In the new media environment, the binary of instrumentality and finality bursts (see Chapter 13). Information and communications build networks. They connect. They are material. They are the *new third culture* of the global society (Lash, 2002, p. 68).

We can see such developments in the profession of public relations. We can take as example the fading division between source and medium. The sources have become publishers (through owned and shared media) and the media have become sources (through content creation studios). Strategic interaction takes place in either direction. He who targets is also targeted. Strategic silence is used either way – to reach a target and not to be reached as a target (see Chapter 7). In PR strategy today, the difference between 'means for an end' and 'end in itself' increasingly dissolves. Both fuse in an infinite cycle of non-linear, synchronic inter-mediation.

Notes

1 For the debate and critique of the category of communicative action, see the contributions by Jürgen Habermas, Ernst Tugendhat, and Hans Haferkamp in (Seebass & Tuomela, 1985).
2 According to Harry Frankfurt, the bullshit artist does not lie consciously but rather cannot tell true from false. But bullshitting is actually worse than lying. Truth-tellers and liars are both acutely aware of facts and truths. The bullshit artist, however, has lost all connection with reality. For that reason he is a greater enemy of truth than liars are (Frankfurt, 2009).
3 Karl Marx's opposition of *exchange-value* and *use-value*. Max Weber's *Zweckrational* and *Wertrational*. Jacques Derrida's idea of *différance* is to deconstruct 'the same', that is to destruct the determinate reason of instrumentality and open up indeterminacy so that one can raise again the ultimate question of meaning of life (Lash, 2002, p. 68).

References

Baudrillard, J. (2001). *Selected writings* (2nd edn). Stanford, CA: Stanford University Press.

Baudrillard, J. (2012). *The ecstasy of communication.* Los Angeles, CA: Semiotext(e).

Baurmann, M. (1985). Understanding as an aim and aims of understanding. In G. Seebass & R. Toumela (Eds.), *Social action* (pp. 187–196). Dodrecht: D. Riedel Publishing.

Bentele, G., & Wehmeier, S. (2007). Applying sociology to public relations: A commentary. *Public Relations Review, 33*(3), 294–300.

Bourdieu, P. (1977). The economics of linguistic exchanges. *Social Science Information, 16*(6), 645–668.

Burkart, R. (2007). On Jürgen Habermas and public relations. *Public Relations Review, 33*(3), 249–254.

Burton, B. (2007). *Inside spin: The dark underbelly of the PR industry.* Sydney, NSW: Allen & Unwin.

Deleuze, G. (1995). Postscript on control societies. In G. Deleuze (Ed.), *Negotiations: 1972–1990* (pp. 177–182). New York: Columbia University Press.

Derrida, J. (2004). *Dissemination.* London: Continuum.

Fairclough, N. (2001). *Language and power* (2nd edn). London: Pearson Education.

Foucault, M. (2003). *Society must be defended: Lectures at the College de France 1975–76.* London: Penguin.

Frankfurt, H. G. (2009). *On bullshit.* Princeton, NJ: Princeton University Press.

Fraser, N. (1985). What's critical about Critical Theory? The case of Habermas and gender. *New German Critique, 35,* 97–131.

Fraser, N. (1990). Rethinking the public sphere: A contribution to the critique of actually existing democracy. *Social Text, 25–26,* 56–80.

Goffman, E. (1959). *The presentation of self in everyday life.* Garden City: Anchor.

Goffman, E. (2005). *Interaction ritual: Essays in face to face behavior.* New Brunswick, NJ: Transaction Publishers.

Haberman, M. (2016, 19–20 March). Obama barracks for Clinton. *The Sydney Morning Herald.*

Habermas, J. (1970). On systematically distorted communication. *Inquiry, 13*(1–4), 205–218.

Habermas, J. (1974). The public sphere: An encyclopedia article. *New German Critique, 3 (Autumn 1974),* 49–55.

Habermas, J. (1985). Remarks on the concept of communicative action. In G. Seebass & R. Toumela (Eds.), *Social action* (pp. 151–178). Dordrecht: D. Reidel Publishing.

Habermas, J. (1987). *The theory of communicative action (vol. 2): Lifeworld and System: A critique of functionalist reason.* Boston, MA: Beacon Press.

Habermas, J. (2009). *Europe: The faltering project.* Cambridge: Polity.

Hobbs, M. (2016). The sociology of spin: An investigation into the uses, practices and consequences of political communication. *Journal of Sociology, 52*(2), 371–386.

Jalbert, P. L. (1994). Structures of the 'unsaid'. *Theory, Culture & Society, 11 (1994),* 127–160.

Kant, I. (1952). *The critique of judgement* (Vol. 314). Oxford: Oxford University Press.

Lamme, M. O., & Russell, K. M. (2010). Removing the spin: Toward a new theory of public relations history. *Journalism & Communication Monographs, 11*(4), 279–361.

Lash, S. (2002). *Critique of information.* London: Sage.

Leitch, S., & Neilson, D. (2001). Bringing publics into public relations: New theoretical frameworks for practice. In R. Heath (Ed.), *Handbook of public relations* (pp. 127–138). Thousand Oaks, CA: Sage.

Mickey, T. J. (2003). *Deconstructing public relations: Public relations criticism.* Mahwah, NJ: Lawrence Erlbaum.

Mouffe, C. (1999). Deliberative democracy or agonistic pluralism? *Social Research, 66*(3), 745–758.

Munshi, D., & Kurian, P. (2005). Imperializing spin cycles: A postcolonial look at public relations, greenwashing, and the separation of publics. *Public Relations Review, 31*(4), 513–520.

Roper, J. (2005). Symmetrical communication: Excellent public relations or a strategy for hegemony? *Journal of Public Relations Research, 17*(1), 69–86.

Seebass, G., & Tuomela, R. (Eds.). (1985). *Social action.* Dordrecht: D. Reidel Publishing.

Smith, J. (2016). Could Hillary's smile cost her the election? Twitter mocks Clinton's 'creepy grandma' grin as she smirks her way through presidential debate. *Daily Mail Australia.* Retrieved 12 June 2017, from www.dailymail.co.uk/news/article-3854016/Could-Hillary-s-smile-cost-election-Twitter-mocks-Clinton-s-creepy-grandma-grin-smirks-way-presidential-debate.html – ixzz4di8ouW5h.

Sumpter, R., & Tankard Jr, J. W. (1994). The spin doctor: An alternative model of public relations. *Public Relations Review, 20*(1), 19–27.

Tiffen, R. (2004, 23 October). Under (spin) doctor's orders. *The Age.* Retrieved 12 June 2017, from www.theage.com.au/handheld/articles/2004/10/20/1097951764549.html.

Tugendhat, E. (1985). Habermas on communicative action. In G. Seebass & R. Toumela (Eds.), *Social action* (pp. 179–186). Dordrecht: D. Reidel Publishing.

Zakaria, F. (2016). The unbearable stench of Trump's B.S. *Washington Post.* Retrieved 12 June 2017, from www.washingtonpost.com/opinions/the-unbearable-stench-of-trumps-bs/2016/08/04/aa5d2798-5a6e-11e6-831d-0324760ca856_story.html?utm_term=.945da4afee41.

Part IV

Indirect communication

6 Silence and invisibility

The sayable and the seeable

In everyday life we often talk about silence and invisibility synonymously. We often use silence as a *spatial metaphor*. 'Silence filled with sound'. 'Sweet silence' – but not 'silent sweetness' (Shen & Cohen, 1998). I do it in places too. PR vernacular does it. For example, we easily replace 'increasing the visibility' with 'having the voice heard'. We talk about 'invisible people' such as the poor, homeless, refugees and sometimes even women and, at the same time, we mean people who are voiceless, silent. Other metaphors such as 'having a place at the table' and 'raising the profile' have both visible and audible dimensions. Silence extends in images. We can talk about silent pictures (Brighenti, 2007; Franke, 2012; Kwiatkowska, 1997; Lester & Hutchins, 2012; Mey, 1997). Metaphors are real. They rest on true experiences. Our random replacements of silence and invisibility reflect the spatial-temporal unity of human interaction. The Modern Age had a *synesthetic* effect on sight and hearing. It gave certain legitimacy to the fusion of both senses and their joined dominance over other ones such as smell, touch and taste (Howes, 2010).

Recently, the actor Richard Gere experienced the change of luck in being someone and no-one. He played a homeless man in *Time Out of Mind*. When he had a test day at New York's *Grand Central Station*, only two passers-by recognised him. A kind-hearted French tourist even offered him her leftover pizza. His take from that day:

> If I'm on the red carpet, there are people screaming, wanting an autograph, wanting to make eye contact. In this situation, this guy is not seen. For me personally, it was a very profound lesson in how superficial it is. When I had the homeless haircut, the homeless clothes, the homeless stance – I had this *stillness* [my italics] I was out of queue with the rhythm of the world.
>
> (Freydkin, 2015)

As long as we use silence as a spatial metaphor, we do not have a problem with seeing invisibility as stillness. Conversely, the visible – the image, vision and especially video – has become a powerful, almost supernatural tool of 'breaking silence' and 'telling the truth'. *Video advocacy*, for example, fits perfectly into the bestselling epistemology of the visual as ultimate validation. A short audio-visual with an artless plot can stir the imagination of broad publics. A revealing image has an immediate and unmatched impact. It makes distant and unseen events present. Shared on platforms such as YouTube or Facebook, visual evidences strategically transform a distant horror into a sympathetic cause and channel sentiment into action (Torchin, 2006): Abu Ghraib; The WikiLeaks video of collateral murder in Iraq; Alan Kurdi, the drowned Syrian toddler;[1] Tamir Rice, the 15-year black teen shot by police. A video, even shot by lay people and without an aesthetic merit (i.e. smartphone crowdsourcing), can not only report but also create critical media events. It can provide visual testimony and a moral storyline, which broader publics can easily follow (Gregory, 2006).

Eileen Pittaway, Director of the *UNSW Centre for Refugee Research* (CRR) and one of the founders of the *Australian Refugee Rights Alliance* (ARRA), goes every year to Geneva for the Executive Committee Meeting of the *UN High Commissioner for Refugees*. In one of her trips to a refugee camp, she happened to have a video camera. She took a video and showed it later in the *Geneva Palais,* to the top of UN. She told me: 'Everyone was shocked, "Oh my God, what should we do, how can we change this?...". The short video has done more in terms of advocacy than all the pages and books I've ever written' (Personal interview, 10 November 2007). This probably summarises best the PR value of a visual.[2]

Yet in many respects, silence and invisibility are also different and even opposite categories. Non-metaphorically speaking, visibility and invisibility are spatial. Sound and silence are temporal. The former are states; the latter are processes. Visibility and invisibility seem to be more direct – either you see something or not. They do not have the many degrees of indirectness of the said and unsaid. Indirect discourse, for example, forms from what is left in the endless chain of saying and hearing of what is said and heard. Of course, visibility can also be mediated, stored and distorted. Our ways of seeing are also more or less indirect – that is socially constructed (Berger, 1972; Brighenti, 2007). But seeing and saying belong to different semantic orders.

Foucault, for example, postulates that visibility and sound dovetail in defining each historical formation (Foucault, 1972). Yet he sticks to the logocentric understanding of discourse. He is adamant that we cannot directly compare the *sayable* (articulated) with the *seeable* (visible). For him the visible is the luminous, non-discursive environment. It is the light-being – just as there is language-being (Foucault, 1973). The articulable is the discursive, including the sayable and readable. The visible is a prerequisite for the sayable – it makes it possible (McKinlay & Starkey, 1998). The seeable and sayable are not isomorphic to each other. They do not correspond in substance. They are different qualities. As dimensions, they do cross but not touch each other. They determine each other but they are not the same. Only an abstract *diagram*, as a theoretical tool or ideal type, can connect them as a line produced by two coordinates (Foucault, 2003).

Foucault gives us no doubt about the priority of the discursive over the non-discursive. No reduction of the visible to the articulable is possible or worth trying (Deleuze, 2006). This is, so to speak, Foucault's meta-theory. Yet one can only appreciate the combined and critical use of the spatial and visible argumentation in his theory. I think, for example, of the asymmetry between visibility and invisibility (added by imposed silence) in Bertram's Panopticon. I would also refer to the French subtitle of *The Birth of the Clinique*, which reads 'une archéologie du *regard médical*' [my italics]. *Medical gaze* is not 'medical perception'. As a relational category, the medical gaze is impersonal, disciplinary. It reflects the 'triumph of vision' in science, which – in medical examination or autopsy – 'sees' hitherto invisible links between symptoms and their possible conditions and causes. At the same time, the depersonalised medical gaze makes *invisible* the individual living body. Its personal, sexual and private distinctions disappear with the institutionalisation of intimately disinterested doctor–patient relations (ethics) (Foucault, 1973).

Yet we need additional tools to reproduce the interplay between invisibility and silence. Such means are, for example, the categories of presence and absence. They mediate between the spatial and temporal dimensions of indirect communication.

Presence and absence

Absence is not lack of communication. 'The family barbeque where the recently divorced father-in-law is not there speaks volumes' (Personal interview, 9 April 2013, with Grant Butler, Managing Director of *Editor Group*.) The presence of an army or the police is often enough to send a clear message.[3] One does not need to talk. The mere fact of someone being or not being there 'speaks for itself'. This is extremely persuasive. One cannot argue with such silence.

We notice an absence within a situation of communication, not outside it. We define and recognise an absence not in isolation, not as such but against its opposite of *presence* – or the other way around. We recognise absence as non-presence – and vice versa. That is why presence and absence are equally communicative. He who cannot be present cannot be absent. Absence and presence constitute one and the same communication event, which only appears in unique time-spaces – in concrete *chronotopes*,[4] in Mikhail Bakhtin's terminology (2010). Chronotopes are richer and more dynamic than static binaries. Absence and presence co-constitute each other. They exist simultaneously as 'self-contained opposites' (Clair, 1993). There is *absence of presence* and *presence of absence*, the joint work of which is somewhat 'ghostly' (Wylie, 2009).

Absence and presence are critical forms of indirect communication, which straddle space and time. This is important. Absence and presence emerge from that tension as forms of mediation. For example, absence is not the spatial version of silence. Presence may be silent as well. There is a value – such as loss, strain, sign and perhaps message – in an absence. Conversely, absentees may resist dominance and 'vote with their feet'. One can be present but 'out of reach'. One can be absent, but not 'leaving us alone'. We make people absent – even when they stand next to us – to deny them their claim of space, which they occupy physically but not publically. Invisibility trumps evidence, delegitimises. Absence demarks zones of control, where other people, ideas and discourses do not belong (Jones, 2012; Jones, Robinson, & Turner, 2012).

What is visible is present. What is invisible is absent. But one can feel its presence nevertheless. I have already discussed that false equation of visibility with veracity (see Chapter 1). The most drastic example of the 'out of sight, out of mind' strategy I can give, is the current 'border protection' policy of the Australian government. A whole section of the public sphere in Australia was closed and militarised (Dimitrov, 2008). A bipartisan policy makes refugees invisible not only physically but also discursively. For example, it reframes the refugee issue as that of 'people smugglers'. Put in an agent–patient relation, the smugglers appear as the active agent and the immigrants as the passive patient. From that angle the government is fighting the 'business model' of the people smugglers. It does not defend the human right of the asylum seekers. Never mind that there is no business model with demand but no supply (Dimitrov, 2014). Political semantics has rendered refugees 'sediments of other people's actions'. They are not 'auctori' – the 'authors of their life trajectories' (Bauman, 2002, pp. 343–344). Not only off-shore detention centre fences but also language has removed the 'boat people'; made them invisible.

> A Chinese tale, told by Mencius, illustrates the effect of presence: 'A king sees an ox on its way to sacrifice. He is moved to pity for it and orders that a sheep is used in its place. He confesses he did so because he could see the ox, but not the sheep'.
>
> (Perelman, 1982, p. 35)

The Internet has widened the rift between presence and space. Unlike face-to-face conversation, online communication no longer equates *proximity* with presence and *distance* with absence. The distant ones may be present on screen and those next to us, even in the same room, may be absent (Miller, 2012). *Presence at a distance* produces disembodied and anonymous agents. At the same time, distance no longer silences and proximity no longer privileges. Digital absence and presence relate and partly overcome the physical, geographical and even the social. For example, they partly offset the costs of travel – the 'tyranny of the distance' in the Australian case. Today it becomes more obvious that distance and proximity have – and always have had – social, political and ethical dimensions (Silverstone, 2003).

Image and representation

How do images represent objects and subjects? Subjects can be represented by images. But how do they signify others and also themselves? Who is visible and who is not in that chain of speaking without words for others and for themselves? The ways images and imaging represent, especially in the era of digital media, is one of the biggest ontological and epistemological issues, which marks the divide between modern and postmodern approaches in communication. But it also has significant implications for the PR profession.

Communicators are mediators who represent others. Representation is indirect communication. But images are deceivingly direct. They look *flat* – as if the signifier and signified are pressed to each other and have become the same. Thus they can hide ideologies, values, interests and intentions even better than words. Invisibility gives away even less than silence. Images construct both visibility *and* invisibility. This fact poses political and ethical questions to every PR practitioner.

Signs reflect both their producer's interest and the object to be represented. Constitutive here is the tension between the meanings of existing signs and the need to produce new signs. Because signs form systems of meaning, there is nothing else to start from but the old signs. Those are the 'normal' ones that 'make sense' and seem 'universal'. Signs are *motivated* from both points of view – of the object and subject. *Interest* selects the characteristics to be represented. Interest is the articulation and realisation of a relationship to an object. It includes multiple factors such as individual and group positioning, intentions and strategies, situational imperatives and structures of power. Signification takes place in collective and historic way, not in individual and isolated face-to-face communication.

The criterial aspect of selecting one characteristic form a signified and making it an apt signifier is the process of construction of *metaphor*. The link between what is selected from the signified and isolated – sometimes at an unimaginable distance – as signifier seems arbitrary only when the conditions, its production and the criterial aspect of the interests remain invisible. Critical reading starts when the observer sees through that presumed arbitrariness, and then, they make visible the *criterial* relation between motivated object and subject.

> The relation of signifier to signified, in all human semiotic systems is always motivated, and it is never arbitrary.... 'Interest' leads the producer of the sign to focus on a particular characteristic of an object or event (whether in an object or event in the physical or in the social/cultural, semiotic world) to make that criterial characteristic of the object or event, that is to make it basis of the production of the signified. [In that sense] all signs are metaphors [and] no sign is innocent.
>
> (Kress, 1993, p. 174)

An everyday, mundane text is equally, if not more, ideologically saturated than an overt political programme. A junk mail is not less political – it is just more indirect – than a protest leaflet. The unsaid, the silently assumed, the taken for granted – the invisible that is present – has the highest ideological impact and not what is noisily stated, affirmed or argued.

From a semiotic point of view, *recognition* also depends on the criterial relation between motivated subject and object. The critical question: Does a group self-represent as a subject? Or is it only represented as an object? 'Gaining visibility' as an object is not good enough. It could even be only part of the silencing of that object – if it is a group. Does gaining visibility also support finding one's own voice? Not the voice of the representer – the voice of the represented? Because the voice of the representer may at the same time overwrite – hush up, suppress – the voice of the represented – are the represented only listening to those who talk on their behalf? Is that their role? Foucault fumed about the 'indignity of speaking for others' (Foucault, 1980). And Guy Debord criticised the separation of publicity from the public and transformation of capital into image. In the 'spectacle' he found the alienation of the object of signification from its subject (1994).

John Berger sees the whole history of Western European painting as a display of woman as the desired object by man – the spectator-owner of a picture. In that regard, the new époque of reproduction and publicity has not changed much. 'That art makes inequality seem noble and hierarchies seem thrilling' (Berger, 1972, p. 29). Nudity, he adds, is not nakedness. Nakedness is revealing oneself as a subject. Nudity is putting on display someone's body as an object. It is *visibility that makes the invisible*. The display turns into disguise. 'Nudity is a form of dress' (Berger, 1972, p. 54).

Baudrillard makes a radical step in the opposite direction. When the (male) subject paints the (female) object, nakedness and nudity may reflect the relation. But in our mediated hyper-reality, there is the reverse determination of objects working on the subjects. In those relations, all *visual has become pornography*. Pornography is the fascination with absolute transparency, with the close up. Nothing is hidden. But no seduction is left either.

> In truth we never *really* look at these images. Looking implies the object viewed covers and uncovers itself, that it disappears at every instant, for looking involves a kind of oscillation. The body is already there *without even the faintest glimmer of a possible absence* [italics of J. B.], in the state of radical presence. In an image certain parts are visible, while others are not; visible parts render the others invisible, and a rhythm of emergence and secrecy sets in, a kind of watermark of the imaginary. While here everything is of equal visibility, everything shares the same shallow space. And fascination comes precisely from this disembodiment.
>
> (Baudrillard, 2012, p. 33)

Baudrillard refers here to Octavio Paz' 'aesthetic of disembodiment' – passion of gaze without an object, of a gaze without an image. Paz writes about Baudelaire's take on Wagner's musing as *disembodiment of presence*. Sensations of 'altitude and voluptuousness' are associated with the loss of body. 'The feeling of being at a frontier: space extends so that in fact it is invisible and inconceivable: non-space, non-time' (Paz, 1992, p. 60). Baudrillard generalises that in the 'radical presence' of the image that says everything and reveals nothing – 'an image where there is nothing to see' (p. 32). 'Nothing takes place, and yet we are saturated by it' (Baudrillard, 2012, p. 34).

Radical proximity and presence of the image expel silence because silence secures the distance from which the subject reconciles past, presence and future. Coincidence is the work of silence. Absolute presence suspends silence because it disembodies time into a series of instances. It is not lived silence any longer. It is, perhaps, the Internet noise – the remnants of silence, which will stay mummified there forever. When we are fascinated, we are hearing but not listening, looking but not seeing. Appearances lead to appearances, not to meaning. Sidelines sliding, not going deeper.

Yet there is a difference between an original painting and an advertised – promoted – image. For Berger, the original one is silent, in a quaint way. Silence permeates the surface. In stillness, traces of the painter's immediate gestures become alive. The time distance disappears. That is, the act of painting of the picture and act of looking at it become one. 'In this special sense, all paintings are contemporary' (Berger, 1972, p. 31).

Advertising produces high-visibility objects. It sharpens the recognition. It focuses the look. Its effect is an instant identification of an object as figure; the pleasure can come later (Brighenti, 2007). 'Publicity images also belong to the moment', says Berger, 'in the sense of that they must be continually renewed and made up-to-date. Yet they never speak of the present' (1972, p. 130). The present is by definition insufficient. It only offers ephemeral images and future tense. Publicity images feed upon the real and serve the spectators with dreams, which only make them more unsatisfied – and unhappy – with the present. Their desirable future replicates the enviable presence of others. That future is endlessly deferred.

> How then does publicity remain credible – or credible enough to exert the influence it does? It remains credible because the truthfulness of publicity is judged, not by the real fulfilment of its promises, but by the relevance of its phantasies to those of the spectator-buyer. Its essential application is not to reality but to day-dreams.
>
> (Berger, 1972)

Feminist and postmodernist approaches tap into Berger's problematisation of the object–subject asymmetry in the representation of women. Visibility is neither disinterested, nor indifferent. Important is not only what representations say about women but also what representation *does* to women (Owens, 1985). If signification is motivated (from both object and subject) and interested (from both producer and consumer), the result is a *privileged signifier*.

A privileged signifier imposes the standards of the privileged viewer (man) and deletes – denies – the difference of the viewed (woman) as a *lack* (of what man has). The symbol of phallus, for example, signifies the (lack of) sexual difference by how man *sights* woman. Raised ('aufgehoben', in the sense of Hegel,

Adorno and Lacan) from a signified to a signifier, the phallus has the potence to present a woman just as a man but only less perfect and lacking his strength. That way, a privileged signifier delivers the credibility and legitimacy of an 'objective' and 'transparent' image.

Being represented – and without access to self-representation – ties vision to power. Visibility here amounts to silencing. Even if the man's vision strips and lays bare a woman, it does *not unveil* her. This is what Berger means when he distinguishes between nakedness and nudity: *more visibility for the object of representation makes it only more invisible as a subject of representation.* And vice versa. 'The phallus can play its role only when veiled', says Lacan.[5]

Images are vehicles of indirect communication. What is visible is the sign. The signified is invisible. Even when the phallus is the right signified to become a signifier, its raising (*aufhebung*) makes it identical with itself (fully visible) only in appearance. The power – 'potence' – of an image, what it 'initiates' and 'inaugurates', is what lies beneath its surface. Visibility is the toy, invisibility – the playground of imagination.

Mediated invisibility and power

Although it is not a zero-sum game, visibility and invisibility are unequally distributed, sometimes the one at the expense of other. That is some become more visible while others become less. In other words, the tension between visibility and invisibility may reflect and actively mediate inequalities of power, recognition, prestige, competition and so on.

Invisibility, however, is not necessarily an attribute of lower social positions or lack of power. Invisibility may also protect wealth and hide control. And visibility may disable and disempower. The Panopticum for example, reverses the principle of the dungeon. 'Full lighting and the eye of a supervisor capture better than darkness, which ultimately protected. Visibility is a trap', says Foucault (1977, p. 200). In the disciplinary society, the surveyance of prisoners, women, children or workers imposes a new way of control and self-control – even by the mere awareness that one is watched.

There is a long post-Foucauldian thread of theories of subjugating by making visible. Deleuze' 'society of control' does not watch individual people but systematically tracks flows of capital and information (Deleuze, 1990). Haggerty and Ericson see in the pervasiveness of 'surveillant assemblages' a shift from public safety, urban regulation and virtual education to embedded, automatic and impersonal control of data flows (2000, p. 619). Invisibility, on the contrary, becomes a sign of luxury, privilege and power. Part of the unfavourable image of the PR industry is associated with what Scott Cutlip named *The Unseen Power* (1994). 'Faceless', 'machine men' (despite the feminisation of the profession) influence the society by backroom deals, away from the scrutiny of the public eye (Mills, 1986).

Strategy is always asymmetric. As choreography of public attention, public relations deals with complex arrangements of asymmetries between visibilities and invisibilities. A two-way symmetric strategy does not exist. Engagement and dialogue, for example, are not ends but only means (tactics) for achieving asymmetric (strategic) ends. Through new technologies and the Internet, both visibility and invisibility – similar to presence and absence – are mediated. They are freed from the spatial and temporal properties of here and now (Thompson, 2005, 2011). They are situated, thus, also subject of strategy. Strategy secedes when the asymmetry between visibility and invisibility normalises. In *Relations in Public*, Goffman analyses 'normal appearances' as representing the state of invisibility. The normal is invisible, transparent. The exception from the normal, the deviant, the dangerous and alarming is visible, opaque (Goffman, 2009). The normal as invisible is 'unmarked, unnoticed, unthematized, untheorized' (Brighenti, 2007, p. 326).

In *mediated visibility*, we see not only those who are co-present – we see that they see us. We also see those who are absent and do not see us. And, at the same time, mediated vision can also achieve the opposite, as in the discussed cases of invisible people. There is *mediated invisibility*, too. It can make those who are the co-present (next to us, here and now) invisible and absent even when we can see them – as they can see us.

As with silence and non-silence, invisibility is often the other side of visibility. In other words, their link is not disjunction (either/or) but conjunction (and/and). As with the unsaid, the visible may hide or point at an invisible meaning. In that regard, we can talk about *silent images* – visual signs that tell more than or are different from what they show. Those silent pictures are *not* just *extensions* of silence in multimodal settings, where the invisible has a supporting role to the silent (Jaworski, 1993, 1997). This view is still language-centred, logocentrist.

We should not forget that, for Foucault, the visible is a precondition for the sayable – not an enclosure. Marshall McLuhan emphasises the primacy of the visual to the verbal in written texts due to the polysemic character of typographic technologies (1994).[6] Images and logos can do more than words to display the global unity and durability of a brand, remaining at the same time silent on the differences in the concrete experiences with that brand (Lury, 1999). From a semiotic point of view, silence is a property not of each mode separately – like 'unsaid' in the verbal, 'unseen' in the visual and 'pause/noise' in the musical modes. Silence is a property of the discourse itself. The multimodal discourse is a system of meanings, which is 'above' the modes. Yet it cannot be produced – realised, modified, negated – other than by the use of modes and media (Kress & van Leeuwen, 2001).

Both visibility and invisibility, including their effects, are ambivalent. They are not directly or automatically tied with power. The exercise of power is also situational, strategic. It is an exercise in selecting and activating in/visibilities (Brighenti, 2007, p. 339). Strategic in that regard is not only the decision which position to make visible and which not, but also the extent and measure of in/visibility. For example, gaining super-visibility may be detrimental. The super-visibility of a brand may weaken it into a generic one. Too much recognition may amount to loss of recognition (Low & Blois, 2002). The strategy of branding by putting the best foot forward may backfire. A generic brand represents not only the signified particular company but also becomes a universal signifier for a range of products or a whole industry. A signified, singled out as signifier, loses its strategic quality of differentiation.

Mediated super-visibility may also correspond with almost full political invisibility. Such are, for example, the experiences of marginalised groups in Western rural landscapes (Milbourne & Cloke, 2013; Robinson & Gardner, 2004). The *discursive absence* of Muslims there is due to their exclusion from popular imaginations of idyllised rural space. Small Muslim communities remain hidden, silent and 'subterranean' with makeshift mosques behind front shops (Jones, 2012). This surface-absence, however, may be interpreted as 'clandestine' and 'sinister', especially when an open request for building a mosque or religious school is made. Then, the overreaction of the traditionally white community may lead to mediated super-visibility of Muslims 'swamping' and 'Islamising' a community 'under siege' (McGrath, 2014).

In a paradoxic way, the principle of creating a generic brand works also here. The media, for example, use a higher level of linguistic *abstractness* when they describe migrants and other minorities. Higher abstractness not only dehumanises a group but also assigns 'inherent' and 'natural' features to its behaviour – not to its situation (Geschke, Sassenberg, Ruhrmann & Sommer, 2015). Differences get lost. Self-representation is deleted. As a result, one can easier take the concrete for general and the signified for a signifier. 'They do not integrate'; 'They keep to themselves'; 'They are sneaky'; 'Muslims are terrorists'; 'Radical Islamism' has become a collocation – not 'Radical Christianity' – the worst, not the best represents the rest. This is generic branding, just upside down.

Notes

1 In the UK and Australia, that September 2015 event triggered a political process that led to an increased intake of Syrian refugees by those countries. Both Prime Ministers, David Cameron and Tony Abbott, expressed their 'shock' from seeing that image. Mr Cameron 'felt deeply moved'. Mr Abbott felt about the images of the lifeless boy 'very sad'. In the same breath, he added that such images only confirm that other countries had to adopt his tough policy of stopping asylum seekers arriving by boat (Knott, 2015). There is something eerie about the inevitability of the 'shocked' cliché that politicians and leaders use by default. They have already been privy to what has been shown. They have been familiar with it. The only news was the sudden access of the public to it. Is seeing so exclusive in comparison to other senses, including hearing, so that reading or listening to reports does not shock but seeing a visual does? Or does not the shock come from another direction: the relational effect of the visual event? Are the representatives shocked from seeing the picture or rather from seeing how many others are seeing it – seeing it *and* watching others seeing them seeing it? As Marcel Duchamp once observed, 'One can look at seeing but one can't hear hearing' (Buskirk & Nixon, 1996, p. 112).

2 Here are some recent examples of consequential video advocacy by the Australian public TV broadcaster ABC. In February 2015, the *Four Corners* programme screened an undercover footage from the *Animal Liberation Queensland* and *Animals Australia*

that showed wide practices in the multimillion-dollar greyhound industry of training with life bites and mass killings of the underperforming dogs (Meldrum-Hanna & Clark, 2015). In July 2016, after a Special Commission of Inquiry found evidence of systematic cruelty, New South Wales became the first Australian state to shut down greyhound racing (Godfrey, 2016). (This ban, however, was reversed again in 2017.) In June 2016, the *7:30 Report* programme showed Vietnamese abattoirs bludgeoning what appears to be Australian live export cattle with sledgehammers. Undercover investigators hired by *Animals Australia* filmed the vision (Thomas, Robinson, & Armitage, 2016). The Federal Government instantly launched an inquiry. This time, the industry self-imposed a ban of live exports to three Vietnamese abattoirs, without waiting for the results from the investigation (Thomsen, 2016a). In 2011, and in similar circumstances, the Australian Labor government temporary banned exports of live cattle to Indonesia, which caused a political backlash on the relations between both countries. In July 2016, again the *Four Corners* programme of ABC showed CCTV footage from the Northern Territories Don Dale juvenile justice detention centre, where Aboriginal boys as young as ten and 13 a locked up, kept in solitary confinement, stripped naked, assaulted and tear-gassed. A take from that visual – a boy, hooded, shackled, strapped to a chair and left alone – went viral in Australia and around the world (Meldrum-Hanna, Fallon & Worthington, 2016). The next day the Prime Minister, Malcolm Turnbull, announced a royal commission into the child protection and youth detention in the Northern Territory (Thomsen, 2016b). Yet this quick move did not stifle the public outrage. It set not the end but only the beginning of a chain of momentous events. They stared with the complaints of Aboriginal organisations that they had not been consulted; the resignation of the royal commissioner, Former Northern Territory chief justice Brian Martin, in less than a week after his nomination; and the new 'more balanced' appointment of, this time, two co-commissioners into the inquiry: former Queensland Supreme Court Justice, Margaret White, and the Aboriginal and Torres Strait Island Social Justice Commissioner at the Human Rights Commission, Mick Gooda (Owens, 2016). Again, a few ministers, politicians and servants who had seen the two-year-old video in the past were equally 'shocked', as the public that saw it for the first time.

3 On a lighter note, Tom Peters muses about 'showing up': 'There's a Woody Allen one-liner I love: "Eighty percent of success is showing up". (I reckon 85 percent)' (1994, p. 31).

4 Bakhtin develops the concept of chronotope as time-space configuration in his essay *Forms of time and of the chronotope in the novel* (2010). Its critical value is in the heightened awareness of the prevalence of *spatial metaphors* in Western languages, which – both in everyday life and science – fix and flatten diachronic events to 'sites' and 'places'. Others such as Roland Barthes, Michel Foucault, George Lakoff, James Scott and Adam Jaworski have also paid special attention to how unchecked spatial metaphors exercise power and form knowledge, relations and identity. Silence, which is both diachronic and synchronic – also falls victim to that metaphorical reduction in phrases such as 'zone of silence', 'grave silence', 'void of silence' and 'temples of silence'. For this analysis, it is vital to deconstruct the spatial metaphor of silence and reconstruct its time-space dynamics.

5 The whole citation from his 'The signification of the phallus':

> The phallus can play its role only when veiled, that is to say, as itself a sign of the latency with which any signifiable is struck, when it is raised (*aufgehoben*) to the function of the signifier. The phallus is the signifier of this *Aufhebung* itself, which inaugurates (initiates) by its disappearance.
>
> (Lacan, 2002, p. 692)

6 Jacques Derrida also prioritises the method of *deconstruction* as confronting written texts through written texts for similar reasons: the hierarchy of sensual perceptions and power of the visual order of signs, especially the implicit inequalities programmed in

binomial constructs (Derrida, 1996; Derrida, Caws & Caws, 1982). Phillip McGuire discusses the *open silences* in Shakespeare's plays (1985). He points at various places where the text 'withdraws', shuts up and lets the director and actors choose how to interpret and play a certain situation. Those open silences, McGuire states, are deliberate and strategic, and not accidental gaps left by the different and incomplete texts of the plays that have survived. Shakespeare was the author but also the director, actor and producer of plays. His point of view was the 'living improvisation' subject to changing context and interpretation, and not the dogma of a text frozen in time. Silence allows a play to prevail over the text. Or, to put it differently, the script is not the text but the act. McGuire criticises a tradition of scholars who try to understand Shakespeare by taking his texts literally and, at the same time, problematises the limits of the said in the multimodal setting of the stage and constantly changing context of performers and publics. There are lessons for public relations strategy too. Message strategies, for example, should not be confused with text writing. Open silences in the scripts of message delivery should allow both freedom of interpretation and awareness of the limits of saying in a multimodal performance.

References

Bakhtin, M. M. (2010). *The dialogic imagination: Four essays* (Vol. 1). Austin, TX: University of Texas Press.

Baudrillard, J. (2012). *The ecstasy of communication*. Los Angeles, CA: Semiotext(e).

Bauman, Z. (2002). In the lowly nowherevilles of liquid modernity: Comments on and around Agier. *Ethnography, 3*, 343–349.

Berger, J. (1972). *Ways of seeing*. London: BBC, Penguin.

Brighenti, A. (2007). Visibility a category for the social sciences. *Current Sociology, 55*(3), 323–342.

Buskirk, M., & Nixon, M. (1996). *The Duchamp effect*. Cambridge, MA: MIT Press.

Clair, R. P. (1993). *Organising silence: A world of possibilities*. New York: State University of New York Press.

Cutlip, S. (1994). *The unseen power: Public relations, a history*. Hillsdale, NJ: Lawrence Erlbaum Associates.

Debord, G. (1994). *The society of the spectacle*. New York: Zone Books.

Deleuze, G. (1990). Postscript on the societies of control. *October, 59*(Winter 1992), 3–7.

Deleuze, G. (2006). *Foucault*. London: Bloomsbury.

Derrida, J. (1996). Remarks on deconstruction and pragmatism. In C. Mouffe (Ed.), *Deconstruction and Pragmatism* (p. 84). London: Routledge.

Derrida, J., Caws, P. & Caws, M. A. (1982). Sending: On representation. *Social Research, 42*(2, Summer), 294–326.

Dimitrov, R. (2008). Acting strategically: Skilled communication by Australian refugee advocacy groups. *Global Media Journal, 2*(2). Retrieved 12 June 2017, from http://stc.uws.edu.au/gmjau/iss2_2008/Roumen_Dimitrov v2_2 2008.html.

Dimitrov, R. (2014). 'Does this guy ever shut up?' The discourse of the 2013 Australian Election. *Global Media Journal: Australian Edition, 8*(2).

Foucault, M. (1972). *The archaeology of knowledge*. London: Routledge.

Foucault, M. (1973). *The birth of the clinique: An archaeology of medical perception*. London: Tavistock Publications.

Foucault, M. (1977). *Discipline and punish: The birth of the prison*. London: Penguin.

Foucault, M. (1980). Intellectuals and power: A conversation between Michel Foucault and Gill Deleuze. In M. Foucault (Ed.), *Language, counter-memory, practice: Selected essays and interviews* (pp. 205–217). Ithaca, NY: Cornell University Press.

Foucault, M. (2003). *Society must be defended: Lectures at the College de France 1975–76*. London: Penguin.

Franke, W. (2012). Apophatic paths: Modern and contemporary poetics and aesthetics of nothing. *Angelaki, 17*(3), 7–16.

Freydkin, D. (2015). How Richard Gere went from sexy to invisible. *USA Today*. Retrieved 12 June 2017, from www.usatoday.com/story/life/movies/2015/09/08/how-richard-gere-went-sexy-invisible-time-out-mind/71645774/.

Geschke, D., Sassenberg, K., Ruhrmann, G., & Sommer, D. (2015). Effects of linguistic abstractness in the mass media. *Journal of Media Psychology, 22*(3), 99–104.

Godfrey, M. (2016). NSW greyhound racing industry to be shut down from 2017. *Daily Telegraph*. Retrieved 12 June 2017, from www.dailytelegraph.com.au/news/nsw/nsw-greyhound-racing-industry-to-be-shut-down-from-2017/news-story/3d45e451862a987 3d3ae506afdcd8458.

Goffman, E. (2009). *Relations in public*. New Brunswick, NJ: Transaction Publishers.

Gregory, S. (2006). Transnational storytelling: Human rights, WITNESS, and video advocacy. *American Anthropologist, March 2006, 108*(1), 195–204.

Haggerty, K. D., & Ericson, R. V. (2000). The surveillant assemblage. *British Journal of Sociology, 51*(4), 605–622.

Howes, D. (2010). *Sensual relations: Engaging the senses in culture and social theory*. Ann Arbor, MI: University of Michigan Press.

Jaworski, A. (1993). *The power of silence: Social and pragmatic perspectives*. Newbury Park, CA: Sage.

Jaworski, A. (Ed.). (1997). *Silence: interdisciplinary perspectives* (Vol. 10). Berlin; New York: Mouton de Gruyter.

Jones, R. D. (2012). Negotiating absence and presence: rural Muslims and 'subterranean' sacred spaces. *Space and Polity, 16*(3), 335–350.

Jones, R. D., Robinson, J. & Turner, J. (2012). Introduction. Between absence and presence: Geographies of hiding, invisibility and silence. *Space and Polity, 16*(3), 257–263.

Knott, M. (2015). Drowned Syrian toddler: Tony Abbott says 'tragic' picture a reminder of need to stop boats. *The Sydney Morning Herald*. Retrieved 12 June 2017, from www.smh.com.au/federal-politics/political-news/drowned-syrian-toddler-tony-abbott-says-tragic-picture-a-reminder-of-need-to-stop-boats-20150903-gjevx5.html.

Kress, G. (1993). Against arbitrariness: The social production of the sign as a foundational issue in critical discourse analysis. *Discourse & Society, 4*(2), 169–191.

Kress, G., & van Leeuwen, T. (2001). *Multimodal discourse: The modes and media of contemporary communication*. London: Edward Arnold.

Kwiatkowska, A. (1997). Silence across modalities. In A. Jaworski (Ed.), *Silence: Interdisciplinary perspectives* (pp. 329–337). Berlin; New York: Mouton de Gruyter.

Lacan, J. (2002). *Écrits: A selection (translated by Bruce Fink)*. New York: Norton.

Lester, L., & Hutchins, B. (2012). The power of the unseen: environmental conflict, the media and invisibility. *Media, Culture & Society, 34*(7), 847–863.

Low, J., & Blois, K. (2002). The evolution of generic brands in industrial markets: the challenges to owners of brand equity. *Industrial Marketing Management, 31*(5), 385–392.

Lury, C. (1999). Marking time with Nike: The illusion of the durable. *Public Culture, 11*(3), 499–526.

McGrath, G. (2014). Anti-Islamic group moves to stop mosque. *Camden-Narellan Advertiser*. Retrieved 12 June 2017, from www.camdenadvertiser.com.au/story/2062242/anti-islamic-group-moves-to-stop-mosque/.

McGuire, P. C. (1985). *Speechless dialect: Shakespeare's open silences*: Berkeley, CA: University of California Press.

McKinlay, A., & Starkey, K. (1998). Managing Foucault: Foucault, management and organization theory. In A. McKinlay & K. Starkey (Eds.), *Foucault, management and organization theory* (pp. 1–13). London: Sage.

McLuhan, M. (1994). *Understanding media: The extensions of man*. Cambridge, MA: MIT Press.

Meldrum-Hanna, C., & Clark, S. (2015). Making a killing. *ABC Four Corners*. Retrieved 12 June 2017, from www.abc.net.au/4corners/stories/2015/02/16/4178920.htm.

Meldrum-Hanna, C., Fallon, M., & Worthington, E. (2016). Australia's shame. *ABC Four Corners*. Retrieved 12 June 2017, from www.abc.net.au/4corners/stories/2016/07/25/4504895.htm.

Mey, J. L. (1997). The invisible man: Of silence and comets: Reflections on a cover picture. *Journal of Pragmatics, 27*(3), 387–392.

Milbourne, P., & Cloke, P. J. (Eds.). (2013). *International perspectives on rural homelessness*. New York; London: Routledge.

Miller, V. (2012). A crisis of presence: On-line culture and being in the world. *Space and Polity, 16*(3), 265–285.

Mills, S. (1986). *The new machine men: Polls and persuasion in Australian politics*. Ringwood, Victoria: Penguin.

Owens, C. (Ed.) (1985). *The discourse of others: Feminists and postmodernism*. New York: The New Press.

Owens, J. (2016). Mick Gooda and Margaret White to be NT royal commissioners. *The Australian*. Retrieved 12 June 2017, from www.theaustralian.com.au/national-affairs/brian-martin-reconsiders-leading-nt-royal-commission/news-story/17efce1242090aee1edd0394713588b0.

Paz, O. (1992). Bauddelaire as art critic: Presence and present. In O. Paz (Ed.), *On poets and others* (pp. 50–65). London: Paladin.

Perelman, C. (1982). *The realm of rhetoric*. Notre Dame, IN: University of Notre Dame Press.

Peters, T. (1994). *The pursuit of Wow! Every person's guide to topsy-turvy times*. New York: Vintage Books.

Robinson, V., & Gardner, H. (2004). Unravelling a stereotype: The lived experience of black and minority ethnic people in rural Wales. In N. Chakrabourti & J. Garland (Eds.), *Rural racism* (pp. 85–107). Cullompton, Devon: Willan.

Shen, Y., & Cohen, M. (1998). How come silence is sweet but sweetness is not silent: A cognitive account of directionality in poetic synaesthesia. *Language and Literature, 7*(2), 123–140.

Silverstone, R. (2003). Proper distance: Towards an ethics for cyberspace. In G. Liestol, A. Morrison & R. Terie (Eds.), *Digital media revisited* (pp. 469–491). Cambridge, MA: MIT Press.

Thomas, J., Robinson, L., & Armitage, R. (2016). 'Australian cattle' being bludgeoned to death in Vietnam sparks Government investigation. *ABC 7:30 Report*. Retrieved 12 June 2017, from www.abc.net.au/news/2016-06-16/australian-cattle-bludgeoned-with-sledgehammer-in-vietnam/7516326.

Thompson, J. B. (2005). The new visibility. *Theory, Culture & Society, 22*(6), 31–51.

Thompson, J. B. (2011). Shifting boundaries of public and private life. *Theory, Culture & Society, 28*(4), 49–70.

Thomsen, S. (2016a, 17 June). Here are the terms of reference for the royal commission into the Northern Territory's juvenile detention system. *Business Insider.* Retrieved 12 June 2017, from www.businessinsider.com.au/here-are-the-terms-of-reference-for-the-royal-commission-into-the-northern-territorys-juvenile-detention-system-2016-7.

Thomsen, S. (2016b, 28 July). Live cattle exports to Vietnam have been banned after more animal cruelty allegations. *Business Insider.* Retrieved 12 June 2017, from www.businessinsider.com.au/live-cattle-exports-to-vietnam-have-been-banned-after-more-animal-cruelty-allegations-2016-6.

Torchin, L. (2006). Ravished Armenia: Visual media, humanitarian advocacy, and the formation of witnessing publics. *American Anthropologist, 108*(1), 214–220.

Wylie, J. (2009). Landscape, absence and the geographies of love. *Transactions of the Institute of British Geographers, 34*(3), 275–289.

7   Communication and silence

Silencing communication

PR practitioners are using silence all the time. They do that not only *tactically*, between instances of speaking – refusing, for example, to make a comment or to give a story legs. More importantly, they are silent in speaking and speaking in silence. They are silent *strategically*.

Strategic silence – as any communication strategy – is a form of *indirect communication*. For example, third party endorsement and word of mouth are effects of strategic communication. We tacitly let someone who is more credible than we are take ownership of our message. We step back and allow someone who is more authoritative to vouch for us. *As strategic communication, PR is essentially indirect communication.*

The failure of the discipline of PR to outline and integrate the category of silence into its theory, is partly due to the lack of a multi-layered macro-model of indirect communication. I would suggest that such a model could help better understand and perhaps define anew the role of PR as *choreography of public attention through indirect communication.*

In defence of PR, I should say that communication studies discovered the effects and significance of silence relatively late. In religion and philosophy, silence has always loomed large, especially as critique of profane epistemology (see Chapter 13). As a modern communications problem, however, silence has a relatively short career. It probably starts with the ground-breaking, although still moral-religious, work of Max Picard *The World of Silence* (1952). Most approaches and authors from which I borrow ideas clash with entrenched Western biases against silence. A tradition in Western thinking, which roots in Enlightenment, regards language and eloquent speaking as the crown of civilisation (Mann, 1927). Word breaks the silence as light breaks the darkness. The virtues of *eloquent silence* were realised much later (Ephratt, 2008).

The stigma of silence also rests on the legitimate democratic-liberal suspicion of the muzzling effects of oppression – of *silencing communication*. In this book, I also discuss various forms of *complicit silence*. It protects the mutual interest of collaborating agents, including of journalists and PR practitioners (see Chapters 3, 14). Progressive scholars study oppressed groups such as employees,

women or ethnic minorities as largely silent and invisible. Emancipative political communication can help such groups find their 'voice', 'gain visibility', get
'recognition' and 'place at the table' (Edwards, 2017; Greenberg & Edwards,
2009). Silencing communication is bad. It subjugates and censors. The silence of
those who cannot speak for themselves. The silence of women. The silence of
the Catholic Church about children's sexual abuse. In Australia, the conservative
government declared its policy of intercepting and returning boats with refugees
at high seas an 'operational matter'. Through the establishment of a *Border
Force*, it criminalised a humanitarian issue, paramilitarised part of the public
service and imposed informational blackout on the movements of asylum seekers
(Barns & Newhouse, 2015). The refugee advocates and inquisitive media have
been successfully silenced. Both the refugee issue and civil society have
retreated. 'Bad silence' is real.

But there is also an *ideological bias* against silence, which serves the capitalist markets. The *machine metaphor*, for example, equates silence with *malfunction* (Scollon, 1985). In the (pre-Brexit and pre-Trumpian) transition from
national productive to global financial markets, capital transactions have sped
up. Silence is increasingly associated with inefficient pause and idle disfluency.
The bureaucratic rationality of 'maximising winning and minimising losses'
does not accept any slowing down or grinding to a halt. It suspects subversion in
any abating of noise, in any 'give us a break'. As attribution theorists suggest,
the metaphor of silence as malfunction has evolved from a specific socio-cultural
way of thinking and acting into a naturalised worldview in global capitalism. An
accidental hegemon in history (Marx) has attributed it to other groups as 'universal truth' (Argyris & Schon, 1974).

Silence as the opposite of speed: 'Speed kills' has become a rule of thumb in
political communication. The mastery of campaigning seems to depend on how
quickly we respond to the attacks of opponents (*'re-buttal'*) or, better, pre-empt
such attacks (*'pre-buttal'*) (Gaber, 2000). 'Silent' is just another derogative for
'slow'. The first one who manages to comment on a news influences it most. The
first interpretation of a fact envelops, packages it. It becomes part of the fact; it
gives it a spin. Slower commentators must interpret not only the fact but also its
frame. Even if they attack that frame, they only reinforce it (Lakoff, 2004, 2010).

The former Prime Minister of Australia, John Howard, was a master of such
first-past-the-post appropriation of facts. He was the first federal leader who
campaigned permanently (Blumenthal, 1982; Sparrow & Turner, 2001). He gave
more time to communicating than to governing. He adjusted his working day to
the 24 hours new cycle. Every morning his team analysed the chance of any
early news in a blog or newspaper to become *the* evening TV news. In the early
afternoon, Howard went to a talkback radio – always accompanied by camera-
men – and 'unexpectedly' commented on news that has not happened on TV yet
(Sinodinos, 2007). That way, he either primed it as news or framed it in advance.
And, in addition, the broadcasters already had a visual. If you want to be
powerful, you'd better be quick. You do not waste time in silence. Slow communication is inefficient. The machine metaphor works here in full steam.

Silencing communication, however, turns out to be a relativist and superficial term. Its meaning depends on its uses. It is value-laden, judgemental and subjective. It is bad if the opponent silences us. But it is good if we silence the opponent. No deeper measure should apply. 'Silencing' presupposes that those who are 'silenced' have not been silent in the past or that someone does not allow them to speak. It assumes an artificial and forced from outside setback from a natural state of free speech. This may be the case, as in the *Border Force* example above. But such regressive and unambiguous category automatically excludes the majority of oppressed groups, who are either officially expected not to talk or use silence to resist and have their way in everyday life (de Certeau, 1984; Clegg, Courpasson & Phillips, 2006; Scott, 2008a, 2008b).

'Silencing' may 'disempower'. But silence can also empower. In other words, power relations are possibly but not necessarily between those who are privileged to speak and those who are pressed to remain silent. It could be the opposite. Silence could be the best asset – and strongest strategy – of power. One does not need to look further but at George Orwell's Big Brother (1949), Michel Foucault's 'panopticon' (1977) or Giles Deleuze' 'control society' (1995). Modern power controls the population 'scientifically' by making it a visible and audible subject of permanent survey. Those are still relations of imbalanced power, but the opposite of 'silencing communication'. Silence and invisibility become either attributes of 'softening' power or 'weapons of the weak' who use caginess and camouflage to stay out of its reach. Many recent publications keenly declare and explore the *power of silence* (Clair, 1993; Glenn, 2004; Jaworski, 1993; Kenny, 2011; Kurzon, 1992; Malhotra & Rowe, 2013; Medina, 2004; Trouillot, 1995).

Communicative silence

For those and other reasons argued later, I prefer the alternative term of *communicative silence*. It still includes applications such as silencing communication. But its meaning is deeper, beneath the surface of its objective appearances. *Strategic silences* are also concrete applications of communicative silence. Once we have clarified what communicative silence is – or what it is *not* – it will be easier to move to its strategic uses. Here, I use 'silence' as the shortcut for 'communicative silence'. I qualify 'silence' only when the meanings of both terms do not converge.

There is no abstract silence. Silence as such does not exist. Any taxonomy of silences would be futile. Even the 'collected silences' of Doctor Murke, the radio journalist from the story of the same name by Heinrich Böll, were tape cuts with all chance silences of his interviewees, which only he could hear and appreciate (Böll, 1966). Equally, there is no absolute silence. The regulations of absolute silence in the Solitary Prison in the penal colony in eighteenth century Tasmania were designed to break the felon-self through silence and sort of exorcising the 'criminal' out of the 'worst offenders' bodies (Hughes, 1987). But even the complete and most extreme use of silence,[1] could not entirely destroy all social relations between prisoners and between prisoners and warders (Frow, 1999).

Communicative silence does not prevent hearing. On the contrary, it makes people listen. John Cage rejected the notion of absolute silence (Cage, 1961). In 1957, the pianist David Tudor performed his 'silent piece' *4'33* for the first time. For 4 minutes and 33 seconds, he made no sound. Cage recalls the premiere:

> There is no such thing as silence. What they thought was silence, because they didn't know how to listen, was full of accidental sounds. You could hear the wind stirring outside during the first movement. During the second, raindrops began pattering the roof, and during the third the people themselves made all kinds of interesting sounds as they talked or walked out.
>
> (Kostelanez, 2003, p. 71)

Silencing communication is a *relative* term. (Communicative) silence is a *relational* category. We define silence only in relation to something else, to non-silence. The reverse move is also possible. In Gestalt psychology terms (I will often use them), silence can not only be figure (determinate) to background (determinant) but also background to figure (Neubauer, 1987). In other words, *silence can also determine what non-silence is* – this will be an important aspect of strategic silence. In speech and writing, the unsaid is defined in relation to the said. And vice versa. In a discourse, the presupposed (not mentioned because taken for granted) is defined in relation to the stated (explicitly expressed). And vice versa. There is no pure silence. Even 'the artist who creates silence or emptiness', says Susan Sontag, 'must produce something dialectical: a full void, an enriching emptiness, a resonating and eloquent silence' (1982, p. 187).

Structural silence

For Niklas Luhmann one cannot separate speech from silence because both together secure the main function of *communication as a paradox* (1994, pp. 26–27). I will call it functional or *structural silence*, a condition of any communication. It is different from strategic silence, which is always situational and depends on purpose, context and problem solving. The paradox of communication: we produce the unity of what is different, the coincidence of communication and non-communication. Communication does not tell [*mitteilen*] the world; it divides [*einteilen*] it. It says what it says and it does not say what it does not say. It differentiates. Both saying and not saying produce a cut – as caesura, an emphasis, a boundary. A function of silence is to tell one thought from another. That way silence sets the pace and rhythm of thinking. When we communicate, we reduce the world to what we point at and observe. We are not only silent about the rest, but we use silence to set inner boundaries. Silence lends clarity to speech by destroying continuity (Bruneau, 1973, pp. 18–19).

Communication structures silence. National discourses, media and events determine what is appropriate to say and what is not. In official commemorations, for example, some people are remembered as heroes and some are let out of history. But silence also structures communication. Silence is no longer a communicative effect but rather agency of change when an Aboriginal woman refuses to speak for her whole life (Mushin & Gardner, 2009) or world leaders march silently against terrorism in Paris (Philips, 1985).

Luhmann believes the world is *incommunicable*. Paradoxical communication projects the world as unity of difference. It is not the world, but a system of meanings – a discourse about the world. Communicable is only what is described and observed. Even when we thematise incommunicability, we communicate by indexing it but not transcending or removing it. Luhmann mocks those who do not see silence as communication:

> This not only means to opt for silence within the distinction between speaking and silence, but to avoid the distinction as such, so that the problem does not arise on the first place – the problem that one 'brakes the silence' by way of (paradoxical, inspired) speech. But then, doesn't one still have the problem that in a world in which one speaks, silence is possible only within self-drawn boundaries, i.e. as the production of difference?
>
> (1994, p. 27)

The production of difference is central for understanding silence. Luhmann conceptualises it from the perspective of structural functionalism. His major concern is how systems of meaning reduce the complexity of the world and 'allow' us to think and act 'rationally' – as if world and sign are the same. His approach to 'difference in unity' remains highly abstract and cybernetic. Foucault (1981) and other post-structuralist thinkers, notably Derrida (1982) and Deleuze (2006), advanced the *productive* aspect of difference – not as negation of identity but as potential for genesis.

Double articulation

But what Foucault also ventured – and others such as postmodernists, feminists, constructivists and neo-Marxists also echoed – was militant accent on *difference* in direct assault on unity. They replaced practice with discourse or plurality of discourses with the presumption of an *arbitrary* relation between signifier and signified.[2] Putting the *difference* front and centre, they are critical of any 'unity' as totality or determinant. They allow theoretical freedom for the 'perpetual slippage of meaning', decoupling difference from the determination of unity.

Stuart Hall's concept of *articulation*, which derives from Louis Althusser's dialectics of difference and unity, offers a materialist alternative to the obsession with discursive differences. I find it essential for the understanding of strategic silence. Hall defines articulation as somewhat (but not fully) arbitrary *'fixing'* of the differences between observable practices. Ideologies, for example, are such articulations. They fix meaning through 'establishing, by selection and combination, a chain of equivalence' (Hall, 1985, p. 93).

As I will argue later, there are chains of equivalence, *interchangeability*, not only between contents but also between forms of communication. My main concern is with silence as *form and process* rather than as content and structure – not when we talk *about* silence but when we *are* silent in our talk. Within a discourse, one could make various (but not an unlimited number of) choices to express the same meaning either through sound or silence. For example, where the Pentecostal church worships God with joyful noise, the Quakers revere it in silence (Maltz, 1985). People can make protest by serious silence or repetitious chanting (Jaworski, 1993, p. 39f.). In Germany, the fans mourned the death of the football legend Udo Lattek in an unusual way. Instead of one-minute silence, they commemorated him with one-minute applause (Norden, 2015). Mourning found equivalent expressions through both silence and applause. When high sensations are in play, whether pleasant or unpleasant, they are likely to demand either extreme noise or extreme silence in a state of 'absence of cognitive control' (Bruneau, 1973, p. 21).

For Hall, equivalence is *somewhat but not entirely random*. Discursive and extra-discursive practices set limits to the interchange of meanings. With the concept of articulation, Hall wants to restore the *unity* in difference, without giving too much to mechanical determinism. For example, one cannot exhaustively explain sexual differences (and racial and cultural and many other differences, for that matter) with economic differences – the argument feminist theories rightly hold against orthodox Marxism (Heath, 1990). Against the poststructuralist approach of no 'necessary no correspondence' between, say, the ideology of a group and its economic, social and political positions, Hall offers the alternative view of '*no necessary correspondence*' (1985, p. 95).

As a black man, Hall mentions his experience of 'blackness' as a child in his native Jamaica and later as adult in Britain. In Jamaica, there were many 'fine' differences and 'steps' of blackness, overdetermined by multiple structures. In that chain of equivalence, Hall distinguished himself as a member of a 'not so black' and relatively 'well-off' group. In Britain, in contrast, all blacks are equal. There is no distinction or hierarchy within the group; the chain of equivalence is stiff and total. The difference (and inequality) was only external: between the unequal chains of 'black' and 'white'. In both countries, he was positioned in discourses of race and racial inequality. The articulation in those discourses, however, attributed to him different contents (identities), positions and relations within more (Jamaica) or less subtle and benign (Britain) differences in the unity of race.[3]

The articulation constructed through practice is not guaranteed.[4] But with that term, Hall overcomes the teleology that boils down to *full correspondence* between the effects of a practice and its origin. Teleological is, for example the way PR evaluates a campaign by measuring the results against its objectives. Articulation presupposes a more indeterminate, open-ended and contingent approach to discourse and change. It acknowledges the relative autonomy of practice without fetishising the signifier (immediacy, presence) or the signified (dehumanism, fatalism). The lesson for PR campaigns through building coalitions between diverse groups:

By developing practices which articulate differences into a collective will, or by generating discourse which condenses a range of different conditions, the dispersed conditions of practice of different social groups *can* [italics by S. H.] be effectively drawn together in ways which make those social forces not simply a class 'in itself', positioned by some other relations over which it has no control, *but also* [italics by S. H.] capable of establishing new collective projects.

(Hall, 1985, p. 96)

Articulation is important in PR practice both as *analysis*, which establishes the chain of equivalence, and *strategy*, which breaks or reconnects or elongates those chains (Fairclough, 2001). Silence is instrumental in both emphasising differences and deleting them. It is a means of moving the boundaries of difference in unity and unity in difference. This is the discursive work of PR.

Communicative silence is paradox; it is dialectical. Communication is silent and not silent at the same time. In discourse, said and unsaid dovetail in articulating variances and similarities between group practices. In Hall's *'double articulation'*, silence is *an act* but also *a relation*. As conversationalists would say, silence is *'collusion'* (Tannen, 1985). It is not one-sided, it must be maintained between people, it must be communal (Ferguson, 2011). Silence is more or less *noticed* as communication. It is an articulation that is *not granted but possible*.

As double articulation between structure and practice – as agency, silence is not only defined as communication within and by a situation of communication. It also co-defines a situation as a communicative one. It is not passive. It can be a determinant, not only a determined. We listen to silences when we (decide we) communicate and we do not listen to voices when we (decide we) do not communicate. In the situation of communication, we let – we call – silence to work on us. 'We never encounter silence itself, but only its effects on us' (Bindeman, 1981). *Active communication*[5] is the state of silence that takes effect.

Notes

1 The Separate Prison – a perfect Panopticon – was for the worst of the worst convicts who offended while in Port Arthur. In 1884, punishment of the body through flogging gave way to punishment of the soul through solitary confinement and silence. Prisoners 'must never read aloud, sing, whistle, dance or make any other noise in their Cells, exercise yards, corridors or Chapel' (Tasmania Convict Department, 1868). Designed as a cross enclosed by a circle, [the Solitary Prison] consisted of three wings of single cells and, in the fourth wing, a chapel in which prisoners were enclosed in separate tiered stalls, cut off from sight of each other. Punishment was by confinement in the totally dark 'dumb cells' in which all sense of the passage of time, and indeed almost all sensory experience, were lost. The universal rule of silence meant that neither prisoners nor guards were allowed to speak, orders being given by the sounding of a bell or by hand signals, or, in the chapel, by a mechanical device displaying the number of the prisoner whose turn it was to enter or to leave. Warders wore felt slippers in the corridors to muffle any sound they made as they patrolled. Meals were served to

prisoners in their cells; in public spaces such as the corridors and the exercise yards they moved only with their faces covered by a 'beak' with eyeholes, which extended as a flexible visor from their caps. Work, too – tailoring, shoemaking, the picking of oakum – was performed in solitude in the cells' (Frow, 1999). In Australia, prison officers did not start talk to inmates until 1998. It was sanctioned as prison offence and corruption (Dapin, 2017).

2 The modernist avant-garde (Julia Kristeva, Roland Barthes) sought to 'free' the signifier, the subject of representation, and postmodernists such as Jean-Francois Lyotard, Jean Baudrillard, Jacques Derrida did the opposite, fought the 'tyranny of the signifier' and thematised the representative fictions of the signified, the object (Owens, 1985).

3 To stay for a moment in the same field: One of my first research projects was about ethnicity and youth in my country of origin, Bulgaria. I remember some striking findings. The majority of Bulgarians discriminated minorities, such as the Turkish one, ethnically. But the majority and all other minorities, including the Turkish one, discriminated the Roma minority racially. Those were two different chains of equivalence, with different articulations of dissimilarity in unity. In a neighbouring country, Romania, there was no such distinction between the ethnic Roma and the socially poor. Members of the 'white' majority who slid down the social ladder and landed at the bottom could become Roma. In the unity of this space of dispossession, social and racial differences disappeared. A chain of equivalence between poverty and discrimination emerged. For the well-off, you are Roma. Yet there is a silver lining in this unlikely equivalence. Once a Roma person, one is welcomed by the solidarity and inclusive safety net of the Roma people. In Western countries with no significant Roma minority, those who fall socially fall hard, and there is no similar alternative (no equivalence) to make your landing softer or safer.

4 There is a *'double articulation'* between structure and practice: structure is both the result of previous practices and 'given condition' for the new ones (Hall, 1985, p. 95). In this respect, Hall is close to Anthony Giddens' theory of *structuration*, which gives primacy neither to structure nor to agency (Giddens, 1984). Hall emphasises the difference of practices in unity:

> It is important that an articulation between different practices does not mean that they become identical or that one is dissolved into the other. Each retains its distinct determinations and conditions of existence. However, once an articulation is made, the two practices can function together, not as 'immediate identity' (in the language of Marx's 1857 Introduction) but as 'distinctions within a unity'
>
> (1985, pp. 113–114)

5 An observation from the practice of psychoanalysis: 'In general, therapists indicated that they would use silence with clients who were actively problem solving, but they would not use silence with very disturbed clients' (Hill, Thompson & Ladany, 2003, p. 513).

References

Argyris, C., & Schon, D. A. (1974). *Theory in practice: Increasing professional effectiveness*. San Francisco, CA: Jossey-Bass.

Barns, G., & Newhouse, G. (2015). Border Force Act: Detention secrecy just got worse. *ABC News*. Retrieved 12 June 2017, from www.abc.net.au/news/2015-05-28/barns-newhouse-detention-centre-secrecy-just-got-even-worse/6501086.

Bindeman, S. L. (1981). *Heidegger and Wittgenstein: The poetics of silence*. Washington, DC: University Press of America.

Blumenthal, S. (1982). *The permanent campaign* (2nd edn). New York: Touchstone Books.

Böll, H. (1966). Doktor Murkes gesammeltes Schweigen. In H. Böll (Ed.), *Nicht nur zur Weinachtszeit. Satiren* (pp. 87–112). München: Deutsches Taschenbuch Verlag.

Bruneau, T. J. (1973). Communicative silences: Forms and functions. *Journal of Communication, 23*(1), 17–46.

Cage, J. (1961). *Silence* (pp. 18–27, 109). Middleton, CT: Wesleyan University Press.

Clair, R. P. (1993). *Organising silence: A world of possibilities.* New York: State University of New York Press.

Clegg, S., Courpasson, D. & Phillips, N. (2006). *Power and organisations.* Los Angeles, CA: Sage.

Dapin, M. (2017, 4 March). Doing time. *Good Weekend (The Sydney Morning Herald),* pp. 14–17.

de Certeau, M. (1984). *The practice of everyday life.* Berkeley, CA: University of California Press.

Deleuze, G. (1995). Postscript on control societies. In G. Deleuze (Ed.), *Negotiations: 1972–1990* (pp. 177–182). New York: Columbia University Press.

Deleuze, G. (2006). *Nietzsche and philosophy.* New York: Columbia University Press.

Derrida, J. (1982). *Margins of philosophy.* Chicago, IL: University of Chicago Press.

Edwards, L. (2017). Public relations, voice and recognition: A case study [electronic version]. *Media, Culture & Society.* Retrieved 12 June 2017, from https://doi.org/10.1177/0163443717705000.

Ephratt, M. (2008). The functions of silence. *Journal of Pragmatics, 40*(11), 1909–1938.

Fairclough, N. (2001). *Language and power* (2nd edn). London: Pearson Education.

Ferguson, K. (2011). Silence: A politics. In C. Glenn & K. Ratcliffe (Eds.), *Silence and listening as rhetorical acts* (pp. 113–129). Carbondale, IL: Southern Illinois University Press.

Foucault, M. (1977). *Discipline and punish: The birth of the prison.* London: Penguin.

Foucault, M. (1981). The order of discourse. In R. Young (Ed.), *Uniting the text: A poststructuralist reader* (pp. 51–78). Boston: Routledge & Kegan Paul.

Frow, J. (1999). In the penal colony. *Australian Humanities Review* (April 1999). Retrieved 12 June 2017, from www.australianhumanitiesreview.org/archive/Issue-April-1999/frow3a.html – footnote 14.

Gaber, I. (2000). Government by spin: An analysis of the process. *Media, Culture & Society, 22*(4), 507–518.

Giddens, A. (1984). *The constitution of society: Outline of the theory of structuration.* Berkeley, CA: University of California Press.

Glenn, C. (2004). *Unspoken: A rhetoric of silence.* Carbondale, IL: South Illinois University Press.

Greenberg, J., & Edwards, M. S. (Eds.). (2009). *Voice and silence in organisations.* Bingley, UK: Emerald.

Hall, S. (1985). Signification, representation, ideology: Althusser and the post-structuralist debates. *Critical Studies in Media Communication, 2*(2), 91–114.

Heath, S. (1990). The ethics of sexual difference. *Discourse & Communication, 12*(2), 128–153.

Hill, C. E., Thompson, B. J. & Ladany, N. (2003). Therapist use of silence in therapy: A survey. *Journal of Clinical Psychology, 59*(4), 513–524.

Hughes, R. (1987). *The fatal shore: A history of transportation of convicts to Australia, 1797–1868.* London: Collins.

Jaworski, A. (1993). *The power of silence: Social and pragmatic perspectives.* Newbury Park, CA: Sage.

Kenny, C. (2011). *The power of silence: Silent communication in daily life.* London: Karnac.

Kostelanez, R. (2003). *Conversing with John Cage.* New York: Routledge.

Kurzon, D. (1992). When silence may mean power. *Journal of Pragmatics, 18*(1), 92–95.

Lakoff, G. (2004). *Don't think of an elephant! Know your values and frame the debate.* White River Junction, VT: Chelsea Green Publishing.

Lakoff, G. (2010). Why it matters how we frame the environment. *Environmental Communication, 4*(1), 70–81.

Luhmann, N. (1994). Speaking and silence. *New German Critique, 61*(Winter), 25–37.

Malhotra, S., & Rowe, A. C. (Eds.). (2013). *Silence, feminism, power: Reflections at the edges of sound.* New York: Palgrave Macmillan.

Maltz, D. N. (1985). Joyful noise and reverent silence: The signification of noise in Pentecostal worship. In D. Tannen & M. Saville-Troike (Eds.), *Perspectives on silence* (pp. 113–138). Norwood, NJ: Ablex Publishing.

Mann, T. (1927). *The magic mountain.* New York: The Modern Library.

Medina, J. (2004). The meanings of silence: Wittgensteinian contextualism and polyphony. *Inquiry, 47*(6), 562–579.

Mushin, I., & Gardner, R. (2009). Silence is talk: Conversational silence in Australian Aboriginal talk-in-interaction. *Journal of Pragmatics, 41*(10), 2033–2052.

Neubauer, D. (1987). *Problematizing studies of international discourse: Reading between the silences.* Paper presented at the Department of Communication, Ohio State University, 29 January.

Norden, C. (2015). Applaus statt Schweigen: Neue Trauerkultur im Fußball. *Szh.* Retrieved 12 June 2017, from www.shz.de/sport/fussball/applaus-statt-schweigen-neue-trauerkultur-im-fussball-id8884851.html.

Orwell, G. (1949). *Nineteen eighty-four.* Boston: Houghton Mifflin Harcourt.

Owens, C. (Ed.) (1985). *The discourse of others: Feminists and postmodernism.* New York: The New Press.

Philips, S. U. (1985). Interaction structured though talk and interaction structured through silence. In D. Tannen & M. Saville-Troike (Eds.), *Perspectives on silence* (pp. 205–213). Norwood, NJ: Ablex Publishing.

Picard, M. (1952). *The world of silence* (Vol. 6067). South Bend, IN: Regnery/Gateway.

Scollon, R. (1985). The machine stops: Silence in the metaphor of malfunction. In D. Tannen & M. Saville-Troike (Eds.), *Perspectives on silence* (pp. 21–30). Norwood, NJ: Ablex Publishing.

Scott, J. C. (2008a). Everyday forms of resistance. *Copenhagen Journal of Asian Studies, 4*(1), 33.

Scott, J. C. (2008b). *Weapons of the weak: Everyday forms of peasant resistance.* New Haven, CT: Yale University Press.

Sinodinos, A. (2007, 26 November). Storytelling the secret to a happy ending. *Sydney Morning Herald.*

Sontag, S. (1982). The aesthetics of silence. In S. Sontag (Ed.), *A Susan Sontag reader* (pp. 181–204). New York: Farrar/Straus/Giroux.

Sparrow, N., & Turner, J. (2001). The permanent campaign. The integration of market research techniques in developing strategies in a more uncertain political climate. *European Journal of Marketing, 35*(9/10), 984–1002.

Tannen, D. (1985). Silence: Anything but. In D. Tannen & M. Saville-Troike (Eds.), *Perspectives on silence* (pp. 93–111). Norwood, NJ: Ablex Publishing.

Tasmania Convict Department. (1868). *Regulations for separate prison. Rules and regulations for the penal settlement on Tasman's peninsula. Selections. Extracts from Port Arthur Approved Regulations* Retrieved 12 June 2017, from http://nla.gov.au/nla.obj-97640875/view.

Trouillot, M.-R. (1995). *Silencing the past: Power and production of history.* Boston, MA: Beacon Press.

8   The ladder of indirect communication

Strategy and silence

I will recap, in a few words, where we have arrived now, before moving on further.

Public relations uses silence as form – not as content. It does not talk *about* silence; it talks *through* silence. There is more. Silence constitutes not only *some* forms of indirectness – not only the most indirect and strategic ones. There is silence in *any* indirect communication. As *structural* silence, it is present in *all* forms. As strategic *silence*, it constitutes only *some* of them. Silence is not only a *possible* but also a *necessary* condition of indirect communication. Public relations capitalises on its strategic potential.

Both strategic communication and communicative silence are forms of indirect communication. In combination, as *strategic silence*, they make up the highest and most extreme forms of indirect communication. Those forms, however, function not at the margins but at the centre of the global societies. Thus, I believe PR uses strategic silence not as some exotic tool but as essential and core strategy in packages with others.

Empirically, there are various degrees and types of silence. Hence it is appropriate to talk about *silences in plural*. I am trying to do it wherever I discuss not the theoretical category but rather various practices of silence.

Now, indirectness is endless. So are the degrees and types of silence. For the purpose of my research, I have selected a limited number of degrees – and some types of silence within them – of indirect communication. They are not *the* levels of indirectness per se. As with silence, abstract or absolute indirectness does not exist. I will call the succession of those degrees the *ladder of indirectness*. The logic that binds the few rungs up the ladder makes sense only in context of the goal hierarchy of my study in the field of PR and communication strategies. From any other theoretical and disciplinary angle such selection and order of terms may appear – justifiably – random.

Every rung contains a pair of alternative categories, an opposition. One of them, the more indirect one, serves as the base for the next rung up. In a way, the scheme of the ladder is functions as an algorithm. At any rung we make a choice between two alternatives. We chose that one, which inside it contains

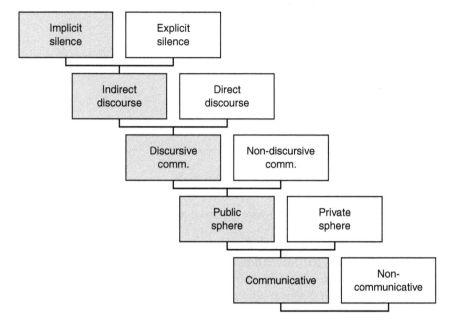

Figure 8.1 The ladder of indirectness.

further degrees and categories of indirectness. To make visualisation easier, I have chosen the concept of a ladder, which is closer to the pyramidal object-diagram. We choose one of two categories and go up, and then we do the same again, and so on. I could have equally used other types of diagram – of circles enclosed one in another, for example – but I find this one especially clear. In the next chapter, *Strategic silences*, I will discuss some of those types of silence, which one can allocate higher or lower, that is at any rung of the ladder of indirectness.

Communication and non-communication

At the base of the ladder, the first opposition is between *communicative* and *non-communicative silence*. Not all silences are communicative. Silence may be negation or absence of communication.[1] Communicative silence takes place in an established, and recognised by all participants, *situation of communication*. In the city, strangers pass by without saying a word. But they are not silent in the communicative sense of that term. They are not in the situation of communication. Passing by is usually a communicative *non-event*. People who walk and talk on the street most likely use a mobile phone handset. They are in a communicative situation with a distant other but not with those who pass nearby. But even when we hear them clearly, we are not listening to them and they are not talking to us.

Silencing communication is still communication. One may actively ostracise others, give them the silent treatment and snub them on public forums (see Chapters 13, 16). But one still communicates – even when one does not utter a sound.

But communication is neither the only nor the most efficient way to silence others. Economic redistribution of capital and wealth manufactures the material inequalities and barriers in communication. Marketing forces determine in stealth: (1) who has access to communication and who not; (2) who can afford it and who not; and (3) who controls those who decide about (1) and (2). One does not argue with those who are silent. One does not have a contact with them. One does not even have to know of their existence. Dispossession of communications access and resources is material but intangible. It is liquid, like money. And like radiation, the affected cannot smell it or feel it.

The current battle for the privatisation and centralisation of telecommunications data, for example, is fierce. But it is capitalism, not communication. Elio D'Amato, CEO of *Lincoln Indicators*, explains why the biggest *telcos* are bidding with outrageously large amounts of money – spending that cannot be rationalised or justified with fundamentals analysis – to acquire and eat out the smaller ones:

> The telecommunication sector is in the state of flux. There's corporate activity everywhere you look. And ultimately, it's all about gaining access to the distribution of data. And companies are tripping over themselves in order to establish strong data points because the world is becoming more and more connected and those who control the data flow are going to be able to control the significant part of all our daily life. And this is why like those are seen above the odds in terms of the acquisition prices, but fair if you consider what the long-term prospects are.
>
> (Fullerton, 2015)

The telcos cannibalism hits the users privately, not publicly. It takes place through market transactions far away and safely isolated from everyday communication. The victims are not among those who have fought with digits. The victims are left incommunicado. It is business strategy, not PR strategy.

Non-communicative silence such as restricted access to information (i.e. digital divide, data collonialisation, invasion of privacy) is a powerful socioeconomic and political factor. It affects communication through non-communication. It engineers the forums of communication; it leaves others act in those forums. PR practitioners influence communication (output) and non-communication (outcome) through communication. They work with communicative silence.

Communicative silence is more indirect than non-communicative silence. Thus, I select communicative silence and exclude non-communicative silence for my further analysis. (But non-communicative silence will be persistently returning through the backdoor.) The next and higher degrees of indirectness are levels of communicative silence.

Public and private communication

One can split communicative silence into public and private silences. Professional communicators are agents of the public sphere. They are public communicators. Public communication is more indirect than private communication. Public silence is more indirect than private silence. My concern is with strategies of *public silence*.

I take from Jürgen Habermas the basic aspects and levels of indirectness of the public sphere (1974, 1989). As a system of communication, the liberal-democratic public sphere mediates exchanges of information between *amateur strangers*. As such, it is *inclusive*. Everyone can access its forums – both the galleries and the arenas – without any precondition. Exclusive are the private relations such as kinship, friendship and specialised clubs. The public sphere language is inclusive. It is simple, context-poor and relevant to all lay-people who personally do not know one another. The public language may look easy, but it is not 'natural', not private. It is somewhat 'artificial' – a *meta-language*. It is not what people start with at home. It takes effort and time and experience and wisdom to learn how to speak and even more of those to learn how to remain silent in public. Specialised, expert languages are exclusive. But public communicators, including journalists and PR practitioners, *specialise in the unspecialised language of the public sphere* (Fuchs, Gerhards & Neidhardt, 1992).

Not only professional communicators but also all other citizens should be able to influence the public agenda by knowing how to speak is public. Some examples follow: if academics, like all experts, want to extend their impact outside their discursive community and directly engage in civil and political life, they have to know not to translate their specialised language into the public vernacular. They have to know how to 'communicate on the sidewalk'. One can only laugh at the futile attempts of measuring the impact of scientific work in a self-referential manner (i.e. by citations in other scholarly publications) within the scientific enclaves of the public sphere – which are rather exclusive (despite attempts at public access and open publishing) and quasi-private. The real, *public* impact of academics it is outside academia.

For Habermas, this is not only a question of communicative competence but also of democratic values (1970). If I, for example, publish an opinion piece in a newspaper and eagerly underline my academic title and ask the readers to believe me because I am more educated than they are and as a professor I know things they do not know, then my argumentation is not only vain but also autocratic. I do not 'bracket' but brandish my supposed superiority. I am imposing my privilege by silencing the readers.

At this moment, when I write this page, there is an issue being discussed in the US press: Is it time to call President Trump mentally ill? Some psychologists are suggesting that Trump shows symptoms of 'schizophrenia', 'narcissistic personality disorder', 'paranoia', 'megalomania' and so on (Friedman, 2017). But is it moral to use professional knowledge as a political weapon against a man who they have never examined – not personally, thoroughly and with his consent? And the answer is: No, it is not! This does not mean scholars should remain silent on politics. Unfortunately, comparatively few know (that they do not know) when and how to do it. But the psychologists who venture to speak about Trump should offer the public their relevant knowledge – not their untested diagnosis. The argument, 'Believe me, I am a psychiatrist – he has psychosis' does not hold more water than, say, my claim that I am not a violent man because I have a wife and a daughter. By the way, many American presidents have suffered during their lifetime from psychiatric disorders, depression, anxiety, bipolar disorder and alcohol abuse. In fact, ten of them have shown symptoms of mental illness while they were in office.

> You can be psychiatrically ill and be perfectly competent, just as you can be mentally healthy but totally unfit.... There is one last reason we should avoid psychiatrically labelling our leaders: It lets them off the moral hook. Not all misbehaviour reflects psychopathology; the fact is that ordinary human meanness and incompetence are far more common than mental illness. We should not be in the business of medicalizing bad actors.
>
> (Friedman, 2017)

Within the public sphere, there are various *levels* of indirect communication. For example the least indirect public conversations take place in the lift, park or pub. People more or less spontaneously talk to one another in what Goffman (1961) calls '*encounters*' and Luhmann (1986) calls 'communication au trottoir'. Some social media forums also belong here. But even at this level of high freedom of speech and low political correctness, loose talk is full with public silences – from formal small talk to instinctive skirting of 'indiscreet' and 'too private' questions such as – in Australia, for example – those of religion, ethnos and politics.

A more structured and mediated level of communication is that of '*gatherings*' – of planned meetings, events and assemblies. This is the domain of communication as management function. Gatherings provide for organisation as self-thematisation (Gerhards & Neidhardt, 1991). Each meeting has a theme. Each theme is a frame. A frame helps the audience to self-select. Only those who relate to the issue come to the meeting. 'Global warming' and 'getting the country back' are not only common themes but also code words and phrases, which would attract certain publics and put off other. Similarly, a hashtag organises audiences through 'ambient affiliation' – users get together in relation to a topic, which reflects their emotional and evaluative orientation (Zappavigna, 2011, 2012). Publics reconstruct themselves through physical or virtual presence as well as through expressive contributions from the floor.

And the highest and more indirect degree of public communication is of the *communication society* (Lash, 2002; Strydom, 1999). Global financial markets and new digital technologies have stimulated the new and already leading industry of communication solutions, B2B services, and hybrid media, which connect at distance and in an instant. Public silences expand in the vast empty spaces and in the utter lack of time. Indirectness is so high that physical presence – face-to-face encounters or institutionalised gatherings – is no longer needed. Absent, disembodied and simulated publics and individuals interact in highly abstract way.

At this highest level of mediation, indirectness verges on infinity. One sees here also the highest degree of *representation*. We still see that in the legacy media – print and TV, despite their digitalisation. Fewer people speak on behalf of those who are silent. Or is it the other way round: more people are silent because fewer speak for them? The professional ideology of journalism is the ideology of journalist professionalism (Dimitrov, 2014). Only few 'real' professionals have the skills and entitlement, including the right to remain silent, to represent their readers and sources. The social media have seriously challenged but not entirely removed that 'quality journalism' last line of defence. But what the new digital technologies have dramatically accelerated was the blurring of the borderlines between public and private, present and absent, and re-presented and presented (see Chapter 8). At this highest level of indirect public communication, representation verges on simulation. The digital media have only amplified the effect of hyper-reality.

Public relations operates at all three levels. Therefore, it is much more than media management. But it is management of communication. It is also *communication of management*. Gatherings as organising through self-thematising shows, for example, how discursive strategies are also action strategies – how a frame, for example, determines not only what to talk and not to talk about, but also with whom to get together and whom to let out of the affair.

As any public communication, public relations is facing the crisis of representation in the communications society. The more indirect – and this also means abstract, anonymous and hyper-real – communication is the more questionable the main function of PR becomes as relationships builder. The relationships we talk about in the profession remain concrete, personalised and present. This is another reason to look at the potential of encounters and gatherings for that purpose. Indirectness and mediation are not the same. Those forms of communication are still more direct, interpersonal, but, in the digital era, also more mediated, interactive. There is more noise in the channel, which disturbs the relations. And silence is the curator of noise (see Chapter 19).

But simulation has not replaced representation, as postmodernists believe – not entirely and perhaps not at all. It has just covered it with layers of meaning. Due to their sheer multiplication, they appear random. But they are not. As Hall says, there is no necessary correspondence. But there is one. Media signification is as material, interested and motivated as it has ever been. Yet the link between the current multi-modal, virtual and real-time representations and the represented – including underlying ideologies, hegemonic discourses and master narratives – has become extremely oblique or invisible to many. No wonder why that some, including scholars (constructivists, postmodernists), deem it non-existent.

Discursive and non-discursive

Public silence in turn is discursive and non-discursive. *Discursive* means here more than 'linguistic'. I use the *semiotic* definition of multimodal discourse. Therefore, my notion of silence *extends* to other systems (modes) of meaning such as image, music, rhythm and gesture (Kress, Leite-Garcia & van Leeuwen, 1997; Kress & van Leeuwen, 2001).

In the 1960s and 1970s, it was the 'turn to language' that inspired functional linguistics, pragmatics and critical discourse analysis (Hodge, 2012). In this tradition, the discursive has been the linguistic and the non-discursive the extra-linguistic. Many do still work in that paradigm and produce notable results. At the end of the Millennium, however, it was the 'complexity turn' (Urry, 2003) or the 'semiotic turn' (Kress & van Leeuwen, 2001). It sought to re-conceptualise discourses as significations of though and action anchored in practice. In that approach, discourses are not only linguistic constructs. They are systems of meaning, which encompass many modes and media. Multiple systems of signs such as images, music and gesture can carry and express a single discourse. Correspondingly, the notion of discursive silence has extended to non-linguistic and multimodal functions of silence.

In his essay *Politics and the study of discourse*, Foucault distinguishes between *intra*-discursive (internal transformation), *inter*-discursive (one discourse changes or annihilates another) and *extra*-discursive transformation (by factors outside a discourse) (1991, p. 58). Discursive here means both intra-discursive (see Chapter 13) and inter-discursive (see Chapter 18). But which one is more transformative? Foucault favours the *exogen* change, which results from the clash between discourses, to the *endogen* one, which gradually takes place within a discourse. Roughly, it is the 'either/or' logic against 'and/and', non-linear against linear development, disruption versus continuity, revolution against evolution and, again, strategy against tactic. Substantial historical changes take place not within a discourse but rather *between* discourses. Some replace, cannibalise, and annihilate others. Changes are mostly abrupt, discontinuous, and non-linear.[2]

The *non-discursive*, the other side in the opposition, is still within the realm of signification. Extra-discursive representation is *practical*. But discourses are practices too. The difference is not between meaning and practice, but between the practices of signification. I align with theories, which regard the discursive as the *re-presented* (Keane, 2003; Lash, 2002). It is the symbolic, lasting. A novel, for example, impacts through interpretation and contemplation. In contrast, the non-discursive is the *presented*. It is the indexical, immediate. It is information: as quick as a mouse click. It comes and goes. It seems not to have any lasting effect after the moment – but it has. Along similar lines, Charles Peirce (1998), for example, distinguishes between symbol, icon and index. Indices are signs that are closest to the situation. Pronouns, for example, do not make sense without our knowledge of their concrete antecedents.

Indexes – from viral kitten videos to survivors TV shows – are the most direct and motivated type of presentation. But they are motivated by the *object* rather than the subject. Indexes are the closest signification to reality. Unlike symbols and images, they are irreducible, last signs of reality. There is not sign beyond their sign, no meaning beyond their meaning. Indices are also the last frontier of difference. For Heidegger and Derrida, they are all that remains after pheno-menological reduction. They present the coveted finality in deconstruction, Der-rida's *différance* (Derrida, Caws & Caws, 1982). There is no articulation, no difference in unity, without indexing. It is strictly context-bound and temporal. An index is a moment, but one cannot confuse that moment with another one. We will see how it goes. It is immediate, unpredictable – no trace of past and no hint of future. Barracking for your team, Internet browsing, calming your baby, chasing up a bargain, reality shows, electronic messaging, tweets, 'likes' and emojis are indexical. Indices signal without discoursing.

Both symbols and indices have a role in critical thinking. One can critique the unimaginativeness of the indexical through the all-inclusiveness of the symbolic. The symbolic is multivocal; the indexical is not. The symbol is more open to the listener. The index is more true to the speaker. Indices resist symbols, including discourses. 'The excess of the reduction is in the index: the excess of the sym-bolic is in the real' (Lash, 2002, p. 11). There is a school of thought, which con-siders real politics as the critique of the symbolic. Dominance, including ideology and hegemony, is symbolic. The resistance should come through the reality. One should use index as critique of symbol (Derrida, 1996; Žižek, 1989).

Re-presentation is *propaganda*; presentation is *promotion*. Hill and Knowlton propagated the justification of war in the Persian Gulf in 1990. The proofs they fabricated were more than symbolic – they were 'fake news'. The *Daesh* pro-duced decapitation videos to promote their horror. The death on the videos was iconic, indexical – it was real.[3] Propaganda is rooted in fixed ideas, promotion – in shifting realities. Yet this does not mean that the former is fake and the latter real – as the example above may mislead. Both discursive and non-discursive practices, re-presentation and presentation are equally potent and powerful resources for strategic communication.

Professional communicators do both – they re-present and present. Strategic silence wields both symbolic and promotional clout. In discourses, silence topi-calises, frames, backgrounds, presupposes, deletes, and so on. In indices, silence reduces communication to a single gesture, image, motion, signal, hint, cue and so on. The difference, however, is again in the degree of mediation. *Discursive communication is more indirect than non-discursive communication.* Therefore, my next pair of categories up the ladder of indirectness rests on discursive silence, although one should not forget the important part indexicality plays in the rise of promotional cultures (Davis, 2013; Wernick, 1991).

Direct and indirect discourse

Discursive silence is multimodal. We can talk about imaging, musical and other discourses. More importantly, discourses overarch modality. A corporate or political website, for example, integrates not only various media such as a

Facebook and Twitter, but uses various modes such as text, video, audio and so on to express a particular discourse. In short, discourses are multimodal.

In this part, however, I would like to flag two important dimensions of the linguistic mode. Spoken discourse can be split into indirect discourse (indirect speech) and direct discourse (direct speech). *Indirect discourse* is, so to speak, the structural memory of a language. It contains forms of meaning and interpretation, which massive and repetitive use has been 'crystallised', 'rounded', and polished – internalised, in one word. We use them all the way. Yet they are too close to see them. In a Foucauldian fashion, we can say that they communicate through us rather than we communicate through them.

Indirect discourse is objectified, normalised and trans-contextual. It is what sets up the direct discourse – speaking and dialogue in real time – and what remains from it. In that respect, history 'uses' indirect discourse as repository. As such, it is not only temporary storage but also a selective mechanism. It separates the wheat from the chaff. It links the past with the future.

It is the *rationale* of public language. But is it *rational*? Habermas would say, 'Yes'. Rationality is the essence of public language. Luhmann would say, 'No'. *Simplicity*, not rationality makes it to the lowest common denominator of collective experiences (see their debate in Habermas, Luhmann & Luhmann, 1974). Constructivists would say, 'Both' (Mumby, 1997; van Ruler, 2005). People deem rational what is simple and relevant to all. Heuristics do work just fine here. Conspiracy theories, for example, are rational when they abridge knowledge gaps and help make sense of the unknown world. Immigrants taking our jobs is simpler to understand than automation of labour and global financial flows.

But I would also link indirect discourse with Mikhail Bakhtin's analysis of the discursively 'rationalised' national languages (see Chapter 8). And I would also compare it with Foucault's 'regimes of truth'. For the latter truth is not outside thinking and power. It is not what but rather *how* we think about *as to how true* a statement is. Through regimes of truth power constrains, regulates, sanctions, valorises and assigns the status of those who are charged with saying what counts as true (Foucault, 1977, pp. 112–113).

Of course, communicators and speakers have to learn the art of direct discourse. Whole branches of discourse theory are devoted to conversational and direct speech analysis (Cameron, 2001; Kurzon, 2013; Mushin & Gardner, 2009; Shiffrin, 1994; Tannen, 1984). But the difference between indirect and direct discourse is, again, also a difference between strategy and tactics. This is important in PR practice. Although much more difficult, changing a discourse is more strategic than just adjusting to it.

Explicit and implicit

And, lastly, indirect discourse splits into implicit and explicit communication. *Implicit* silence, in that regard, is more indirect than explicit silence. In the logic of this book, it is the most indirect form of communication. It perches at the highest rung of the ladder of indirectness.

Explicit silence is more direct. It is the silence that speaks for itself. The meaning of what a speaker says without words is roughly the meaning of what he expects the listener to understand. Implicit silence is more ambiguous. What is meant is different from what is said. Presupposition, implicature, sarcasm, irony and innuendo are tactics of implicit silence. Insinuation, for example, works that way: if accused of what he means, the speaker can always hide behind what he says.

In the next section, I discuss in more detail the last two and highest degrees of indirect communication – indirect discourse as well as explicit and implicit silence. Those are also the degrees of indirectness, which harbour most of the strategic silences.

Notes

1 'Communication' is the preferred word to 'utterance' or 'self-expression' to avoid any slant to solipsism (Gilkey, 1983).
2 Foucault's preference of external and discontinuous (inter-discursive or extra-discursive) discursive change puts him in a broad tradition of diverse approaches – from Thomas Kuhn's 'paradigmatic' change (Kuhn, 1970) to George Lakoff's 'frame replacement' (Lakoff, 2004), and from Jürgen Habermas' 'Lebenswelt' modifying the system from outside (Habermas, 1981) to Alain Touraine's 'social movements' (Touraine, 1988), which create an environment of change for the inherently static state.
3 I would like to thank Jordi Xifra for that idea. Look forward to his upcoming book on public relations and death.

References

Cameron, D. (2001). *Working with spoken discourse*. London: Sage.

Davis, A. (2013). *Promotional cultures: The rise and spread of advertising, public relations, marketing and branding*. Cambridge: Polity Press.

Derrida, J. (1996). Remarks on deconstruction and pragmatism. In C. Mouffe (Ed.), *Deconstruction and pragmatism* (p. 84). London: Routledge.

Derrida, J., Caws, P. & Caws, M. A. (1982). Sending: On representation. *Social Research*, *49*(2, Summer), 294–326.

Dimitrov, R. (2014). Do social media spell the end of journalism as a profession? *Global Media Journal: Australian Edition, 8*(1).

Foucault, M. (1977). The political function of the intellectual. *Radical Philosophy, 17*(Summer), 12–14.

Foucault, M. (1991). Politics as the study of discourse. In G. Burchell, C. Gordon, & P. Miller (Eds.), *The Foucault effect: Studies in governmentality. With two lectures and an interview with Michel Foucault* (pp. 53–72). Chicago, IL: The University of Chicago Press.

Friedman, R. A. (2017). Is it time to call Trump mentally ill? *New York Times*. Retrieved 12 June 2017, from www.nytimes.com/2017/02/17/opinion/is-it-time-to-call-trump-mentally-ill.html?_r=0.

Fuchs, D., Gerhards, J. & Neidhardt, F. (1992). Oeffentliche kommunicationsbereitschaft. Ein test zentraler bestandteils der theorie der schweidespirale. *Zeitschrift fuer Soziologie, 21*, 284–295.

Fullerton, T. (2015). Elio D'Amato speaks to the business. *ABC The Business*. Retrieved 12 June 2017, from www.abc.net.au/news/2015-05-14/elio-damato-speaks-to-the-business/6471138.

Gerhards, J., & Neidhardt, F. (1991). *Strukturen und funktionen moderner Oeffentlichkeit: fragestellungen und ansaetze*. Berlin: Wissenschaftszentrum Berlin fur Sozial Forschung gGmbH (Wzb).

Gilkey, L. (1983). The political meaning of silence. *Philosophy Today, 27*(2), 128–132.

Goffman, E. (1961). *Encounters: Two studies in the sociology of interaction*. Indianapolis, IN: Bobbs-Merrill.

Habermas, J. (1970). Towards a theory of communicative competence. *Inquiry, 13*(1–4), 360–375.

Habermas, J. (1974). The public sphere: An encyclopedia article. *New German Critique, 3*(Autumn), 49–55.

Habermas, J. (1981). New social movements. *Telos, 49*, 33–37.

Habermas, J. (1989). *The structural transformation of the public sphere: An inquiry into a category of bourgeois society*. Cambridge: Polity.

Habermas, J., Luhmann, N. & Luhmann, N. (1974). *Theorie der Gesellschaft oder Sozialtechnologie: was leistet die Systemforschung?* [Theory of society or social technology: What does systems' research do?]. Frankfurt am Main: Suhrkamp.

Hodge, B. (2012). Ideology, identity, interaction: Contradictions and challenges for critical discourse analysis. *Critical Approaches to Discourse Analyses Across Disciplines, 5*(2), 1–18.

Keane, W. (2003). Semiotics and the social analysis of material things. *Language & Communication, 23*(3), 409–425.

Kress, G., Leite-Garcia, R. & van Leeuwen, T. (1997). Discourse semiotics. In T. A. van Dijk (Ed.), *Discourse studies: A multidisciplinary introduction* (pp. 257–291). London: Sage.

Kress, G., & van Leeuwen, T. (2001). *Multimodal discourse: The modes and media of contemporary communication*. London: Edward Arnold.

Kuhn, T. S. (1970). *The structure of scientific revolutions* (2nd edn). Chicago, IL: The University of Chicago Press.

Kurzon, D. (2013). Analysis of silence in interaction. In C. A. Chapelle (Ed.), *The encyclopedia of applied linguistics*: Oxford: Blackwell.

Lakoff, G. (2004). *Don't think of an elephant! Know your values and frame the debate*. White River Junction, VT: Chelsea Green Publishing.

Lash, S. (2002). *Critique of information*. London: Sage.

Luhmann, N. (1986). *Ökologische Kommunikation. Kann die moderne Gesellschaft sich auf ökologische Gefahren einstellen?*. Opladen: Westdeutscher Verlag.

Mumby, D. K. (1997). Modernism, postmodernism, and communication studies: A rereading of an ongoing debate. *Communication Theory, 7*(1), 1–28.

Mushin, I., & Gardner, R. (2009). Silence is talk: Conversational silence in Australian Aboriginal talk-in-interaction. *Journal of Pragmatics, 41*(10), 2033–2052.

Peirce, C. S. (1998). *The essential Peirce: Selected philosophical writings. 2 vols. The Peirce Project*. (Vol. 2). Bloomington, IN: Indiana University Press.

Shiffrin, D. (1994). *Approaches to discourses*. Oxford: Blackwell.

Strydom, P. (1999). Triple contingency The theoretical problem of the public in communication societies. *Philosophy & Social Criticism, 25*(2), 1–25.

Tannen, D. (1984). *Conversational style: Analyzing talk among friends*. Norwood, NJ: Ablex Publishing.

Touraine, A. (1988). *The return of the actor: Social theory in postindustrial society.* Minneapolis, MN: University of Minnesota Press.

Urry, J. (2003). *Global complexity.* London: Sage.

van Ruler, B. (2005). Constructionism theory. In R. L. Heath (Ed.). *Encyclopedia of public relations* (Vol. 1, pp. 184–186): London: Sage.

Wernick, A. (1991). *Promotional culture: Advertising, ideology and symbolic expression.* London: Sage.

Zappavigna, M. (2011). Ambient affiliation: A linguistic perspective on Twitter. *New Media & Society, 13*(5), 788–806.

Zappavigna, M. (2012). *Discourse of Twitter and Social Media.* London: Continuum.

Žižek, S. (1989). *The sublime object of ideology.* London: Verso.

9   Indirect discourse

Speech acts

PR is increasingly aware of its work as discursive practice. It deals with discourse maintenance and change. In a Foucauldian sense, PR strategies and tactics are discourse technologies (Leitch & Motion, 2007; Motion & Leitch, 2007). Discursive technologies and practices are contingent on other social practices. Discourses mediate social action (Scollon & Scollon, 2001, p. 545).

New developments in humanities such as functional linguistics, pragmatics and semiotics have shifted the view on discourse from a purely cognitive system of meanings to a structure and process of *speech acts* (Austin, 1975). Words and signs as 'performatives' have an 'illocutory force' (Grice, 1975). They presuppose and trigger not only ideas and knowledge but also judgement, will, action and power (Kurzon, 1992; Wilson, 2006). Language, for example, is neither just a speech code nor merely transmission of information. It is a form of practice.

> To order, question, promise, or affirm is not to inform someone about a command, doubt, engagement, or assertion but to effectuate these specific, immanent, and necessarily implicit acts.... The meaning and syntax of language can no longer be defined independently of the speech acts they presuppose.
>
> (Deleuze & Guattari, 1987, p. 90)

Discourse analysts have problematised the link between what is said and what is meant in 'these specific, immanent, and necessarily implicit acts'. This is central for the understanding of both PR as 'effectuating communication' and silence as indirect 'speech act' (Fairclough, 1992, 2001; Jalbert, 1994).

Consider the following dialogue:

A.: Where are you going?
B.: I'll be right back.

A simple question and a simple answer. Yet we do not know the context of that conversation. When I ask my students to figure what was going on, the only material they can retrieve is from the text. That is the only option they have is an *intra-linguistic* one. They look for an 'inherent' and literal meaning, a meaning those few words and phrases carry 'universally', outside any context. We will see that indirect discourses internalise social conditions and historical contexts. Connotative meanings become denotative. It looks like words and phrases are independent, pure and speak for themselves. But they have already been multiply determined in practice and from outside. We have to uncover what they do not say, to articulate their silences to make visible their discursive and social construction.

Regarding the example above, an intra-linguistic interpretation of the chat between A. and B. does not make sense. A guess closest to mind is that the dialogue – if this is a dialogue – is about understanding. A. asks for information and B. gives that information. This is the first, inside-out, *grammarian* attempt at interpretation. The meaning of a text is expected to come from its elements and structure. A pure grammarian perspective seeks for the 'essence' of utterances (including silences) in their lexical and semantic order. But even so, there are contradictions in that 'pure logic'. A.'s question is about place. B.'s answer is about time. Does this mean B. does not understand the question? Does it also mean A. does not understand the answer? Or is B. refusing to answer the question? Or is B. answering the question by not answering the question? One needs to fill in the extra-linguist context (Gee, 2011) to indicate what is going on. This is what PR research as discourse analysis is doing.

Fortunately, ordinary people are not grammarians. In a real situation and when they are familiar with the context, they instantly grasp the meaning of what looks confusing and illogical on paper. People instinctively fill in context even when we do not know much. What they do not know they may assume based on other experiences. Usually they take it for granted – after the Grice's maxims of *relevance* (1975) – that there is sanity and good reason for what people say to one another. People are motivated to find meaning in any exchange until proving the opposite. Maintaining the situation of communication alive, including the social norms and roles in it, is more important – but more routinised and less conscious – than what they actually talk about.

The first that comes to my mind to fill in the context of the chat above is the plot of a trivial domestic dispute between wife and husband. For example, A. (the wife) is not quite happy with B. (her husband). Her question, 'Where are you going?' may not be a question at all. It may express: (1) a tacit disapproval that he runs away from some duty at home and perhaps not for the first time. 'Oh, not again!' It also may be a signal stronger than opinion: (2) an unspoken order not to do it. 'Enough is enough'. Similarly, his answer may not be an answer in terms of giving information, telling her something what she does not know. It may be: (3) an act of resistance – an appeal to her finally to recognise the normality of their small disagreement. 'Much ado about nothing'. Or it may also be: (4) a tongue-in-cheek dismissal of the relevance of her notice. 'You are holding me from coming back sooner'. Filling in the extra-linguistic context of a text may reveal the conversation as a sequence of communication acts, in which both interlocutors strategically try to achieve certain outcomes.

Indirectness – oiled through various silences (from 1 to 4) – helps A. and B. not to discharge each other from the face-off they have to have and, at the same time, to cool off their close – warm but not heated – bond as husband and wife. Of course others my fill in the context differently. The point is silences mediate speech acts as indirect communications.

Now, it is the reader's turn. Please fill in the context and articulate the silences in:

A.: How was last night?
B.: I found my umbrella in the fridge.

Silence as indirect discourse

I will discuss indirect discourse in two different aspects. The first reflects the ability of discourses to tackle contents indirectly instead of head-on. The second aspect looks into forms of discourse as indirect speech and opposite to direct speech. Correspondingly, I first focus on silence as *indirectness in* (any) *discourse*. Then I move to silence in *indirect discourse*, the most established and consequential discourse in a national public sphere.

Within a discourse:

> Silence is the extreme manifestation of indirectness. If indirectness is a matter of saying one thing and meaning another, silence can be matter of saying nothing and meaning something. Like indirectness, silence has two benefits in rapport and defensiveness. The rapport benefit comes from being understood without putting one's meaning on record so that understanding is seen as result not of putting meanings into words ... but rather as the greater understanding of shared, experience and intimacy, the deeper sense of 'speaking the same language'.... The defensive value of silence comes from omitting to say something negative – not confronting potentially divisive information, or being able later to deny having meant what may not be received well.
>
> (Tannen, 1985, p. 97)

For Deborah Tannen, there are two principal goals of human communication, which silence achieves: to be *connected* and to be *independent*. Similarly, Penelope Brown and Stephen Levinson distinguish two main types of saving face – of *politeness* (1987). Positive politeness serves the need to be approved by others. Negative politeness avoids imposition on others. In direct interaction, face saving employs indirect communication, including various strategies of silence (Goffman, 1955, 2005). In politeness, silence can attend to addressee's both positive face (i.e. listening and not speaking, ellipsis) and negative face (i.e. silent deference, emotional neutrality) (Sifianou, 1997).

Goffman, Tannen, Brown and Levinson offer an abstract model of interaction between two. Mikhail Bakhtin's concept of dialogue is more socialised. Bakhtin presumes the differentiation of multiple voices not only between the interlocutors. There is a third voice, which reflects the collective input of the public sphere. And there are multiple voices inside the subjectivity of an individual. Our voice is not only ours. It is already an answer to another voice. In that sense, there is no first voice. Every voice is a second one (Bakhtin, 1986, 2010). This is how Bakhtin sees the main functions of communication such as connectedness and independence (Tannen, 1985) or difference and unity. He integrates indirectness in collective consciousness and internal dialogue.

Silence facilitates a paradox – the said, which is not meant, and the unsaid, which is meant. Silence cannot only be a 'matter of saying nothing and meaning something', as Tannen observes. The opposite could also be true. In his groundbreaking *The history of sexuality*, Foucault studied the *transformation of silence into discourse* in the seventeenth and eighteenth centuries (1990). The post-Victorians found a way of talking 'institutionally' and 'scientifically' about sexual desire in order to subjugate it. Foucault called that type of verbose silence *exhaustive representation*. The proliferation of academic, educational and policy discourses about sex served a momentous shift of power: *indirect discourse has replaced direct repression*. The early modern world was moving towards the more efficient technologies of indirect and soft – discursive that is – power.

Indirect discourse has also another meaning: *indirect speech* as opposite to *direct speech*. Direct discourse is incidental, situational, close to context and practice. Indirect discourse, however, is the enduring one, closer to structure, history and culture.

For Bakhtin there is a third voice and no first voice. Deleuze and Guattari go further, 'There is no individual enunciation' (1987, p. 92). Any statement, any 'order-words' – that is words as performatives – imply 'collective assemblages'. Those are social, impersonal and multiple constructs. They do not differentiate between the subjects of a discourse. They rather 'assemble' all present voices, all possible word-choices – 'the languages in a language' (p. 93). They call this *indirect discourse*. It is publically spoken and written. It necessarily goes from a second party to a third party, neither of whom is seen (p. 89). I am saying what I have heard that someone was saying. It is the lowest common denominator of shared collective experience that has crystallised in idiomatic, impersonal and actionable language.

More abstract and rigid, indirect discourse institutionalises the moral from (hi-)story of a nation.[1] Indirect discourse is hardest to change. Of course, national discourses are subjects of myriad internal and external communication strategies. But as I have already stressed, using the discourse for change (tactic) is easier and more common than changing the discourse (strategy). PR practitioners are keenly aware of the dilemma: either the discourse works for you or you work against the discourse.

Indirect discourse is determined by the circumstances and context of its production. Here, authors as different as Marx, Foucault, Bourdieu, Hall, Benveniste and Deleuze are in an agreement. In both direct and indirect discourse, words as performatives are not self-referential. They are socially devoted to certain actions and effects. One cannot explain them without the extra-linguistic imperatives and practices from which they derive their 'illocutory force' (Benveniste, 1971). Language in its entirety is indirect discourse. Pragmatics is 'a politics of language' (Deleuze & Guattari, 1987, pp. 96–97).

In the 1920s, Valentin N. Vološinov suggested a philosophy of language.[2] He was influenced by Ferdinand Saussure's structural linguistics but also critical of the 'absolute literalness' of the 'grammarians'. In his momentous book, Vološinov gives special prominence to indirect discourse. He sees analysis as its 'heart and soul'.

> All the emotive-affectual features of speech, in so far as they are expressed not in the content but in the form of a message, do not pass intact into indirect discourse. They are transited from form into content, and only in that shape do they enter into the construction of indirect discourse.... Thus, for example, the direct utterance, 'Well done! What an achievement!' cannot be registered in indirect discourse as, 'He said that well done and what an achievement'. Rather, we expect: 'He said that that had been done very well and was a real achievement'. Or: 'He said', delightedly, 'that that had been done well and was a real achievement'.
>
> (Vološinov, 1973, pp. 128–129)

All silences, ellipses and omissions possible in direct discourse on emotive-affectual grounds, cannot be any longer tolerated in their original forms. Indirect discourse is, in a way, more mediative and 'cooler', but not necessarily less emotive-affective. Yet it is another genre or modality, in which messages – including their silences – must find their fitting translation and reconstruction. The distinctive features of indirect discourse are pertinent to the mastery of all promotional cultures, including PR. For example, how much of the dull and ineffective stuff we watch in commercials is due to the confusion between indirect corporate discourse and direct speech form? Either the protagonists on the screen speak in corporate jargon that is alien to the everyday life vernacular or company representatives insult the audiences by addressing them as gullible and brainless 'loved ones' with a fake diction taken from the worst children programmes. Mechanical, literal transposition does not work. Indirect discourse 'hears' differently, 'answers' differently, and 'obeys' differently to order-words. For example, only long chains of indirect discourse may lead to third party endorsement and word of mouth.

Referent and style

Vološinov distinguishes between two directions, which the analytical tendency of indirect discourse can take: referent-analysing and texture-analysing. Analysing as converting forms into contents does not mean academic analysis, although it may well be. Indirect discourse is analytical in a sense of *reporting about reporting*. When we do that, so Vološinov says, we focus our attention on two different objects. *Referent-analysing* fixes the ideational position of the speaker. It is what he says, what he refers to – the 'referent' in his terminology. Yet we can re-direct our gaze toward the speaker – the agency of direct discourse. This is *texture-analysing*. It observes not only the referent, but, more importantly, the manner, style and way of expression. If we oversimplify those two projections, we may roughly reduce them to 'theme' and 'style'.

The referent-analysing level does not 'hear'. It 'passes' by anything that does not have thematic significance. That is why it makes an 'excellent means of *linear-style* speech reporting' (Vološinov, 1973, p. 130). The texture-analysing modification, however, incorporates into indirect discourse the subjective and stylistic physiognomy of the message, including the specific words and expressions. Here is also the authorial angle. The speaker who represents other speakers 'makes strange' their representations, 'suits himself', inserts his own attitude, and adds shades, colours and social comments. For Vološhinov, the texture-analysing style is a *non-linear* way of reporting, rooted in cultures of critical and realistic individualism such as the Russian one. In contrast, the referent-analysing, linear perspective is predominant in Western cultures shaped by Enlightenment and rationalist type of individualism – especially the French one.[3]

I am tempted here to make a parallel between Vološinov's theme and style and my analysis of 'the message as the story' and 'the messenger as the story' (see Chapter 3). I think also of the shift from 'issue' to 'image politics' in the turn towards political marketing in the 1970s and 1980s (Lees-Marshment, 2001; Newman, 1999; Schweiger & Adami, 1999). Theme and style also correspond with Shanto Iyengar's differentiation between 'thematic' (focus on societal and political actors) and 'episodic fames' (emphasis on individual victims, use of pro-establishment heuristics) in the news media (Iyengar, 2009). Today, the tabloid and social media formats pursue their grabs and click-baits by personality politics rather than policy analysis – looking at 'style' rather than 'theme'. It is sort of an anti-Enlightenment reversal of public language, 'acting' less French and more Russian.

Metamessages

On the texture-analysing side of indirect discourse, we see the function of silence in *metamessages*. As the *First Axiom of Communication* suggests, 'One cannot not communicate' (Watzlawick, Bevelas & Jackson, 1998).[4] What a speaker says and what not, how he says it and how not, are not only deliberate choices he makes to suit the expectations of an audience. Wittingly or unwittingly, he also communicates his whole social persona, including his habitual ways of communicating, over which he has little or no control (Bateson, 1972). To take the axiom to a new level: *We cannot not communicate a metamessage.* In other words, the public not only hears *what* we want to tell it (according to our definition of situation of communication) but it also hears – (and sees!) – *how* we tell it (according to its definition of the situation of communication). Ultimately, the public judges a speaker against not only what he says but also what he shows.

Metalanguage is silent. Silence mixes with voice either way. It supports or contradicts it. It may conceal or reveal. Indirect discourse is difficult to navigate, and so metalanguage.

There is *metamessage* in the metalanguage. Professional communicators watch and include it in their message strategies. A metamessage could have positive or negative effects on the speaker. In a metamessage, the indirect clues of the social status and orientation of the speaker are often more powerful than their direct statements and appeals (Bourdieu, 1977). Yet unaware metamessages may also unwittingly 'betray' what a messenger does not want to say but cannot conceal. This is, for example, a disadvantage in advertised content. The metamessage is first in the genre itself. Someone has paid for the message. The metamessage also does not leave any doubt about whom the message serves. But public relations is also not immune to the unintended effects of metamessages. An example I have already discussed is when the message is not silent about (the hidden process of) its production (see Chapter 3).

The former Polish President, Lech Walesa, usurped a big chunk of broadcast time in his frequent appearances on the national TV (Jakubowicz, 1996). He believed – and this was not rare attitude in Eastern Europe in the 1990s – that he who has the TV has the power. Yet being all over the place on air did not serve him the way he expected. The public could not prevent Walesa from appearing on 'his' TV as often as he wanted, but Walesa could not prevent the audience from seeing not only what he wanted to show. He poorly understood the treachery waters of the medium and magnifying glass effects of the screen. Instead of dominating the agenda and imposing his authority, his rather high-handed and abrasive style alienated the viewers. The more they were watching him, the less they were listening to him (Millard, 1998).

One cannot not metacommunicate. So the question is not whether but how to do it. The metamessage is the most indirect, silent part of the message. *Any message is also a messenger of a metamessage.* The metamessage is often overlooked, although, potentially, it is the most powerful part of the message. It could be either a bliss or menace in PR practice. A bliss, when the metamessage goes undetected under the radar of the addressee. And a menace, when it is just a slip of the tongue by the speaker. A bliss, because the metamessage does not appear as deliberate and instrumental as the message. This makes it especially efficient. And a menace, because undervalued and uncontrolled, a metamessage may work as a counter-message against the intended one. In this case, the communicator acts like a driver who simultaneously pushes both the accelerator and the breaks of his car.

Notes

1 I align here with academics who do not find evidence against the thesis that public spheres are still national rather than international. For example, there is still reasonable doubt about the existence not only of a global but even of a European public sphere (Benson, 2001; Bentele & Nothhaft, 2010; Dahlgren, 2005; Koopmans & Pfetsch, 2003; Volkmer, 2003).

2 Today, it is almost certain that Mikhail Bakhtin has written a couple of books under the names of his associates Vološhinov and Medvedev, including the book I quote here, *Marxism and the Philosophy of Language* (Vološinov, 1973). Sergey Bocharov, the collection editor of Bakhtin, gives various proofs (including Bakhtin's admissions from conversations with him) for those collaborations, which allowed Bakhtin, especially after his arrest, to publish although under another names (Bocharov, 1994). Bakhtin's wish, however, was not to alter the names of the authors and to let those books live as historical facts.

3 Vološinov states that the Western type of referent-analysing has no parallel in Russian literary language. This explains the absolute predominance of texture-analysing over referent-analysing modification in Russian (Vološinov, 1973, p. 132). Those are important cultural differences between the public spheres in the West and East, which the Habermas' model has not incorporated but which are significant from a PR perspective.

4 I have already discussed why abstract rules like this axiom are true only partially and only in in situations of communication, in which the main participants are expecting and anticipating communication. The shifting boundaries of that very definition – whether there is situation of communication or not, who should speak and who should listen – are themselves a strategic battle front, and not only, not even primarily, a question of whether the message comes across or not.

References

Austin, W. J. (1975). *How to do things with words: The William James Lectures delivered at Harvard University in 1955*. Oxford: Oxford Scholarship Online.

Bakhtin, M. (1986). *Speech genres and other late essays*. Austin, TX: University of Texas Press.

Bakhtin, M. M. (2010). *The dialogic imagination: Four essays* (Vol. 1). Austin TX: University of Texas Press.

Bateson, G. (1972). *Steps to an ecology of mind*. Chicago, IL: University of Chicago Press.

Benson, R. (2001). *The mediated public sphere: A model for cross-national research?* Berkeley, CA: University of California Press.

Bentele, G., & Nothhaft, H. (2010). Strategic communication and the public sphere from a European perspective. *International Journal of Strategic Communication, 4*(2), 93–116.

Benveniste, E. (1971). *Problems in general linguistics* (Vol. 8). Coral Gables, FL: University of Miami Press.

Bocharov, S. (1994). Conversations with Bakhtin. *Publications of the Modern Language Association of America, 109*(5), 1009–1024.

Bourdieu, P. (1977). The economics of linguistic exchanges. *Social Science Information, 16*(6), 645–668.

Brown, P., & Levinson, S. C. (1987). *Politeness: Some universals in language usage* (Vol. 4). Cambridge: Cambridge University Press.

Dahlgren, P. (2005). The Internet, public spheres, and political communication: Dispersion and deliberation. *Political Communication, 22*, 147–162.

Deleuze, G., & Guattari, F. (1987). *A thousand plateaus: Capitalism and schizophrenia*. London: Bloomsbury.

Fairclough, N. (1992). *Discourse and social change*. Cambridge: Polity Press.

Fairclough, N. (2001). *Language and power* (2nd edn). London: Pearson Education.

Foucault, M. (1990). *The will to knowledge: The history of sexuality* (Vol. 1). London: Penguin.

Gee, J. P. (2011). *How to do discourse analysis: A toolkit.* New York: Routledge.

Goffman, E. (1955). On face-work: An analysis of ritual elements in social interaction. *Psychiatry, 18*(3), 213–231.

Goffman, E. (2005). *Interaction ritual: Essays in face to face behavior.* New Brunswick, NJ: Aldine Transaction.

Grice, H. P. (1975). Logic and conversation. In P. Cole & J. L. Morgan (Ed.), *Syntax and semantics* (pp. 41–58). New York: Academic Press.

Iyengar, S. (2009). How framing influences understanding of public issues (An interview). *FrameWorks Institute.* Retrieved 12 June 2017, from www.frameworksinstitute. org/assets/files/iyengarinterview2009.pdf.

Jakubowicz, K. (1996). Television and elections in post-1989 Poland: How powerful is the medium? In D. L. Swanson & P. Mancini (Eds.). *Politics, media, and modern democracy. An international study of innovations in electoral campaigning and their consequences.* Westport, CN: Praeger.

Jalbert, P. L. (1994). Structures of the 'unsaid'. *Theory, Culture & Society, 11,* 127–160.

Koopmans, R., & Pfetsch, B. (2003). *Towards a Europeanised public sphere? Comparing political actors and the media in Germany, ARENA Working Paper 23/2003.* Retrieved 12 June 2017, from www.sv.uio.no/arena/english/research/publications/ arena-working-papers/2001-2010/2003/wp03_23.pdf.

Kurzon, D. (1992). When silence may mean power. *Journal of Pragmatics, 18*(1), 92–95.

Lees-Marshment, J. (2001). The marriage of politics and marketing. *Political Studies, 49,* 692–713.

Leitch, S., & Motion, J. (2007). Retooling the corporate brand: A Foucauldian perspective on normalisation and differentiation. *Journal of Brand Management, 15*(1), 71–80.

Millard, F. (1998). Democratization and the media in Poland 1989–97. *Democratization, 5*(2), 85–105.

Motion, J., & Leitch, S. (2007). A toolbox for public relations: The oeuvre of Michel Foucault. *Public Relations Review, 33*(3), 263–268.

Newman, B. W. (1999). *The mass marketing of politics. Democracy in an age of manufactured images.* Thousand Oaks, CA: Sage.

Schweiger, G., & Adami, M. (1999). The non-verbal image of politicians and political parties. In B. W. Newman (Ed.), *Handbook of political marketing* (pp. 347–364). Thousand Oaks, CA: Sage.

Scollon, R., & Scollon, S. W. (2001). Discourse and intercultural communication. In D. Schiffrin, D. Tannen, & A. E. Hamilton (Eds.), *The handbook of discourse analysis* (pp. 538–547). Malden, MA: Blackwell.

Sifianou, M. (1997). Silence and politeness. In A. Jaworski (Ed.), *Silence: Interdisciplinary perspectives* (pp. 63–84). Berlin; New York: Mouton de Gruyter.

Tannen, D. (1985). Silence: Anything but. In D. Tannen & M. Saville-Troike (Eds.), *Perspectives on silence* (pp. 93–111). Norwood, NJ: Ablex Publishing.

Volkmer, I. (2003). The global network society and the global public sphere. *Development, 46*(1), 9–16.

Vološinov, V. N. (1973). *Marxism and the philosophy of language.* New York; London: Seminar Press.

Watzlawick, P., Bevelas, J. B. & Jackson, D. D. (1998). *Pragmatics of human communication: A study of interactional patterns, pathologies and paradoxes.* New York: Norton.

Wilson, J. (2006). Power and pragmatics. In K. Brown (Ed.), *Encyclopedia of language & linguistics.* London: Elsevier.

10 Explicit and implicit silence

Explicit silence

Moving to the next and highest level, one can break down indirect discourse into *explicit* and *implicit* communication strategies. Explicit silences are '*notable silences*'. Barry Brummett (1980) gives an example of strategic silence, when he discusses *presidential silences.* He focuses on the US President, Jimmy Carter's conspicuous absences from public life. In July 1979, for ten days, Carter cancelled a major speech on the rising costs and decreasing availability of oil. Instead, he withdrew into his Camp David residence, where he held a 'domestic summit', consulted aids, met locals but did not talk publically about the worsening energy crisis.

Brummett is a key author for the goals of this analysis. He is one of the few communication scholars,[1] who have offered a definition of *strategic silence.* His definition, however, is a very specific one. He studies *presidential silences* as cases of *political* strategic silence. But what strategic silence is not political?

Brummett assigns to strategic silence three major features: (1) it *violates expectations;* (2) it always attributes a predicable set of meanings such as '*mystery, uncertainty, passivity and relinquishment*'; and (3) it is *intentional* and *directed* at an audience (1980, p. 290).

I find the first aspect, violation of expectations, important. It is pertinent to the definition of *explicit silence*, but not of implicit silence. Explicit silence is *notable* silence that *violates* the expectations of a public for verbal communication. Instead it receives non-verbal communication. But is silence here only lack of talk or also lack of communication? To make sense of this silence, the public is pushed out of its comfort zone and tacitly asked to re-define and broaden its expectation of communication – to include silence as part of it. This is a big ask – and risk. But it is strategic. Risk and strategy often go hand in hand. The President offers his silence as a different – he hopes a better – medium for a different message. But would the public be able to process that shift of medium and message? Would it tolerate that violation? Would it be willing – according to the Grice's principle of relevance – to walk the extra mile and find a sound reason in what does not make sense? Would it be able to 'decode' the presidential silence as communication instead of the lack of such?

Explicit silence is *conversational* silence (Bilmes, 1994). The President is expected to talk, but he does not. And this is remarkable. Publics interpret each notable silence regardless of whether it is intended or not. A silence becomes notable when it constitutes something like an exception, deviation or disruption. Silences, which are formal (i.e. of the subordinate) or customary (i.e. out of respect), are not strategic.[2] Normative, ritual, institutional, role-bound, unmarked, and other silences are expected and therefore not notable. They remain an inarticulate background of other non-silent events.

Many presidential silences are strategic. Abraham Lincoln's prolonged silence before his *Gettysburg Address*, which purpose was to prevent not only the country but also (and perhaps more importantly) the Republican party from early splitting on the inevitability of the imminent war with the Border slave states, is a classic example of strategic silence (Black, 1994; Gunderson, 1961). Strategic is also the *near silence* of the 'minimum comment' (Brummett, 1980, p. 295). In 1979, Senator Edward Kennedy tersely and repeatedly denied his intention to run for president. This is one of the most universal uses (if there is such) of strategic silence. He who denies running for a leader position until the time has come does not give the rivals the munitions to subvert him as the 'presumptive' frontrunner. Silence keeps one's powder dry.

Variations of this near silence often mark the boundary between strategy and tactic. Such are the techniques of 'small target' and 'keeping low profile' (see Chapter 13), when more public attention would inevitably inflict more political damage (Sparrow & Turner, 2001). In the short term, such tactics may serve as camouflage to survive the contest. But in the long run, because strategy requires more than reflex, they may turn self-defeating.[3]

The second part of Brummett's definition of strategic silence – that it attributes a predictable set of meanings such as 'mystery, uncertainty, passivity and relinquishment' – is unconvincing. Brummett presumes that presidential silences do not fully need to rely on context. There is something metaphysical in the political stature (if not charisma) of the President. Perhaps he knows something the people do not know. Perhaps the perceived weakness of the President conceals his real strength. Perhaps he is holding his winning cards to his chest. Perhaps Carter was not speaking because he was listening. Perhaps his strategic silence 'received at least one desirable attributed meaning, that of creating an image of receiving communication even if he gave none out' (Brummett, 1980, p. 300).

Mystery is a convenient substitute for explanation. Linking silence with mystic has been an entrenched bias in the Western cultural traditions. Mystical is what cannot be expressed in words. What cannot be expressed in words is mystical (Bindeman, 1981; Streng, 1983). Brummett chooses metaphysics to practice. He presupposes invariable and predicable attributions to presidential silences. Such constants do not exist. There are no equal silences – not even presidential ones. No strategic silence should be taken out of the conditions and context of its production. One should explore the presuppositions of Brummett's presuppositions. In the President Carter's example, 'mystery' and 'uncertainty' may indicate disorientation. In the end his strategic silence failed. It did not create more suspense. It rather broke the rule of relevance. Meaningful communication was no longer taking place. The public saw Carter as 'weak' and 'wavering yet again'. By the way, it is risky to build a positive category based on a negative case. What was wrong: President Carter's strategic silence or its Brummett's definition?

The third aspect of it – that strategic silence is 'intentional' and 'directed' towards audiences – is not wrong. Of course, people and organisations intend, formulate, plan and direct strategies toward audiences. Brummett, however, finishes where his analysis should start. His model of communication is abstract, asymmetric and productionist. The speaker, the President in this case, is who creates the meaning. Missing in the analysis are the critical co-determinants – the existing discursive practices, including political strategies, which circulate in collective, impersonal and widely automatised modes (see Chapter 5). In the political public sphere, politicians and communicators are neither the sole nor the main producers of communication strategies. They need at least half of their time to research and adjust to the flow of already excising strategies and use their direction and thrust. What they can do is to 'piggyback' or 'sail into the wind' of that flow. What they cannot is to create or control it.

There are examples of successful presidential silences too. In 1991, when the fall of the Soviet Union was approaching, President George H. W. Bush chose to remain largely silent in response to the critical events around the attempted coup in Moscow and its aftermath. It proved to be the right move. It allowed the disintegration of the USSR to occur without leaving an impression of US interference, which would give the communist hardliners an excuse to rebel against meddling from outside (Harlow, 2014). Other silences, however, such as the failure of President Ronald Reagan in the 1980s to denounce the regime of apartheid in South Africa were more controversial. Even if it was as a provisional strategic choice in the absence of a best choice, many interpreted Reagan's silence as complicit rather than diplomatic (Dugard, 1982; Harlow, 2010).

Explicit silence is a risky strategy because it places much weight on the interpretative capacity of a public, in the presidential case – of many publics. The public, not the speaker has to do the heavy lifting of sense making. The risk is double. The public has to decide what meaning silence caries. But it also has to establish whether it is meaningful in the first place. This is a public relations issue too. It affects the relationship of the person or organisation with a public. Does a notable *silence allow the public to relate to a speaker or not*? Does the public interpret it as a prolonged conversation or as an abrupt escape from it? Because the PR principle remains the same: *No conversation – no relating – no relations*.

Explicit silences may be *explained* or unexplained. The presidential silences discussed above were not explained – at least not to their addressees. And there are degrees of explanation – with anything in between. A speaker may choose to clarify why he has been (was, will be) silent. But is talking about silence still silence? Talking about silence is 'talking'. Silence is especially powerful when self-explanatory. Brummett is right when he counts only *unexplained silence as strategic silence.* Explained silence cannot violate expectations (Brummett, 1980, p. 290). Businesses and governments often go to great lengths in justifying their various silences with 'nothing new', intellectual rights, confidentiality clauses, privacy protection, litigation concerns, operational matters, military secrets and national security. That way, they create and maintain expected silences, which may be a part of broader strategies but are not strategic silences per se.

Implicit silence

In contrast to explicit silence, which is notable, implicit silence is anything but. Its function is quite the opposite. Explicit silence means something that words cannot express. Implicit silence means one thing by saying another. Explicit silence appeals to the consciousness of the public. Implicit silence tries to slip under its radar. Explicit silence takes chances. It challenges the public to be the judge. Implicit silence plays it safe. It relies on truths not worth mentioning because taken for granted. No mentioning – no questioning. Explicit silence clarifies by stillness. Implicit silence obscures by words (Bilmes, 1994, p. 82).

Implicit silence is not passive. Its main function is not to withhold. Implicit silence is active. It directly backgrounds, deletes and backgrounds. But it also indirectly suggests, infers and promotes. As life, in the John Lennon famous quote, is what happens to you while you are making other plans. There is no coincidence that, as the highest form of indirect communication, implicit silence is so complex and elusive that many do not see it as silence. This only confirms its particular power. *Silence is most strategic when it does not look like silence.* It is curious to observe how public relations practice employs implicit silence on a daily basis and as core strategy, but public relations theory has not identified, let alone conceptualised it yet.

Strategies of implicit silence define surging public relations areas such as public diplomacy, litigation and investor public relations. The former Federal Reserve Chairman, Alan Greenspan, has elevated implicit silence to art and science of monetary policy communication. His *Fedspeak* has evolved and institutionalised as second language of all those national and international bank leaders, whose statements may affect global markets (Bligh & Hess, 2007; Farber, 2013). Since Greenspan, monetary policy speeches have become fretworks of strategic silence. Laces of measured remarks are knit to say a little in many words. But they are not entirely hollow. That little matters much. Markets – stock, commodity and currency traders, media pundits – expect direction. The responsibility is enormous.

Explicit silence is out of question. No comment would increase uncertainty and send markets into overdrive. Implicit silence such as 'massaging' the meaning of undeniable facts and not getting caught in 'uncooked' policy decisions informs the statements. 'Obfuscation' is how Greenspan readily called it once. 'Your syntax collapses', he confessed.[4] Consider this statement by Greenspan in 2005 before the US House Financial and Services Committee:

Risk takers have been encouraged by a perceived increase in economic stability to reach out to more distant time horizons. But long periods of relative stability often engender unrealistic expectations of it[s] permanence and, at times, may lead to financial excess and economic stress.

(Holden, 2014)

At first glance, the chairman's language is defensive, merely designed to protect the institution and minimise the risk of unintentional consequences from the bank's communication. Yet, there is more to it. Even when Greenspan admits obfuscation, he obfuscates. His 'revelation' is part of his silence. If his only goal was to say as little as possible – and ideally nothing – that would amount not to a successful strategy but to a failed tactic. The function of Fedspeak is more proactive, although less obvious. It is subtle governance by indirect communication. On the one hand it leaves people with the vague feeling that something significant is said, though beyond their competence. This is image management. On the other hand, the trained eye is able to detect valuable cues. Pundits can still speculate about what the decision-makers really think. This is not due to the fact that is impossible to absolutely hide – especially from vested interests and expertise – actual monetary policy behind a wall of verbose silence. Quite the contrary, it is because this form of doublespeak *is policy*. It is made to influence. Ben Bernanke, who succeeded Greenspan, said in a 2012 speech that 'communication about the Fed's expectations' in regard of the exceptionally low interest rates 'is [after security purchases] a second *new monetary policy tool* [my italics]' (Farber, 2013).

With Fedspeak, central bankers can manipulate not only interest rates. They guide expectations about inflation, growth, unemployment, housing market and more. They use *strategic ambiguity* (see Chapter 16) in the balancing act of remaining vague but also precise, credible and, above all, *manifestly confident* in the fundamentals and overall direction of the economy (Holden, 2014). In that regard, one can also study the forestalling and reassuring language of the *Bank of England* in the aftermath of the UK Brexit vote. Public relations assumes a central role when communications about a policy becomes *the* policy as well.

Fedspeak falls only marginally into the category of *Doublespeak*. Taking the cue from George Orwell's *Newspeak* and *Doublethink*, William Lutz has identified types of doublespeak such as euphemisms (i.e. 'enhanced interrogation'); specialist jargon (i.e. 'quantitative easing'); 'bureaucratese' (i.e. 'downsize'); and inflated language (i.e. 'negative patient care outcome') (1989, 1996). Although Fedspeak brims with Doublespeak, this alone is not enough to make its silences implicit or strategic. Doublespeak usually shows the first function of Fedspeak, verbose defensiveness (saying much and meaning little), but not the second one, silent influence (meaning more than actually saying).

Lutz analyses Doublespeak elements at the lower level of words and phrases in a text. Although Fedspeak makes use of such words and phrases, its magic takes place at the higher level of the whole text and its connection with other texts (inter-contextuality). Doublespeak is impervious to context. Its words and phrases are abstract, like replaceable bricks. Fedspeak is highly sensitive to context. Its constructs are concrete, like transient visions. This difference between levels of discourse translates in PR practice as the distinction between tactic and strategy. In short, Fedspeak is more strategic than Doublespeak.

One can also compare the concept of Doublespeak with that of *Unspeak*[TM]. Steven Poole has written the seminal *Unspeak: How Words Become Weapons, How Weapons Become a Message, and How That Message Becomes Reality* (2006). What is the difference here? Doublespeak pretends it is not saying what it is saying. It is not what you think. It does not mean what it says. Unspeak, on the contrary, does not say what it means. What matters is what is *unsaid*, left out (Jalbert, 1994). Doublespeak openly dissuades; Unspeak 'persuades by stealth'. Doublespeak is lexical. Unspeak is syntactic.[5]

The silences of Unspeak are implicit. It subtly infers meanings, which do not surface as utterances in the conversation. This is not because those meanings are not relevant but because they are taken for granted. The implications then serve as subconscious frames for interpreting other meanings, which are questioned and debated. Unspeak makes wide use of *implicatures* – various discursive tools that shape discourses through implicit silence (Bilmes, 1993; Pop, 2010; Vallauri & Masia, 2014). Poole gives the classic example with the 'pro-life' and 'pro-choice' parties in the abortion debate. As implicature 'pro-life' discourse suggests that the opponents are 'anti-life'. 'Pro-choice', on the contrary, infers that those who are against are sexists who deny women their right to dispose of (and make independent decisions about) their body. 'Tax relief' is another example. It presupposes that tax is a burden. It replicates but does not unmask a dominant neoliberal discourse. Like Doublespeak, Unspeak models words and phrases at lexical level. But those words and phrases are concrete, not abstract. They encapsulate in miniature whole unspoken narratives, which silently impact on the listener's mind the level of text and intertextuality.

Implicit silences that discourse are strategic. In Australia, both the Conservatives and Labor debate *within* the 'tax relief' discourse – not against it. They argue about whether a 'levy' (i.e. on *Medicare*) or 'duty' (i.e. on alcopops) is a tax or not. If it looks less like a tax, it is more likely to pass parliament. They would not argue for 'raising taxes', although this is what both sides actually do. Neither would dare to attack the discourse at syntax level (Dimitrov, 2014). Neither would offer an alternative discourse such as that of justice Oliver Wendell Holmes, Jr., 'I like to pay taxes. With them I buy civilization' (cited in Frankfurter, 1938, p. 495). Neither unspeaks – that is deconstructs – 'tax' as implicature. They need it unspoken for their tactical (for a political advantage), not strategic (for changing the society) struggle.

One cannot underestimate the importance of implicit silences in public relations. Communicators need to know the intended and unintended effects from dealing with the lexical and syntax levels of discourse as well as Fedspeak, Unspeak and other practices of silence. Even when one aligns with a cause, constituency or client at the level of syntax, message and narrative, one may unwittingly undermine their own enterprise at lexical, order-word and code-word level. Communicators must be aware of the power of the unsaid – of whole ideologies, discourses and doctrines settled and hardened as self-evident, 'neutral' and minute 'figures of speech' in public language. When Labour politicians, for example, deny that their 'revenue measures' amount to 'raising taxes', they reinforce the neoliberal discourse of 'tax is a burden'. Which in the long run is self-defeating. They loudly argue in a language, which quietly works against their case.[6]

Framing the mix

Strategic packages contain not only silent and non-silent but also explicit and implicit silence strategies in unique mixes. When a speaker, for example, answers another question, not the question asked by journalists, this technique typically combines explicit and implicit silence. The speaker explicitly does not answer the question. But he implicitly suggests an answer to a question that has not been asked. As I will later argue, the art and science of silence is in influencing the questions, not the answers (see Chapter 19).

Grice's *maxim of relevance* reflects the common rule that all participants in a conversation contributed appropriately (that is in a meaningful manner) to its needs and goals (Grice, 1975). Even when one *flouts* the maxim and skilfully dodges a question by answering another one (through irony, sarcasm, hyperbole), the others are still capable of finding an indirect meaning in the lack of a direct one. I remember I was a kid and our class met with the writer of a children book we had have to read. 'What did you feel when you were writing?' I diligently asked him when my turn came. 'It was hot and the flies were biting', batted out the exasperate author. You can break the rule of relevance, but you cannot escape it (Bilmes, 1994, p. 76). The mix of explicit and implicit silences does not necessarily grind a conversation to a hold. It may be an eloquent interruption that triggers an unexpected interpretation.

I would also like to pick a fresh example from the time of writing these lines. In June 2016, *Politico.com* had learned that *Apple* had privately told US Republican (GOP) leaders that it would not provide funding or other support (like MacBooks) to the party's 2016 presidential convention as it had done in the past. It also conveyed to the GOP leadership that it decided to stay away due to the controversial comments of their presumptive presidential candidate, Donald Trump, about immigrants, minorities and women. This was in response to Trump's verbal attack on the whole tech industry. The candidate then singled out *Apple* for its stance on encryption and called for a boycott of the company's products (Romm, 2016).

This situation of communication involved various silences. *Politico* got the news from 'two sources familiar with the iPhone maker's plans' – not one but two leaks. Leaks are forms of silent communication. Both the source and the media are silent about the source, not the news. But there is no silence between the source and the media. There is silence only between them and their publics (see Chapter 3). *Politico* did not say whether the sources originated from *Apple* or the GOP Headquarters or both. One can only speculate. Both institutions declined to publically comment on the story.

Apple's silent move not to support the 2016 Republican convention was telling. It communicated with body language, not with words. Communication is action; action is communication. A deed or gesture is one of the most efficient tools of explicit silence. 'Their deeds speak for themselves'. 'Don't tell them, show them'. A decisive move – especially if it does not seem designed for public effects but of course is – earns high credibility with no need to explain. Gazing as listening does not need verification. Gazing verifies listening. What is seen validates what is heard (see Chapter 6). If *Apple* had centrally leaked, which is my educated guess, it was strategic. If someone in the Republican Party had leaked, it was rather subversive. Subversive may be strategic or not, depending on the intentions of the source, reputation of the organisation and public resonance the leak gets (see Chapter 18).

The Trump campaign did not respond to the *Politico*'s request for comment. No comment may constitute deferred communication (no meaning involved) or explicit silence (conveying a meaning). This one was deferred communication as the make-up of no communication (averting any meaning). The problem is that the perspective of the campaign was the perspective neither of the media nor of the audiences. No comment is no news. But this is not feeding the imagination of others. The media then present the lack of comment, the silence, as news. No communication from the point of Trump's campaign becomes explicit silence from the point of the media. No comment becomes *hidden* news, and silence – a sign of agreement.[7] That is why the media prefer to see explicit silences even where speakers are left with no choice – where both speaking and being silent are 'worse options' (see Chapter 13).

Trump's silence was also explained silence. His campaign had revoked the press credentials of *Politico* and other news outlets.[8] It was giving them the silent treatment. Trump was making no secret of that. He used the ban as a deterrence to others. The ban explained the silence. It made it explicit from all points of view.

The only verbal reply came from a spokeswoman for the GOP convention: 'We are working with a variety of major tech partners who are focused on being part of the American political process' (Romm, 2016). This was an answer. But answered was another question, not the question *Politico* had asked. *Questions rather than answers frame a discourse*. It was the GOP frame, not the frame of the media. This is already implicit silence. And it is core in public relations discourse.[9] As George Lakoff cautioned: Do not try to change the frame of an opponent. Stick to your own frame. Do not even try to refute what the other contends.

> When we negate a frame, we evoke the frame. Richard Nixon found that the hard way.... He stood before the nation and said, 'I am not a crook'. And everybody thought about him as a crook. This gives us a basic principle of

framing, for when you are arguing against the other side: Do not use their language. Their language picks out a frame – and it won't be the frame you want.

(Lakoff, 2004, p. 3)

First, the GOP answer did not confirm the fact of *Apple*'s withdrawal. No mention of the elephant in the room. No newsworthy admission. Second, the reply only reaffirmed that 'a variety' of tech companies customarily helps the Republican convention. One more or less, what difference does it make? Variety is quality in quantity, not a number. Third, the emphasis was on the democratic process. If you are not part of it, that is your problem. And, finally, the GOP reply used present tense – 'are working' and 'are focussed' – which has stronger modality than the past tense in a question like, 'What happened?'

Extreme examples of answering questions that are not asked are the Kelly-anne Conway's performances before journalists. She is, as I write, Counsellor to the President for Donald Trump and has also been a Republican Party campaign manager, strategist and pollster. The problem, however, is that she always changes the questions to such a degree that her answers are often ridiculously absurd (Vox, 2017). Influencing the questions is serious art and science. Yes, questions do frame. Yes, answers can re-frame. But answers that re-frame still have to make sense in relation to the frame of the question – *as if* they are within the same frame. This silent 'as if' secures the chain of equivalency in the move between non-linear logics. Frames grow slowly and 'naturally' in the public sphere. They are quasi-objective structures of meaning. One cannot ignore or reject them at will or ad-hoc (Lakoff, 2010; Nisbet & Huge, 2006). An old rule in rhetoric posits that a speaker always has to start from the premise of the audience and then subtly lead it toward her or his conclusion (Perelman, 1982).

Explicit and implicit silences work in concert in discursive practice. Silence does not only cover words; words do not only conceal silence. Both words and silences work simultaneously, dialectically, and inseparably. Noisy silences are in contention. Discourses fight one another – frame against frame. They displace – and silence – one another.

Notes

1 Not much in communication studies is published about strategic silence and virtually nothing in the public relations literature. Along Brummett's 'classic', I would point out two other articles that deal with strategic silence in a more systematic way. One is Richard Lentz' *The Search for Strategic Silence: Discovering what Journalism Leaves Out* (1991). His eloquent historical analysis, however, focuses on strategic silences as editorial policies of the US legacy media. (Yet the difference between journalist and PR strategic silence is perhaps smaller than both professions wants us to believe.) And Adam Jaworski, who has for a long time worked about silence, writing one book (1993) and editing another (1997), returned once more to the topic in *Strategies of Silence: Omission and Ambiguity in the Black Book of Polish Censorship* (Jaworski & Galasiński, 2000). Censorship is an important political condition of strategic silence. I believe the content of that article is close not only to people like him and myself, who

have grown in communist East European countries. Just, the soft power of market-based (self-)censorship in the Western word proved to be more efficient and durable than the hard power of government-based coercion.

2 Brummett claims that Gandhi's practice of observing regular period of silence (Merriam, 1975) was meaningful and political but not strategic. That may had been the case in various contexts of his life. But when he fell silent and went on infinite hunger strike until the atrocities between Hindus and Muslims stop, he strategically used physical self-denial, 'dead silence' as the ultimate form of leadership.

3 Strategic silence also occurs when a group or representative delays or refuses to take a verbal action. In 2016, the House Speaker Paul Ryan (R-Wis.) conspicuously protracted his formal backing of the presumptive presidential nominee Donald Trump. His silence was not hostile but, nevertheless, pointed. It was as strategic as the endorsement Ryan eventually gave Trump after one-month holdout (Kane, 2016).

4 In the same interview for the *Chicago Tribune*, he was cheekily self-deprecating.

> What tends to happen is your syntax collapses. All of the sudden you are mumbling. It often works. I created a new language, which we now call Fedspeak. Unless you are expert at it, you can't tell that I didn't say anything.
>
> (Barnhart, 2007)

5 Halliday and Webster have observed that tacit meaning is more common when we move from micro to macro, in language from lexical to grammatical choices. 'Conscious language achieves its creative force mainly by lexical means; and lexical items are semantically close to experience. Unconscious language depends much more for its creative force on grammar – and grammatical categories are far removed from experience' (Halliday & Matthiessen, 2004, p. 303). In my opinion, this delineates a major difference between Doublespeak and Unspeak.

6 Steven Poole's *Unspeak*™ drew the ire of Alastair Campbell, best known as the Director of Communications and Strategy for Prime Minister Tony Blair (from 1997 and 2003). Campbell was instrumental in designing the 'New Labour' strategy and language of the Blair years (Campbell, 2007). Poole richly uses examples of the New Labour vocabulary not only to deconstruct their ideological façade, but also to question their 'newness' in the broader neo-liberal discourse. (In a Foucauldian way, Poole does not distinguish between bad and good government.) This is something rather marginal in his effort but central in Norman Fairclough's critic of Blair and Campbell, in *New Labour, new language* (Fairclough, 2000). Defending his legacy, Campbell attacks the 'hypocrisy' in Poole's 'Paris left-bank ... vague, under-developed, anti-war, anti-corporate, anti-politics agenda', in his book review of Unspeak (Campbell, 2006). From the position of a public relations practitioner, he contends that indirect figures of speech, patterns of the unsaid and implicit meanings are inherently nether good not bad. They are what they are. They are powerful discursive tools everyone can use. In the hands of governments, their concrete use – the values, motives and choices behind them – is what makes them good or bad. For example, Campbell argues, IRA was 'in war' with governments, not governments with the IRA. The success in Northern Ireland was sealed with the IRA declaration that 'war' was over. Or Labour's 'community support officer' should not be dismissed as 'a second-class cadre of policeman'. Politics without words is not the alternative of politics. Politics uses words and silences simultaneously and sometimes synonymously.

7 Not even in court is the right to remain silent treated neutrally. Against the judge's advice, jurors are tempted to suspect and interpret silence as cover-up of guilt (Davis, 2002; Fortunato Jr, 1998; Kurzon, 1995, 2011). Even more so in the 'court of the public opinion'. Australian PR Director Geoffrey Stackhouse chose to name in his blog the entertainer Rolf Harris, when the UK Police had imposed an embargo on that name. He argued, 'Our legal system is based on the presumption of innocence, but sadly [*sic!*] the court of public opinion is not' (Miller, 2013).

8 The media ban included (as of June 2016) *Politico,* the *Washington Post, BuzzFeed, the Des Moines Register* and *The Huffington Post* (Sullivan, 2016).
9 Three days before the 2016 Federal Elections in Australia and just after the media blackout of political ads had started, a radio host asked the Prime Minister, Malcolm Turnbull, whether he wished the opposition leader, Bill Shorten, well. He replied, 'I wish every Australian the best of health' (Murphy, 2016). Implicit silence is always the same, but there are myriad ways of using it. In this case, the PM dodges the *real* meaning of the question, which is *metaphorical* ('well'), and safely plays the fool by replacing it by the meaning of his choice, which is the *literal* one ('health'). His indirect answer also includes a logical (abstract, non-contextual) presupposition: 'I wish every Australian the best health', 'The opposition leader is an Australian', 'Thus I wish the opposition leader the best of health'. The function of such purely logical and deliberately emptied syllogism is to de-individualise and belittle the opponent.

References

Barnhart, B. (2007, 18 May). Fedspeak's new nuances. *The Chicago Tribune.* Retrieved 12 June 2017, from http://articles.chicagotribune.com/2007-05-18/business/0705171 115_1_greenspan-and-bernanke-ben-bernanke-monetary-policy.

Bilmes, J. (1993). Ethnomethodology, culture, and implicature: Toward an empirical pragmatics. *Pragmatics, 3*(4), 387–409.

Bilmes, J. (1994). Constituting silence: Life in the world of total meaning. *Semiotica, 98*(1–2), 73–88.

Bindeman, S. L. (1981). *Heidegger and Wittgenstein: The poetics of silence.* Washington, DC: University Press of America.

Black, E. (1994). Gettysburg and silence. *Quarterly Journal of Speech, 80*(1), 21–36.

Bligh, M. C., & Hess, G. D. (2007). The power of leading subtly: Alan Greenspan, rhetorical leadership, and monetary policy. *Leadership Quarterly, 18*(2), 87–104.

Brummett, B. (1980). Towards a theory of silence as a political strategy. *Quarterly Journal of Speech, 66*(3), 289–303.

Campbell, A. (2006, 11 February). We must talk. *Guardian.* Retrieved 12 June 2017, from www.theguardian.com/books/2006/feb/11/highereducation.alistaircampbell.

Campbell, A. (2007). *The Blair years.* London: Hutchinson.

Davis, T. J. (2002). Conspiracy and credibility: Look who's talking, about what: Law talk and loose talk. *William and Mary Quarterly, 59*(1), 167–174.

Dimitrov, R. (2014). 'Does this guy ever shut up?' The discourse of the 2013 Australian Election. *Global Media Journal: Australian Edition, 8*(2).

Dugard, J. (1982). Silence is not golden. *Foreign Policy, 46,* 37–48.

Fairclough, N. (2000). *New Labour, new language.* London: Routledge.

Farber, A. (2013). Historical echoes: Fedspeak as a second language. *Liberty Street Economics.* Retrieved 12 June 2017, from http://libertystreeteconomics.newyorkfed. org/2013/04/historical-echoes-fedspeak-as-a-second-language.html – .Vd5AJulNOpq.

Fortunato Jr, S. J. (1998). On a judge's duty to speak extrajudicially: Rethinking the strategy of silence. *Georgetown Journal of Legal Ethics, 12,* 679–716.

Frankfurter, F. (1938). Justice Holmes defines the constitution. *Atlantic Monthly, 162*(4), 484–498.

Grice, H. P. (1975). Logic and conversation. In P. Cole & J. L. Morgan (Ed.), *Syntax and semantics* (pp. 41–58). New York: Academic Press.

Gunderson, R. G. (1961). Lincoln and the policy of eloquent silence: November, 1860, to March, 1861. *Quarterly Journal of Speech, 47*(1), 1–9.

Halliday, M. A., & Matthiessen, C. M. (2004). *An introduction to functional grammar* (3rd edn). New York: Routledge.

Harlow, W. F. (2010). Silence as presidential argument in international affairs. *Texas Speech Communication Journal, 35*, 76–95.

Harlow, W. F. (2014). The rhetoric of silence and the collapse of the Soviet Empire. *American Communication Journal, 16*(2), 52–66.

Holden, R. (2014, 24 August). Greenspan's 'uncertainty principle' and the evolution of Fedspeak. *The Conversation*. Retrieved 12 June 2017, from http://theconversation.com/greenspans-uncertainty-principle-and-the-evolution-of-fedspeak-29784

Jalbert, P. L. (1994). Structures of the 'Unsaid'. *Theory, Culture & Society, 11*, 127–160.

Jaworski, A. (1993). *The power of silence: Social and pragmatic perspectives*. Newbury Park, CA: Sage.

Jaworski, A. (Ed.). (1997). *Silence: interdisciplinary perspectives*: Berlin; New York: Mouton de Gruyter.

Jaworski, A., & Galasiński, D. (2000). Strategies of silence: Omission and ambiguity in the Black Book of Polish Censorship. *Semiotica, 131*(1–2), 185–200.

Kane, P. (2016, 2 June). Paul Ryan endorses Donald Trump. *Washington Post*. Retrieved 12 June 2017, from www.washingtonpost.com/news/powerpost/wp/2016/06/02/paul-ryan-endorses-donald-trump/?hpid=hp_hp-top-table-main_trumpryan_lede_330pm%3Ahomepage%2Fstory.

Kurzon, D. (1995). The right of silence: A socio-pragmatic model of interpretation. *Journal of Pragmatics, 23*(1), 55–69.

Kurzon, D. (2011). Speed traps and the right of silence. *Research in Language, 9*(1), 165–176.

Lakoff, G. (2004). *Don't think of an elephant! Know your values and frame the debate*. White River Junction, VT: Chelsea Green Publishing.

Lakoff, G. (2010). Why it matters how we frame the environment. *Environmental Communication, 4*(1), 70–81.

Lentz, R. (1991). The search for strategic silence: Discovering what journalism leaves out. *American Journalism, 8*(1), 10–26.

Lutz, W. (1989). *Doublespeak: From 'revenue enhancement' to 'terminal living': How government, business, advertisers, and others use language to deceive you*. New York: Harper & Row.

Lutz, W. (1996). *The new doublespeak: Why no one knows what anyone's saying anymore*. New York: HarperCollins Publishers.

Merriam, A. H. (1975). Symbolic action in India: Gandhi's nonverbal persuasion. *Quarterly Journal of Speech, 61*(3), 290–306.

Miller, N. (2013, 3 April). To name or not: In age of Twitter, such is dilemma for mainstream media. *The Sydney Morning Herald*, p. 2.

Murphy, K. (2016). Australian election 2016: Radio host tells Turnbull he'll be replaced if he doesn't win well. *Guardian*. Retrieved 12 June 2017, from www.theguardian.com/australia-news/live/2016/jun/30/australian-election-2016-turnbull-claims-a-mandate-and-calls-for-maturity-politics-live.

Nisbet, M. C., & Huge, M. (2006). Where do science debates come from? Understanding attention cycles and framing. In D. Brossard, J. Shanahan, & T. C. Nesbitt (Eds.), *The public, the media and agricultural biotechnology* (pp. 193–230). Cambridge, MA: CAB International.

Perelman, C. (1982). *The realm of rhetoric*. Notre Dame, IN: University of Notre Dame Press.

Poole, S. (2006). *Unspeak^{TM}: How words become weapons, how weapons become a message, and how that message becomes reality.* New York: Grove Press.

Pop, A. (2010). Implicatures derived through maxim flouting in print advertising. A contrastive empirical approach. *Toronto Working Papers in Linguistics, 33*(1).

Romm, T. (2016). Apple won't aid GOP convention over Trump. *Politico.* Retrieved 12 June 2017, from www.politico.com/story/2016/06/apple-wont-aid-gop-convention-over-trump-224513.

Sparrow, N., & Turner, J. (2001). The permanent campaign. The integration of market research techniques in developing strategies in a more uncertain political climate. *European Journal of Marketing, 35*(9/10), 984–1002.

Streng, F. (1983). The ontology of silence and comparative mysticism. *Philosophy Today, 27*(2), 121–127.

Sullivan, M. (2016). Does it matter that Donald Trump has banned us? Not in the way you'd think. *Washington Post.* Retrieved 12 June 2017, from www.washingtonpost.com/lifestyle/style/does-it-matter-that-donald-trump-has-banned-us-not-in-the-way-youd-think/2016/06/14/e11aa0c2-324f-11e6-95c0-2a6873031302_story.html.

Vallauri, E. L., & Masia, V. (2014). Implicitness impact: Measuring texts. *Journal of Pragmatics, 61*, 161–184.

Vox. (2017, 13 February). *Kellyanne Conway's interview tricks, explained.* Retrieved 12 June 2017, from www.youtube.com/watch?v=C-7fzHy3aG0.

Part V

Strategic silences

11 Strategic silences

A definition

In contrast to the rich literature and multiple approaches to *communicative* silence, the paucity of research about *strategic* silence is striking. The few publications, which come close to a definition such as Brummett's piece about presidential (1980) and Lentz's essay (1991) about editorial (both political) strategic silence offer a good starting point. Yet they were written in another epoch, before the social media added their chapter to strategy. And they were also exploring strategic silence from a more general angle of political (government and journalist) communication.

Summing up results from my analysis in the previous chapters and preparing the reader for this one, which particularly deals with strategic silences, I would like to offer a specific definition that I believe is more adequate for PR theory and practice. It favours a particular selection and gradation of strategic silences. It follows a particular logic and escalates toward the most indirect forms of communication. It is based on my belief that, despite its struggle to adapt to the rapidly changing environment, public relations remains the most indirect – and in that sense most strategic – approach in the promotional mix.

The ladder of indirect communication has set the theoretical construct for such definition. Strategy increases the indirectness of communication. And silence increases the indirectness of strategy. That is why strategic silences present extreme forms of indirectness. To reach them, one has to climb to the highest rungs of the ladder.

I will define strategic silences in plural. There are many strategic silences, always empirically unique as cases. But strategic silences are also different as types, depending on features like their objective and degree of indirectness. A definition of a category in plural cannot avoid internal contradictions. Indeed, any of the distinctive meanings in its outline allows nuances, variations and alternatives. The definition is as follows:

Strategic silences are: (1) intentional, directed at audiences; (2) mostly communicative; and (3) discursive practices that take place in (4) situations of communication, (5) at higher degrees of indirectness, which usually entail (6) a shift from speaking to actionable listening.

I will now briefly discuss those six meanings.

Intentional, directed at audiences

Strategic silence is an informed choice on purpose. It is not the opposite of agency. As strategy, it gives agency direction. As strategy, every silence is situational. It is a temporary means for solving a temporary problem, even when the time period may last long. There is no taxonomy of strategies, let alone silent ones. My students learn PR strategy through experiential methods, including problem solving, case study, practical expertise and scenario plays. The execution of a strategy leads toward a durable and, so to speak, trans-situational outcome. The result may be in general the solution of a problem and in particular the creation of a new one. When we no longer have 'a situation', then we no longer have 'strategy'. Then we probably have a 'rule', 'plan' or 'tactic'.

Strategic silence, however, is not just a means. As strategy, it is not a single tactic. It is not like the linguistic techniques of pause, ellipsis or implicature, for example. Strategic silences are compound and global, possibly conceptual (where deliberate research and planning are involved) representations of the means of achieving a goal (or objective, in PR terms). As such, they are not separated or independent from other strategies. They are rather aspects of strategy that also presuppose their opposite in various modes. In a paradox sense, silences are strategic – perhaps most strategic – but also within other, broader and overarching strategies, which are not only silent. But the reverse is also true. There is no strategy without the mediation of silence. Depending on how indirect they are, strategies are more or less silent.

Original intention, however, adapts, socialises and transforms when strategy meets practice. As communication strategies, silences become problem solving practices. They lose authorship, self-correct quasi-automatically and expand as complex relations. They become resources of indirect discourse (see Chapter 9). The objective mechanisms of a society built on markets and profits determine the character of indirect discourse as collective memory and repository of successful practice. Whether for the promotion of a new car or 'promotion development' in an academic carrier or individual self-promotion on Facebook, we use depersonalised, repetitive, and 'polished' by public use strategies of verbose silence. We put our best foot forward. We do no advertise what does not sell – just to get rid of it. We advertise what we do best to represent the rest. Achieving the 'halo effect', the essence of branding (Ries, 2006), we are strategically vocal about one thing and silent about many.

Communicative

Silence is not the opposite of communication. Silence may communicate meaning. It may be content but also a form of communication. It mediates communication, makes it possible. Silence, however, is not only an extreme form of indirectness. Silence *is* indirectness. We fold something and make it smaller, partly invisible. We take turns to make a conversation. A conversation consists of folded silences. Indirect communication – or mediation in a broader sense – takes place when something or someone represents. Representations are folds. They silence the represented to carry its sign over. Even when we represent ourselves, we are speaking (painting, playing, dancing, gesturing and so on) and also silent about us at the same time. This silence is *structural*, not strategic (Luhmann, 1994). It is constant – not situated. There is no communication without representation. Structural silence is a precondition of strategic silence.

Communicators mainly employ silence as communicative strategy. But strategic silence can also be non-communicative – silence that purposefully prevents access to resources, including to communications; the fight of the telcos for a larger chunk of big data. He who controls the data controls the future. It is strategic and silent. But communicative? (See Chapter 7). The silence of disassociation: any communication would only encourage and legitimise unwanted participants (see Chapter 15). More positively it is the silence of secret political negotiations. Any communication with the external world or specific publics would disturb the talks. Public relations practitioners deal with non-communicative strategies on a daily basis. Even as action strategies, such silences may have communicative effects. Nevertheless, they are not core strategies. The profession meets its purpose when it communicates.

Discursive

Strategic communication is discursive and non-discursive. Public relations theory has discovered the power of discourse relatively late. There are many and contradictive approaches to discourse. A broadly accepted distinction, however, marks discourse as a system of interrelated meanings, which are produced, distributed and interpreted in more or less mediated communication – from text reading to personal conversation. The impact of a discourse goes beyond argumentation and persuasion. A discourse shapes not only the superstructure of opinions. More importantly, it frames the base – the thematic order, including issue priorities, upon which those opinions are built. The circulation and hierarchy of themes takes precedence to the circulation and hierarchy of opinions. Themes seem to be value-neutral and unbiased, but they are not. In a rather suggestive and subconscious way, certain themes tacitly lead to certain opinions. An invitation to conversation about '*the* climate change', for example, presupposes – not only through the word 'change' but also through the definite article 'the' – that global warming is real.

Only a few themes – the most significant, urgent, repeating and entertaining issues – do attract and keep the attention of publics. As choreography of public attention, however, public relations makes strategic use not only of the most attractive themes. It is equally interested in unimpressive, bland and boring contents, which deflect and divert that attention. Discursive strategies are invaluable weapons in establishing zones of meanings (Heath, 1993), which drive attention either high or low. (Non-communicative strategies, in contrast, just try to prevent or terminate such zones of meaning.) The discursive toolkit is very rich in that regard. Topicalising, framing, foregrounding and backgrounding, transparent and opaque representation, omission and presupposition, ideal reading positions, modality and mood, implicature and irony – there is a trove of tools that configure attention with non-attention, high with low affinity with truth, presence and absence, remembrance and oblivion.

This two-sided and even-handed discursive approach, which integrates strategic silence, sharply differentiates public relations from other communications such as journalism, marketing and advertising, including negative advertising. It also delivers an additional and sensible argument for why issues management is more central and strategic for PR than crisis communication. Arguing within a discourse is reactive and tactical. Changing a discourse is pro-active and strategic.

In the ladder of indirectness, I put discursive silences at the top as the highest and most sophisticated type of indirect communication. Digitalising the media, however, presents a trend that rather limits the use of discursive communication through textual systems of signs, including narratives and myths. Instead, it works in favour of non-discursive means of communication, including iconic and indexical signs (to use those Peircian terms). In the eighteenth century, for example, discursive fiction such as poetry and novel was the main form of transmitting social experience from one generation to another. Today, it is non-discursive non-fiction such clickable pieces of news and how-to-do information, fleeting comment and opinion and ephemeral ambient affiliation. Experience is transmitted through fragmented, short-lived and de-contextualised means of iconicity and indexicality, which Facebook, Twitter or Snapchat epitomise.

Yet it will be wrong to presume that the social media have driven communications 'backwards' to more primitive, less indirect and pre-discursive forms. Digital and non-discursive strategies of silence embrace a whole new game of 'presence at a distance and absence at the moment', of places that project spaces and real time without history. The shift has been from textual to more pragmatic representations. Discursive silences point inwards, at the blanks of a text, which perhaps hide its essence. Non-discursive silences point outwards, at the (discursive or non-discursive) practices of others, which bear silent witness of the possible sense of a text. Non-discursive and digital silences operate in the realm of hyperrealism. They are oddly practical. Practice is the ultimate, thus silent mediator. Which mediates which in a speech act, for example? The act of speaking or not speaks too.

Situations of communication

Communicative silences are relevant in situations of communication. This is not a trivial statement. Situations of communication include expectations of exchange of information both by speakers and listeners. I disagree with Brummett who defines strategic silence as violation of the expectations of communication. People expect someone to speak, but the person does not. This may be the case with strategies of explicit silence, but not of implicit one. And even with explicit silence, we should not confuse expectations of communication with expectations of speaking. I do not think people are so naïve and 'naturally' discarding silence as the opposite of communication. Of course, there are cultural and historical differences between them in that regard.

People deliberately and regularly flout their own expectations of conversations, as Grice's cooperative principle demonstrates (1975). They know how to hint at the unsaid by other means – linguistic or not. They do it for various reasons. For example, they may use silence as strategy of politeness. Indirect pitch mitigates the impression that they impose profitable action on others. Or they may try to avoid responsibility for what they mean by referring to what they have said, as in strategies of insinuation. Or they may only reinforce the effect of the unsaid in the ears of the listeners (see Chapter 10). 'Wash your hair in sunshine'. This commercial headline for a shampoo may be interpreted as noncooperative and false, violating the expectations of reasonable conversation. Yet it may just be an artful twist of words, which elicits and conveys more and beyond their conventional meanings (Pop, 2010).

I would suggest that strategic silence does not necessarily violate expectations of communication but rather constitutes a second level of those expectations, a level of meta-communication. Unexpected is the shift in the roles and relations within the situation – from communication to meta-communication, from trivia (convention) to creativity (flouting the rules) and from speaking to listening as main agency. Communicators act both *within* and *upon* a situation of communication. In other words, they try to make the best out it but also redefine its boundaries.

We should not be talking only about speakers who do not speak. How about the opposite scenario: A person is speaking but no one is listening? There is no violation of expectations here. But there is no situation of communication either. If we agree with the axiom that one cannot not communicate (see Chapter 10), we have to assume situations of communication, which also depend on whether the listener is listening. Are there, for example, potential situations, for which the speakers are either unaware or unprepared or both? For Bourdieu, a situation of communication does not only depend on internal factors, such as communicative competence, but also on external factors such as the pecking order of symbolic practices. Who is expected and *appropriate* to speak (or not) to whom, how, where, when and under which circumstances?

Degrees of indirectness

There are many strategic silences because there are many degrees of indirectness. In the ladder of indirectness, I have identified the most important types, including their transitions from one rung to another. For example, discursive silence is more indirect than the non-discursive one, and implicit silence is more indirect than the explicit one. The last distinction is critical. Some scholars would possibly disagree that strategic silence goes beyond its explicit manifestations. For them, strategic silence is when someone does not talk on purpose, period. In contrast, implicit silence does not pass the obviousness test. You are either silent or you do talk. Verbose silence seems to be an oxymoron. Indeed, the degree of mediation of implicit silences is so high and their subtle work is so under the radar that they often remain unrecognisable for the naked eye.

But this is the whole point. We would miss many, perhaps the most effective communication strategies in the contemporary society if we ignore the hidden and tacit ones. The more indirect strategies are, the more inclusive they become. Extreme indirectness is not marginal. It does not take place at the fringes of society. On the contrary, it is typical for its core. We use invisible weapons to hit visible targets. We do not see the transparent; we see through it the opaque. What we do not see determines how we see. We use truths taken for granted to question other truths (truths of others). That way, implicit silences serve to naturalise our values, beliefs and actions. Such strategies are hegemonic, mainstream and central.

Actionable listening

Strategic silence as indirect communication moves the emphasis of communication from the speaker to the listener. The more indirect a silence is, the more prominent that shift becomes. In that sense, silence elevates listening as an equal, if not more important part of the conversation. It assigns agency to heeding; it transforms it into actionable listening. As in Shakespeare's open silences, space opens not only for multiple interpretations of the script, but also for free improvisations outside it. Not only in theatre, the essence of staging lies in the play rather than the screenplay, in the performance rather than the text, in the publics rather than the actors, and in the silences that articulate the words.

There is no strategy without risk and surprise. Strategic silences also take chances. They allow but also demand an unusually higher degree of engagement, for which the listeners may not be ready. Does the situation of communication really favour equal participation? What is the added value? Is it worth the interpretative effort? Is the content compelling enough? Is it both interesting *and* of interest? If successful, silence engages a big deal. If not, it puts off and alienates. There is no coincidence that agents also use silence to disengage from some publics and keep them away (see Chapter 15). Ambiguity is inherent to strategic silences (see Chapter 16). This is one more reason to define them in plural. They can do many things and, among them, build relations or destroy them.

References

Brummett, B. (1980). Towards a theory of silence as a political strategy. *Quarterly Journal of Speech, 66*(3), 289–303.

Grice, H. P. (1975). Logic and conversation. In P. Cole & J. L. Morgan (Eds.), *Syntax and semantics* (pp. 41–58). New York: Academic Press.

Heath, R. L. (1993). A rhetorical approach to zones of meaning and organizational prerogatives. *Public Relations Review, 19*(2), 141–155.

Lentz, R. (1991). The search for strategic silence: Discovering what journalism leaves out. *American Journalism, 8*(1), 10–26.

Luhmann, N. (1994). Speaking and silence. *New German Critique, 61*(Winter), 25–37.

Pop, A. (2010). Implicatures derived through maxim flouting in print advertising. A contrastive empirical approach. *Toronto Working Papers in Linguistics, 33*(1).

Ries, A. (2006, 17 April). Understanding marketing psychology and the halo effect. *Advertising Age*. Retrieved 12 June 2017, from http://adage.com/print?article_id=108676.

12 Content provision

Stealth marketing

Content providers is the general term I use to describe the newly emerging intermediaries between businesses, media and the public relations people. Those new agencies are increasingly taking charge of trending promotional practices such as 'content marketing', 'native advertising', 'brand journalism' and 'promoted user endorsement'. They create, re-purpose and curate online content such as articles, lists, charts, audios, videos, infographics, archives and documentaries to drive profitable action. They also present a challenge to the profession of public relations, including to its traditional functions and roles (Hallahan, 2014; Zerfass, Verčič & Wiesenberg, 2016).

In the past, there was a clear demarcation between editorial content, which the consumer paid for, and *interruption*, advertising-based content, which businesses paid for. Interruption advertising is no longer generating sufficient revenue to sustain both the mainstream and niche media. Consumers are losing patience with offline and online advertising – the second perceived even more annoying and intrusive than the first (Austin & Newman, 2015). But how to drive profitable action without interrupting editorial content?

Thanks to digitalisation, the old linear and chronological way of content production – from creation and aggregation to distribution and consumption – has given way to a non-linear and simultaneous coexistence of those activities in real-time (see Chapter 20). Content distributors such as Google, Amazon and Netflix are producing content themselves. Google, for example, is investing $200 million in original TV. Microsoft is adopting the studio module (support of independents for sharing distribution rights) through its Xbox Studio. Many media businesses are using a new strategy looking for direct relationships with consumers on platforms like *iTune*, *YouTube* and *Twitter*. They are no longer obsessed with driving web traffic towards their own company sites (PwC, 2013). At the same time, quintessential online media such as *Daily Beast*, *BuzzFeed* and *Vice* are making the most of their money from promoted content. The legacy media are also following suit.[1]

Content providers take indirect communication to a new level. They have inserted themselves as brokers between businesses and media, whose relations used to be more direct in the past. Similarly, their strategies of content provision are also indirect. The best ones demonstrate mastery in invisibility and silence. The whole purpose of native advertising, for example, is that it does not look like advertising. It camouflages as native narrative. Legal and ethical considerations set limits to full invisibility. Labels such as 'paid for', 'sponsored by' and 'promoted' should disclose the name of the sponsor of the publication. Yet promoted content remains silent about its purpose and message. It is 'the marketing trend that dare not speak its name (unless required)' (Bednarski, 2014). It is 'stealth marketing' (Goodman, 2006), which mimics editorial integrity and genuine conversation.

Other elements of content marketing partly 'compensate' for the visibility of the sponsor. There is the byline, for example. The name of the author – who may be a prominent journalist, influential blogger, independent expert or credible consumer – can individualise and de-corporatise the content. Bylines divert the attention from the promoter's strategic intent to the impartiality of the writer and added value for the reader. A good story is always a good story. Users reward real, human experiences, including of a brand.

Disclosure and labelling standards are struggling to adjust to the complexity of blogging. Instagram and Twitter, for example, frequently use hashtags like '#ad' and '#spon' to denote that the posts are paid for. Yet in the online flow, it is often not hard to omit what is actually promoted. It is impossible to tell, for example, which of DJ Khaled's snaps (that also include his own merchandise) are for profit and which not (Lansky, 2016).

Surely, labelling of content diminishes the effect of silence – of marketing and advertising pretending not to be what they are. It discloses the sponsor, which qualifies the origin and purpose of the content. And it also alerts the user, diminishing the pleasure of reading to an extent. Labelling, like advertising, is an interruption. As such, it is even more boring than real commercials. It does not divert the attention to another sale. It only says, 'This is a sale'. It does not add value; it deducts value. In contrast to traditional online ads, including advertising banners and promoted links, a sponsor disclosure is still rather relevant to the content, part of its design. But it also qualifies it, relativities its direct effect. A qualification is, like some silences, metacommunication. It requires an extra effort to put content in context of its sponsor. But why should users be interested in extra reflection, which would only take the edge off a gripping narrative? Who needs other lights when the stage is lit? And there is also a chance that they have developed 'ad blindness' and just skip such any interruption.

The expectations of younger and older generations also defer in that regard. When older readers discover they have read a 'paid for' piece, they feel disappointed, cheated. The younger consumers, however, seem to be more open – and more indifferent – to stealth marketing. As a Windows generation, they are more comfortable with 'what you see is what you get'. A good play of appearances is fair enough. If news is riveting, advice useful and chat amusing, why should they scratch and get the shine off the surface of smooth content (Austin & Newman, 2015)?

PR – from wholesaler to retailer?

Content marketing encroaches on public relations internally and externally. Internally, many corporations are building their own branding newsrooms. Filled mostly with journalists and designers, those rooms often duplicate and interfere with the public relations departments. Externally, the new agencies are adopting subtle, 'soft selling' and 'no selling' strategies, which have been an unchallenged prerogative of PR for a long time. Marketing *sells*, content marketing *tells* (Hallahan, 2010; Pulizzi, 2014; Strong, 2014).

The content providers are imposing on public relations a structural and functional conversion from *wholesaler* to *retailer* of information. In the traditional binary, the PR practitioner is a (gradually ever more powerful) source of information for the journalist – an information *subsidiary* (Gandy, 1982). The business (through its PR people) supplies and suggests, the media decides and produces. The media is in direct relation with its audiences. Through the media, the business is in indirect relation with its publics. The PR people of the business are in direct relation with the media. Their closeness – if not cosiness – is subject of their mutual – if not complicit – silence. In symbiotic relations, the source is the *wholesaler*, the media the *retailer* (see Chapter 3).

Both companies and media have markedly changed. The rise of digital content providers has substantially altered their relations. In an increasing number of situations, they are no longer between wholesalers and retailers. On the one hand, the businesses have become publishers themselves. Using external studios or internal newsrooms, they are coming in *direct* contact with their audiences. They are converting from wholesalers (through the media) to retailers of information. They are partnering *and* competing with the media, which is new for them. And they are not awfully good at it. The media, on the other, are also changing. Many are becoming suppliers of infrastructure and empty shells for content created somewhere else. The relations between content providers and media increasingly resemble those of producers and distributers.

Consumer advocacy

The relations between content agencies and media companies are not only of difference but also of *sameness*. Both sides have become partners in retail. *They generate revenue by capitalising on the economic consequences of the editorial content they create.*

Content provision is not product placement. There are two main differences. First, product placement can exist in entertainment-based, but not in news-based content. It is confined to 'less serious' areas than news, politics and economics such as music, entertainment, lifestyle, travel and fashion. Second – and this is perhaps more important – product placement does not mix with editorial content well. Again, content creation is about retail, not wholesale. It is the (re-)*creation of a product anew* and *at the point of its sale*, as uncompromised and gripping editorial policy.

Content providers do not only promote corporate interests but also advocate on behalf of consumers. Lachlan Harris is former Press Secretary for the Australian Prime Minister, Kevin Rudd. He co-founded *One Big Switch*, an advocacy group that campaigns to push down electricity prices for households. He explains how his agency uses content provision as advocacy strategy:

> Editorial still has to be good. Compelling editorial is what people want to read and see. The editorial shouldn't change at all in its nature or its intent or its objectivity or the way it delivers the call to action. All that's happening now is that the media companies understand that for them to survive over the longer term, they must monetise the economic consequences that have always existed from the content they create.... It's the act of advocacy in creation that actually maintains the purity of the editorial content. We are working with and teaching media companies how to create new price points for products, new products, using the power of their readership, their audience.... If a media company decided to create, without permission of the electricity providers, genuine competition between them, and deliver an outcome for their audience, which doesn't currently exist, that is consistent with what their objectives have always been. It's an evolution of the [editorial content] model towards an advocacy-based model. But it's still objective, pure editorial content in the interest of their readers.
>
> (Personal interview, 23 February 2015)

The agency of Harris operates in the area of consumer affairs. But one can also add other 'serious' areas of public advocacy such education, health and environment, where product placement is almost non-existent but content provision is on the rise. Electricity or milk prices, childcare or waste disposal – the principle is the same. One does not just sell a product. (Although a purchase has to take place in the end.) One does not even sell the cheapest one. Through informed comparison, content that calls for action taps into the self-interest of the readers as consumers.

But this is only the beginning. The users, if the content is compelling and offers added value to them, take it from there. We see here strategic silence in work. Reading, not writing – listening, not speaking – creates a new price point, a new product. That product may be, for example, an increased pressure on the prices to go down. Anecdotally, that pressure may be vocal. People may speak out against the higher prices. But it is more likely to be silent. Consumers just walk out on the more expensive providers. Markets have their silent ways of correction and sanction (Hirschman, 1970).

Content creation and relationship building

Is content creation relationship building? This is a million-dollar question for public relations now.

Yes, content providers use strategies of implicit silence. The overt purpose of the product is to add value for the reader. It is *telling*. The covert one is to drive profitable action. It is *selling*. The message blends in the story. It dons the story as invisibility cloak that drives it safely home.

I am deliberately avoiding examples of illegal and unethical practices – from writing fake customer endorsements to not disclosing the sponsor of an article. I am interested here in the inherent features of content provision, which do not depend on whether people make good or bad use of it.

Public relations practitioners are struggling to define their roles in the new promotional practices such as content marketing and native advertising. As I have pointed out, the recent structural and functional conversion of PR from wholesaler to retailer is full with new tensions and confusions.

Publicity, for example, is what PR used to be best at. Yet there are differences between publicity and relations building. Even media management is more than publicity work. Content creation, re-purposing and curation may serve for but are not identical with relationships building. Journalists, for once, are not the best builders of relations with, well, journalists!

Stakeholders are more than audiences. PR involves activities in public and in private. Publicity is only a means for the end of relationships building. No publicity is another means. As choreography of public attention, PR uses silence both to engage and disengage publics (see Chapter 15). It also employs non-mediated strategies such as formation of alliances, keeping presence, quiet deeds and philanthropic gestures. Publicity often mixes well with silence. Another 'classic' PR rule (borrowed from literature studies): 'Don't *tell* them, *show* them' (Powell & Cowart, 2003, p. 210).

In such silence, agents grow a precious asset, part of their media capital, which I call 'the PR bonus of non-instrumental integrity'. Refugee activists in Australia, for example, who habitually visited detention centres of 'boat people', accrued such capital as regular, reliable and irreplaceable media sources. Critical for the build-up of their excellent relations with journalists were their actions – not communications. You cannot care *about* the issues publically if you do not care *for* the affected privately (Dimitrov, 2008, p. 198). Paraphrasing McLuhan, the *mediator* is the medium.

Content provision will possibly trigger some kind of renaissance in a pivot of public relations, which universities have increasingly neglected in the last decade: *public relations writing*. Writing well – telling a good story and knowing when to shut up – has been, is and will be, paramount for the profession. Now, we have to convince our Millennial students that writing texts is more than texting. Better job prospects, quicker repayment of the student debt, and *not having to write much* should not be the main motives, false or not, for enrolling in public relations rather than, say, in journalism (see Chapter 2, note 1).

Public relations people are best not at any publicity but – as wholesalers and information subsidiaries – at achieving *free* and *earned media*. Using more indirect strategies, they try to control the process, not the outcomes. In contrast, marketing and advertising professionals use direct strategies. They *pay* to get published. They control the outcomes, not the process.

This difference is critical. And here is the question. What will public relations gain and what will it lose if it adopts content provision as its main feature – if it becomes more like marketing and advertising? What will it accomplish, if the buyer–seller relationship will be reversed – when the information source becomes the buyer and the media outlet the seller (Hallahan, 2014, p. 410)?

There is no simple answer to such questions. No doubt, there have been a growing number of mediators in communications such as the new content agencies. And there has also been an increasing number of institutional agents who target their public directly – as audiences of their own media. They do that, however, through increasingly indirect content strategies, including content marketing and native advertising. And this is the paradox of online communication: the more direct its forms become, the more indirect its contents. This moves the emphasis of strategy from media (form) to message (content).

Public relations people are under pressure to move from the wholesaling to the retailing business. Such change is at least partly unavoidable. Wholesale, however, has always been more strategic than retail, and media management more strategic than content management. In principle, selling the whole is more strategic than selling it in parts. We do not want to reduce the function of public relations to management of direct (tactical) economic transactions and bargains about the price and revenue that content provision would generate. We do not want to see the profession lose its strategic position within the promotional mix.

The position it still occupies allows it to combine two different – and often opposite – logics. The first one is of *being media*. The product here is *output*, the attention of publics, measured by print space, broadcast time, online traffic and so on. And the other logic is of *not being media*. The product here is *outcome*, measured by ROI, sales, membership and other indicators for action. Public relations people mediate between sponsors of communication and stakeholders. Being media (output) is a means for an end that is usually not being media (outcome). And content provision, as direct communication with some stakeholders as media audiences, is only part of that means. As central as it seems to be, it is not conducive to most forms of indirect, strategic communication. It does not reflect most of the PR work with most of the stakeholders most of the time.

The concept of strategic silence delivers some arguments for where public relations should integrate content provision and where not. Implicit silences (invisible intent and message) in a good narrative are nothing new in public relations. Publicity as indirect, soft sell has always been the hallmark of the profession. PR practitioners know how to remain silent while telling a story. They know, for example, how to frame it – what to highlight and what to delete. Publicity, however, is not an end in itself for them. Ultimately, they serve to stakeholders, not to the media. They direct the public attention by both increasing and reducing it. They influence *within* publicity and also *the* publicity. They use silence to buttress *and* bridge its boundaries. This is a more indistinct game – subtler than the competition of appearances such as whose pitch is heard louder and whose brand is more visible. Public relations, like marketing and advertising, serves to goals, which ultimately go beyond publicity. But it, unlike them, does not put its eggs in the one basket of mimicked, paid and published content.

Note

1 Newspapers such as the *New York Times*, *Washington Post*, *Guardian*, *Süddeutsche Zeitung*, *Die Zeit* and *The Sydney Morning Herald* have markedly increased both the number and quality of their 'paid post' formats. (I also use 'advertorials' as a generic term for sponsored content formats.) A recent example is the, celebrated by critics, native ad for the *Netflix* series *Orange is the New Black* posted in *New York Times*. It uses not only text but also video, charts and audio testimonies about female imprisonment in the US (Daziel, 2016).

References

Austin, S., & Newman, N. (2015). *Digital News Report* 2015: Attitudes to sponsored and branded content (native advertising). Retrieved 12 June 2017, from www.digitalnews-report.org/essays/2015/attitudes-to-advertising/.

Bednarski, P. J. (2014,17 January). Native advertising: The marketing trend that dare not speak its name (unless required). *MediaPost.com*. Retrieved 12 June 2017, from www.mediapost.com/publications/article/217622/native-advertising-the-marketing-trend-that-dare.html.

Daziel, M. (2016). Women inmates: Why the male model doesn't work (paid post). *New York Times*. Retrieved 12 June 2017, from http://paidpost.nytimes.com/netflix/women-inmates-separate-but-not-equal.html.

Dimitrov, R. (2008). ChilOut: Strategic communication by small advocacy groups. *Australian Journal of Communication, 34*(3), 129–143.

Gandy, O. H. (1982). *Beyond agenda setting: Information subsidies and public policy.* Norwood, NJ: Ablex Publishing.

Goodman, E. P. (2006). Stealth marketing and editorial integrity. *Texas Law Review, 85*, 83–152.

Hallahan, K. (2010). Being public: Publicity as public relations. In R. L. Heath (Ed.), *Handbook of public relations* (pp. 523–545). Thousand Oaks, CA: Sage.

Hallahan, K. (2014). *Publicity under siege: A critique of content marketing, brand journalism, native advertising and promoted user endorsements as challenges to professional practice and transparency.* Paper presented at the 17th International public relations research conference, University of Miami, FL.

Hirschman A. O. (1970). *Exit, voice, and loyalty: Responses to decline in firms, organizations, and states.* Cambridge, MA: Harvard University Press.

Lansky, S. (2016, 16 May). The self-help sage of Snapchat. *Time*, pp. 34–39.

Powell, L., & Cowart, J. (2003). *Political campaign communication: Inside and out.* Boston, MA: Allyn and Bacon.

Pulizzi, J. (2014). *Epic content marketing. How to tell a different story, break through the clutter and win more customers by marketing less.* New York: McGraw-Hill Education.

PwC. (2013). *Game changer: A new kind of value chain for entertainment and media companies.* Retrieved 12 June 2017, from www.pwc.com/us/en/industry/entertainment-media/publications/assets/pwc-value-chain.pdf.

Strong, F. (2014, 28 January). The soft and subtle PR pitch of content marketing. *Sword and the script blog.* Retrieved 12 June 2017, from www.swordandthescript.com/2014/01/pr-pitch-of-content-marketing/.

Zerfass, A., Verčič, D., & Wiesenberg, M. (2016). The dawn of a new golden age for media relations?: How PR professionals interact with the mass media and use new collaboration practices. *Public Relations Review, 42*(4), 499–508.

13   Silence as negation

Apophatic silence

Alexander Solzhenitsyn's novel *One Day of the Life of Ivan Denisovich*, a Ulysses in a Siberian Gulag camp, ends with the main hero's take on the past day:

> Shukhov went to sleep fully content. He'd had many strokes of luck that day: they hadn't put him in the cells; they hadn't sent the team to the settlement; he'd pinched a bowl of kasha at dinner; the team-leader had fixed the rates well; he'd built a wall and enjoyed doing it; he'd smuggled that bit of hacksaw-blade through; he'd earned something from Tsezar in the evening; he'd bought that tobacco. And he had not fallen ill. He got over it. A day without a dark cloud. Almost a happy day.
>
> There were three thousand six hundred and fifty-three days like that in his stretch. From the first clang of the rail to the last clang of the rail. Three thousand six hundred and fifty-three days.
>
> The three extra days were for leap years.
>
> (Solzhenitsyn, 1970)

Solzhenitsyn's volley of negations serves an almost impossible task. It makes the unimaginable real by saying it has not happened and the menacing inevitable by describing its chance avoidance. Apophasis is a deliberate embrace of the lack of words. It takes strength from the weakness of language. It is a form of explicit rather than implicit silence. We are not silent about the meaning of what we are saying. It is more straightforward than that. We are saying that there is a meaning that cannot be expressed.

Apophasis is a broader concept of linguistic self-negation that points at and carries extra-linguistic connotations. It could be a religious doctrine, literary method or communication strategy. Language admits that it is not an almighty medium, but also reminds us that nothing else can replace it. Language sets the direction but not the destination. It leaves the meaning of an utterance outside the words of the speaker and wholly to the imagination of the listener. Silence is the power that keeps the meaning hovering – like the magnetosphere holds the plasma. And this is important for public relations. Full engagement of a public in a conversation – active and responsible co-creation of meaning – is a prerequisite for relationship building.

The strategy of negation is not necessarily negative. It is not a strategy of utter denial, for example. It is not even mainly negative. Rejecting someone's claim of truth is not its chief thrust. It indirectly carries a positive metamessage – watchfully silent and ever-present. It also raises a claim of truth, but of a subtler and higher order. An attempt to express that truth with the conventional means of language – with any means – would only misread, trivialise or violate that truth. If there is a universal message in apophasis, it is: 'Don't try to define what is worth in life; definitions kill'. Like in the *Bible*: 'You shall not make for yourself a carved image, or any likeness of anything that is in heaven above, or that is in the earth beneath, or that is in the water under the earth' (Exodus 20:4 ESV). And like in Sinead O'Connor's love song: 'Nothing compares 2 U' (1990).

'No comment' is neither apophatic nor strategic. It is tactical silence, a tool of time management. It is concerned not with information, but with the instance of its (non-)communication. 'No comment' leaves the door open for a fact and interpretation to be validated or not. It only means 'no communication here and now'. It neither confirms nor denies. The speaker is saying that he cannot speak. There is something clumsy, awkward in 'No comment'. Any other communication would be better, except not saying even that. This answer is rarely satisfying for those who ask. And then, the mere fact that the speaker is left with no other alternative, is also telling. Seasoned listeners know what to read into that imposition.

Silence discourses

In his *Rhetoric*, Aristotle defines 'kataphasis' and 'apophasis' as 'categorical proportions as either affirmation or denial, saying and unsaying' (Henderson, 2003, p. 10). As rhetorical devices, however, both categories represent logical qualities that include both statement of truth (whether something is or is not) and directive for its communication (whether to bring it up or not). Apophasis (Greek from ἀπόφημι, 'to say no'), for example, may also extend to the denial that one has not or will not say what one is just saying. (Donald Trump, for example, repeatedly reassuring that he would not talk about the extramarital affairs of Bill Clinton.) Thus, it may liaise with other devices such as sarcasm, irony or insinuation.

The kataphatic approach dominates in the Western Christian churches. But this is uneven and not across the board – as the differences between the (apophatic) silent Quaker and (kataphatic) noisy Pentecostal worships show (Maltz, 1985). Kataphasis is also at the root of the European Enlightenment, rationalism and positivism. The apophatic theology, on the other side, is typical for the Orthodox Christianity and other Eastern religions. Yet the history of the European and North American cultures is rich in apophatic projects. They spread from religion and philosophy to poetry and arts (Franke, 2012; Gibbons, 2007; Martin, 1985).

Master Eckhart cautions,

> If you visualise anything or if anything enters your mind, that is not God....
> To speak about God in any simile is to speak of him in an impure mode. But
> whoever speaks of God through nothingness speaks of him to the point.
>
> (Schürmann, 1978, p. 125)

John Milton presents the truth of God as silent truth in his poem *Paradise Lost*: 'His words here ended, but his meek aspect/Silent yet spoke, and breathed immortal love' (Milton, Kastan, & Hughes, 2005, pp. 266–267). Religion and literature meet here in the use of negation as a poetic tool. It is the opposite of Foucault's *exhaustive representation*, the transformation of silence into discourse, where silence is achieved through verbose reasoning about what is not said (1990).

> If discourse is an exhaustive representation that silences by leaving no gaps
> or silence, it says everything and so leaves nothing more to be said. Silence
> is, then, in possession of meaning. Thus it can be said that we are now
> dealing with two forms of exhaustive representation: discourse that silences
> and silence that discourses.
>
> (Sendbuehler, 1994)

The truth of God is a silent truth. It is not just an object of discourse. It *is* the discourse. Christ must not simply speak about truth, but he must also 'speak true' – be the truth he speaks. In apophasis, silence discourses. Apophatic silence is *profound* silence. Meaning emerges from its own depth.

Poetics is, in a way, apophatic. It is creative negation, reflective of the limits of language.[1] It ventures outside language with a view to helping it by destroying it (Franke, 2012). A device of indirect communication, apophasis is not a forthright negation. It alludes to something by denying that it is mentioned.[2] It points at the inadequacy of naming. But it names – quietly, by the fact of no naming. Something is present *by* its absence (Gibbons, 2007).

Small voice and small target

In politics, we use negation to promote ourselves by differentiation. In identity politics, for example, we place emphasis on who we are *not* instead of who we are. It is especially persuasive when we are less popular and recognised than our opponents. Apophatic strategies include: pitting the unknown (hope, freshness) against the known (dead end, boring); aspiration (ideals, values) against experience (disappointments, cynicism); and (unspecified) policies against (specified) spin. 'All talk and no action'. Obama's 'new car smell' (Miller, 2014).

In *Julius Caesar*, Shakespeare's Mark Antony belittles himself as meek orator to distinguish himself from Brutus, the orator in vogue:

I come not, friends, to steal away your hearts.
I am no orator, as Brutus is,
But, as you know me all, a plain blunt man
…
For I have neither wit, nor words, nor worth,
Action, nor utterance, nor the power of speech,
To stir men's blood. I only speak right on.
(Shakespeare, *c.*1599[1988])

Small voice makes us a small target. We should not rush to abandon a discourse, which is not ours but where our target publics are. It is the premise we have to accept and understand. We have to work first there – could be for very long – before we try to move them to our conclusion (Perelman, 1982). Calculated self-negation comes to help. We openly submit to that discourse and tacitly undermine it by *inner* withdrawal. We gradually disown it by diminishing, mocking or falling our role in it. We shift gear and forcefully pull the public out of the premise to our conclusion *only* when our discourse gathers enough torque and has chance for success.

From Mark Antony back to Theresa May. In the contest to replace the Leader of the Conservative Party and Prime Minister, David Cameron, after the UK Brexit vote in 2016, Theresa May gave a speech. In it, she used apophasis to turn the disadvantage of not being one of the winner MPs who had campaigned for UK to leave the EU (especially Michael Gove), into an advantage:

I know I'm not a showy politician. I don't tour the television studios. I don't gossip about people over lunch. I don't go drinking in Parliament's bars. I don't often wear my heart on my sleeve. I just get on with the job in front of me.

(Rentoul, 2016)

In the same speech, May promised that in case she was elected Leader (and thus Prime Minister), a 'boring and competent' government. 'Boring' is a code word for 'small target'. At the same time it reinforces the notion of good government as silent government as the opposite of noisy government. A government that evades the radar of the media not because it is undemocratic, but – if good news is bad news – because there is nothing to report. A government that is not at issue.

'Small voice' is a strategy of silence as old as the world. In ancient Greece, the rhetoric Isocrates claimed that he was not a good orator. He only had a 'small voice'. Some contemporaries and also scholars from later epochs took him at his words. But there is another hypothesis. He used his supposed *mikrophōnia* to distance himself from the figure of the 'great orator' and 'new politician'. Cleon's rantings, for example, notoriously represented the decay of the mores, courts and civil institutions during his time. Witness of noisy and poisonous 'democratic virtues', Isocrates retreated to his silent, unassuming and self-effacing art of writing and teaching. 'A "small voice" is associated with a life of

quietude, responsibility, that is political non-involvement, and with the aban-
doned democratic virtues, above all "moderation"' (Too, 1995, p. 8).[3] Moderation, impish stillness may have – who knows – spared him Socrates' fate.

The PR lesson here is not that if you are, for example, a small business you
have to lower your voice and sink as a target. On the contrary, small businesses
usually occupy niches, which allow them to have a choice. They are usually
boring and trivial subjects of conversation. The media are rarely after them.
They can be easily silent and invisible – if they choose to be. Their problem is
not looking smaller; their problem is looking bigger. It is the optics of blowout.

The lesson is rather for the big corporations and political institutions, which
are under constant, systemic media scrutiny. For them, silence and invisibility as
being outside the media sphere is not an option. They do not have that luxury.
Their problem is that they have to incessantly feed the media cycle. There is no
outside. They can only be silent in what they say and invisible in what they
show. And here strategy, including of small voice and small target, comes into
play for the big ones.

CEOs and politicians often confuse strategy and tactic (Tiffen, 2012). The
need to be constantly winning fixates them on the short-term communication
objectives, including involuntary reactions. They overrate the role of positive
spin. They overreact to tangential issues (see Chapter 20). Strategic silence gives
way to tactical noise. Yet obsession with not losing any battle rarely leads to
winning the war. Small voice, moderation and keeping it cool may protect big
organisations from the detrimental impact of tactical thinking on long-term
decision-making.

The spell of uncompromised reality

Terence Martin explores the negative structures of American literature. For him,
US identity is built on apophasis. 'America is not Britain'. America is a 'blank
sheet'. The New World as the negation of the Old one – from Judd and Melville
to Paine and Whitman (Martin, 1985). He sees the same in advertising. For
example, Seven-Up was for a number of years known as 'Uncola'. It appeared
on TV commercial in 1983 as a beverage with 'No caffeine, no artificial fla-
vours, no artificial colours'. At roughly the same time, Perrier's advertising positioned the mineral water as 'clear' and 'pure':

> Earth's first soft drink. Not manufactured, but created by the earth when it
> was new. [Perrier remains] clear, pure and sparkling, and minus all those
> additives that civilisation has invented. There's no sugar. No artificial sweet-
> ener. No calories. There's no caffeine, no colouring. And Perrier is recom-
> mended for salt-free diets, as well.

'The earth when it was new'. *Brand new*, I would have added. Apophasis is a
strategy of *brand differentiation*. In markets with material saturation, it differentiates ideally. It is anchored in reality, in which we already live. But it is a

perfected, retouched reality – with all wrinkles boldly denied or subtly photoshopped.

Shellharbour is two hours drive from Sydney on the Illawarra South Coast. The visitor's guide touts the paradise to tourists and 'sea changers':

> We admit it, there's a lot that you're used to that you won't find in Shellhar-bour. At first, you won't notice what you are missing, but slowly it'll become very obvious.
>
> For a start, we don't have crowds. Even if we're busy we don't feel jammed up or hassled, because we've got space everywhere....
>
> We don't have parking meters. They're for places with too many people, driving too many cars and not enough spaces to part them. They make you feel like you should not be there, and they make you pay for the privilege of being unwanted.
>
> We don't have traffic jams. They're for people who don't value their own time but like wasting petrol and feeding parking meters.
>
> We don't have air you can see or water you can't see through....
>
> We don't have noise. Well, not the annoying, headache-inducing kind you get from the city traffic, flight paths and heavy industry....
>
> You'll also miss out on feeling stressed and hassled, tired and worn down, put out and put upon.
>
> You see, it's the things we don't have that make us who we are and how well we feel – relaxed, informal, friendly and good humoured.
>
> (South Coast NSW, 2014)

Negated are the symptoms of urban malaise, the fallouts from the marketplace, and the sacrifices one makes to take advantage of the big city. Apophasis human-ises the loss. It wakes up forgotten dreams of childhood. It distils memories and frees from conventions. It appeals with native, stylised and idyllic (if not Utopian) values. The new brand positions itself 'in a void beyond definition'. It addresses the 'grievous need to negate'. It offers an original, uncompromised reality (Martin, 1985, p. 8).

There is a strong link between strategies of negation and relationship build-ing. In the Bakhtin/Vološinov paradigm, emotion and evaluation are essential elements of genuine conversation, which in turn is a prerequisite for actual rela-tions between active publics. Apophasis steps up when high emotion needs representation but finds no words (or other signs). Silence in worship, love, intimacy, mourning, victory and loss symbolises – not only initiates but also celebrates – close bonds. High-value matters, high valence – states of extreme feelings (positive or negative, see Chapter 2) and situations that prompt extra-ordinary measures *test* not only the power of language but also that of relations. Strategies of negation move outside the language to stay inside the relations. If successful, they save the language from itself and the relations for themselves. The language, let alone, does not weaken. But the relations, endowed with silence, appear stronger.

The apophatic turn

Chris Galloway, who has introduced the topic in public relations, argues for a wider adoption of the 'apophatic turn'. Globalisation, de-traditionalisation, increase in mediated experience, pluralisation (and fragmentation) of social positions, and emergence of contingent knowledge assist that turn *inwards*, to a *new reflexivity*. Negation may remove misconcepts that arise from imperfect language. In may claim higher, spiritual (not necessarily metaphysical) grounds by refusing profanation by the uniformed. It conveys a sense of the whole against the 'literal' (positivist) definitions of its parts. He claims, it is more telling and less risky to define public relations though what it is not, instead of what it is (Galloway, 2013).

The apophatic turn marks the transition to modernity and postmodernity. Strategies of negation have always enabled resistance to verbal dominance. In the Soviet Union, aphorisms were an indelible part of such opposition – as the memes in the West today. A pessimist says, 'Life cannot get worse'. An optimist says, 'Yes, it can'. When people had to choose between two things, a typical reply was '*оба хуже*' – 'both are worse' (Golinkin, 2016). We see in such impersonal, automated strategies of negation silence working in cultural-critical and post-modern fashion. Again, no professional strategist or communication scholar can make up such pop-art practices of resistance. Yet they already contain everything the apophatic turn can offer.

In 'both are worse' we see the Bakhtian rejection of the exclusive and authoritarian binary of 'either/or' in favour of the inclusive and carnavalesque 'and/ and' (1984). 'Both are worse' flouts the formal logic of someone's 'natural' choices. We also see the Derrida's rejection and binaries, in which relations of the dominant and dominated are camouflaged as equal alternatives (1996). Proverbial and aphoristic negation subverts logic (of dominance). It is absurd that makes sense. And there is even something from Lyotard's 'différend' – a dispute between parties that cannot be equitably resolved because there is no overarching rule of judgement (1988). (Victims of the holocaust cannot disprove holocaust deniers because they are dead. Australian Aborigines cannot claim native title in a legislative tradition of 'terra nullius'.) 'Both are worse' does not only discard the alternatives as inequitable but also the mere notion of having a choice within a discourse; from which straightjacket we dream to break free.

The apophatic way stresses on the exploration rather than taken for granted and open-ended rather than 'business as usual'. Evaluation then would not be self-referential, autopoetic 'measuring of the outcomes against the objectives' but a constant, spontaneous and spiralling quest of 'learning loops' (Kanter, 2010).

> turning inwards aims not at doing but at undoing, not at constructing but deconstructing. It aims at weakening rather than enhancing the rationalising, calculating, planning dimensions of the self-self relationship.... It focuses less on purposive decision-making process and more on getting rid of the

'tyranny of purposiveness'. Eventually, it aims at the achievement of a void within goals and means, rather than being actively choses, emerge spontaneously. Goals in the apophatic case are neither pre-given/pre-constituted (as in rational choice theory), nor extremely imposed.

(Mouzelis, 2010, p. 273)

Interestingly, the concept of silence as negation makes a case for communicative action (communication before goals) against strategic action (goals before communication). More precisely, it solves its koan – of the type of 'What comes first: the chicken or the egg?' – by merging goals and communication in incessant loops of practice. Yet it does it on terms, which are dissimilar, even opposite to the kataphatic, rationalist argumentation of Habermas. That is why the apophatic approach may help overcome the putative – and false, in my understanding – distinction between communicative and strategic action. As we have seen, silence as negation may retain its experiential, exploratory and creative thrust and, at the same time, serve well as a strategy of communication.

Notes

1 See the use of the apophatic device in literature (Gibbons, 2007; Lorenz, 1989; Martin, 1985) and also in architecture and music (Franke, 2012; Jankelevich, 2003).
2 Insinuation also works that way: 'I am not saying that he is....' If accused of what he means, one can point at what he has said.
3 I would like to thank Chuck Marsh who gave me the idea of silence as 'small voice' and who also made me read the seminal book about rhetoric and Isocrates by Yun Lee Too.

References

Bakhtin, M. M. (1984). *Rabelais and his world* (Vol. 341). Bloomington, IN: Indiana University Press.

Derrida, J. (1996). Remarks on deconstruction and pragmatism. In C. Mouffe (Ed.), *Deconstruction and pragmatism* (p. 84). London: Routledge.

Foucault, M. (1990). *The will to knowledge: The history of sexuality* (Vol. 1). London: Penguin.

Franke, W. (2012). Apophatic paths: Modern and contemporary poetics and aesthetics of nothing. *Angelaki, 17*(3), 7–16.

Galloway, C. J. (2013). Deliver us from definitions: A fresh way of looking at public relations. *Public Relations Inquiry, 2*(2), 147–159.

Gibbons, R. (2007). On apophatic poetics. *American Poetry Review, 36*(6), 19–23.

Golinkin, L. (2016, 28 December). A flashback to my Soviet childhood. *New York Times.* Retrieved 12 June 2017, from http://nyti.ms/2htSKMS.

Henderson, D. (2003). Carl Jung and Thomas Merton: Apophatic and kataphatic traditions in the 20th century. *Studies in Spirituality, 13*, 269–291.

Jankelevich, V. (2003). *Music and the ineffable.* Princeton, NJ: Princeton University Press.

Kanter, B. (2010). *The networked nonprofit: Connecting with social media to drive change.* San Francisco, CA: Jossey-Bass.

Lorenz, O. (1989). *Schweigen in der Dichtung: Hoelderlin – Rilke – Celan.* Goetingen: Vandenhoeck & Ruprecht.

Lyotard, J.-F. (1988). *Le différend: Phrases in dispute* (Vol. 46). Minneapolis, MN: University of Minnesota Press.

Maltz, D. N. (1985). Joyful noise and reverent silence: The signification of noise in Pentecostal worship. In D. Tannen & M. Saville-Troike (Eds.), *Perspectives on silence* (pp. 113–138). Norwood, NJ: Ablex Publishing.

Martin, T. (1985). The negative structures of American literature. *American Literature, 57*(1), 1–22.

Miller, Z. J. (2014). Obama: Voters want 'new car smell' in 2016. *Time*. Retrieved 12 June 2017, from http://time.com/3601329/obama-new-car-election-2016/.

Milton, J., Kastan, D. S. & Hughes, M. Y. (2005). *Paradise lost*. Indianapolis, IN: Hackett Publishing.

Mouzelis, N. (2010). Self and self–other reflexivity: The apophatic dimension. *European Journal of Social Theory, 13*(2), 271–284.

O'Connor, S. (Singer/Producer). (1990, 8 January). *Nothing compares 2 U*. Retrieved 12 June 2017, from www.youtube.com.

Perelman, C. (1982). *The realm of rhetoric*. Notre Dame, IN: University of Notre Dame Press.

Rentoul, J. (2016). Boring and competent Theresa May is what the nation needs after the shock of the Brexit vote. *Independent*. Retrieved 12 June 2017, from www.independent.co.uk/voices/boring-and-competent-theresa-may-is-what-the-nation-needs-after-the-shock-of-the-brexit-vote-a7114531.html.

Schürmann, M. (1978). *Meister Eckhart: Mystic and philosopher*. Bloomington, IN: Indiana University Press.

Sendbuehler, F. (1994). Silence as discourse in Paradise Lost. *GEMCS Conference, Rochester, NY,* 5 November 1994. Retrieved 12 June 2017, from https://facultystaff.richmond.edu/~creamer/silence.html.

Shakespeare, W. (*c*.1599[1988]). The tragedy of Julius Caesar. *The Oxford Shakespeare*. Retrieved 12 June 2017, from www.limpidsoft.com.plays/juliuscesar.pdf.

Solzhenitsyn, A. I. (1970). *One day in the life of Ivan Denisovich*. London: Victor Gollancz.

South Coast NSW. (2014). *Shellharbour: Visitor's guide*.

Tiffen, R. (2012). Spin doctors, news values and public interest – the Bermuda Triangle of policy debate. In M. Ricketson (Ed.), *Australian journalism today* (pp. 16–27). Melbourne, Victoria: Palgrave Macmillan.

Too, Y. L. (1995). *The rhetoric of identity in Isocrates: Text, power, pedagogy*. Cambridge: Cambridge University Press.

14 Complicit silence

Weapons of the weak

Complicit silence is the silence of a weaker party in struggle. Yet the stronger, dominant party does not entirely force it on the weaker. Totally imposed silence – such as an obligation under a non-disclosure agreement – is neither complicit nor strategic. There has to be a situation of choice. Silence must be more or less voluntary. It also has to be not one-sided, but mutual. It is not like, 'I will be talking – not you!' Both the dominant and the dominated have reasons, however different, to remain silent. In history and culture, they can not only swap positions across the vocal/silent divide, also 'bunch' together on one of the sides.

Complicit silence is not a 'truce'. It has not been openly negotiated and advertised in the public discourse. In a sense, it is silent silence – silence in stealth. It is a strategy both (or all) sides use, without to have necessarily agreed – or even talked – about it. The parties are mutually silent not only outwards, to their constituencies, but also inwards, to one another. It is silence based on self-interest and a disposition to avoid any symbolic conflict. Even if both (all) parties are not happy with their relations, they know that they would lose more from a public face-off – regardless of who is stronger and who weaker.

'Complicit' also conveys a political, moral judgement. We are no longer talking about a neutral strategy. It is a tainted strategy – a strategy of silencing or self-silencing. It is unjust, at the expense of something or someone or both. It is habitual, but also unstable. It is calculated but not quite true. Something is not right. Something has to give. There is a build-up of tension in it. It could last so for long – but not for good. It is the calm before the storm.

Normal, everyday struggle is silent. 'Everyday forms of resistance make no headline', says James Scott in *Weapons of the Weak* (2008, p. 36). Living in a Malayan village for a long time, he registered the conflict between state and peasants and rich and poor (two axes of power struggle). The weapons of the weak against those who seek to extract labour, food, tax and interest are ordinary and prosaic: 'foot dragging, dissimilation, desertion, false compliance, pilfering, feigned ignorance, slander, arson, sabotage, and so on' (p. xvi).

Those petty acts are anything but heroic. They are often invisible. They are unremarkable in the long intervals between short dramatic events. They are anti-climax gestures. They are 'grounds' rather than 'figures'. They submerse in unreflected routine. They are 'doxa', in Bourdieu's language (1977). But they buzz with indirect clues. One has to read the faces of the water polo players to figure what is going on under the water. That below-the-surface scuffle remains broadly unreported by news media and research records.

Those acts dodge the limelight. As hidden occurrences, they are *offstage* performances. *Onstage* is the game of official domination. The public sphere only exposes the weak. Anonymity is their safety. The private sphere is their camouflage. A public stoush is the last thing they need. Until they get strong.

Yet the effect of their *Schweikaesc*, cunning unruliness is enormous. States and upper classes – although the rich can also be in uneven struggle with the government – feel their invisible presence. To use Scott's metaphor, those petty acts are like millions of microscopic polyps that, willy-nilly, create a coral reef, on which many ships of state run aground. The guilds of writers and chroniclers remain silent on this common, everyday resistance. They become accomplices in silence. Not to give themselves to public ridicule, the officials are also unlikely to publicise the silent insubordination. Such admission could snowball and hit back as self-fulfilling prophecy. They would rather swallow their embarrassment.

> The nature of the acts themselves and the self-interested muteness of the antagonists thus conspire to create a kind of complicitous silence that all but expunges everyday forms of resistance from the historical record. History and social science, because they are written by an intelligentsia using written records that are also created largely by literate officials, is simply not well equipped to uncover the silent and anonymous forms of class struggle that typify the peasantry. Its practitioners implicitly join the conspiracy of the participants who are themselves, as it were, sworn to secrecy.
>
> (Scott, 2008, pp. 36–37)

Collectively, those speakers and writers form an 'unlikely cabal'. The dominant either speak freely, in Bourdieu's perspective *carelessly* – because their language is the dominant language. Or they impose non-communicative silence about anything that contradicts the master narrative (they also have the coercive means for that) and exposes their hypocrisy. The dominated, however, have to speak – or pretend to speak – the language of the dominant. Yet their distance from the official stage leaves them with many freedoms – not only of the fool. Sometimes, the backstage is where the public is. The dominated use the backstage and everyday tricks to ambiguate and subvert the dominant discourse – from underground ploys to brand jacking. The dominated are even more creative than the dominant because they are forced to communicate more indirectly, using uncommunicative or implicit silence.

I believe that Scott's observations of pre-capitalist forms of everyday struggle are also relevant for the capitalist society. My interest here is in the complicit silences that ensue from the aggregation of individual interests in the market, which still do not amount to public interest. Mutuality does not necessarily lead to publicity. Nowadays, silence is still the offstage performance of the weak.

Publicity is control. Overhearing is how control reaches out. Out or sight is out of control. Performing onstage, however, does not guarantee full control. When elites talk to 'the public', they often talk mostly to themselves.[1] In that regard, public relations is part of the cabal sworn in complicit silence. It is the silence of the relatively strong, of the *sensible minority* who are kidding themselves about the impact of their words. It is also the silence of the relatively weak, of the *silent majority*. Their weapon, according to Baudrillard, is '*actual*, in the present, and sufficient unto itself. It consists in their silence, in their capacity to absorb and neutralise, already superior to any power acting upon them' (1983, p. 3). The strength of the weak is in being impervious to forms of symbolic power, including the finest and most indirect ones such as public education and public relations.

We cannot notch complicit silence direct on the ladder of indirectness, because it is not neutral. It is a modification. It is, so to speak, applied silence with political and moral implications. We judge it from the optics of power struggle, including responsibility and guilt. It is less likely to appear as explicit silence. If the weak are expected to talk, they will. And they usually say exactly what they are supposed to. Their resistance will be in perhaps saying it a bit louder. They do not have the luxury of the powerful to defy expectations and choose not to speak if they wish. That is why complicit silence is rather implicit. One conveys more and differently from what one says. That allows mimicry and camouflage.

Implicit silence reinvents the Aesopian language. Bakhtin studied its use by the Russian radical intelligentsia, whose position in the authoritarian state was economically safe but politically weak. Russian writers took the use of allegory to a new level. The subtext was hidden, multilayered, 'more honest' than the text. Literary language was the 'anti-thesis of "plain-speak" and kind of culturally institutionalized and revered "oblique-speak"'. The reader was 'trained to see non-functional references beneath every functional surface' (Emerson, 2000, pp. 8–9). But Aesopian language was in many respects the opposite of bureaucratese, of Doublespeak. It was hiding what it was telling; it was not pretending it was telling it all. Bakhtin himself used pseudonyms not only to help close associates but also 'as strategies by which he could simultaneously disguise and circulate his ideas' (Farmer, 2001, p. 36).

Aesopian language is carnavalesque, mask-wearing, 'internally polemic', with a 'sideward glance', playing the fool, and deadpan serious (Bakhtin, 1984a, 1984b). Of course both the Malaysian peasants and Russian radicals used its idioms to resist and subvert. But this does not mean they were not complicit. Complicit is just another word for weak. Resisting and collaborating are not necessarily different activities. There are big disadvantages to fight and small advantages to protect. Communication is intervention. It is anything but innocent.

Embarrassment as strategy

The concentration of grocery chains in Australia is one of the highest in the world. Three major grocers have for long dominated the retail: *Coles, Woolworths* and *Metcash*'s *IGA*. Yet new players recently entered the market and started to erode the trio-poly from both ends: *Aldi* is eating out their share from the lower prices end. And from the luxury goods end, the department store David Jones is introducing gourmet food basements (Mitchell, 2015). Aldi is especially worrying them. There is more volume and profit to be made at the lower rather than the upper price range of the market.

Price wars are silent by design. A main tactic is to quietly squeeze the suppliers. It has worked many times in the past. In that country, there is imbalance of power between the few big grossers and many small farmers and contractors. The suppliers, not having much choice, yield to the bullying of the 'big boys', and cut their prices again and again. Pushed to the edge, many are not able to pay their bills. But even in dire straits, they remain silent in hope for last minute concessions.

Business relations are private. Confidentiality conceals the conditions of the contract. Complicit silence, however, is more than private obligation. It is public silence. As such, it is political. Silence keeps appearances. It preserves image and prestige. A *Coals'* supplier! A *Woolworths'* wholesaler!

Complicit, vested silence thrives on the autosuggestion that it is in the self-interest of the monopolist supermarket not to kill the goose that lays golden eggs. Keeping the old suppliers solvent would be for it less costly than seeking for and cultivating of new ones. 'We are in the same boat, aren't we?' 'If you feed the horse enough oats, some will pass through to the road for the sparrows'. Such metaphoric ingredients provide for the social alchemy of the bonding, routine, unperturbed, doxic culpability Bourdieu speaks about:

> Interested relationship is transmuted into a disinterested, gratuitous relationship, overt domination into misrecognized, 'socially recognized' domination, in other words, *legitimate authority* (p. 192).... The most successful ideological effects are those which have no need of words, and ask no more than complicitous silence (p. 188).
>
> (1977)

The material benefits of not speaking publically about the inequalities and struggles in the chain of supply usually outweigh the symbolic benefits of trying to solve private (market) issues through public action. After all, the retailers, wholesalers and producers are only a part of the grocery chain. They personalise in the owners, shareholders and boards of the companies. They organise the secondary redistribution of added value. The primary source remains the commodity of labour – the part of wealth workers and consumers give to them. You do not publically problematise secondary relations of redistribution if that may spill over and affect primary relations of production. And if you, nevertheless, have to do it, then you have to make sure you break your silence the right way. Your attack on a rival in a conflict of interest should best appear as disinterested care for common values.

Aldi's aggressive pricing was undermining *Coles'* 'Down, Down' slogan. Then, *Coles* was still recovering from a legal blow. In 2014, disgruntled contractors brought it before court. The Federal Court fined *Coles* $10 million for 'serious, deliberate and repeated' misconduct toward suppliers, some of which were in financial distress. The supermarket chain had also to compensate 220 suppliers with combined sales of $660 million (Lynch & Low, 2015). The other main rival, Woolworths, was in similar trouble.[2]

The straw that broke the camel's back was the breakdown in negotiations with *Bellamy*, the producer of a popular infant formula. *Bellamy* threatened to pull out its baby milk powder if Coles did not accept price rises. That happened only weeks after a similar stoush with *Arnott's*, the producer of the iconic Tim Tam biscuits.

For the reader unfamiliar with the Australian context: There had been an unprecedented Chinese demand for Australian infant milk brands such as A2 and Bellamy due to their proven quality and also the safety problems with similar products in China. It was still cheaper to buy the baby milk in Australia and send it to China. The big Australian grocers benefited enormously from that unprecedented demand. Although the Australian brands had ramped up their production by many times, the supermarkets were still struggling to keep the shelves stocked. In 2014 and 2015, *Coles*, for example, limited the purchase of *A2* and *Bellamy* formula to two units per customer.

In the face of increasing competition, rising prices was a no-go zone for *Coles*. But it also could not afford losing *Bellamy*. The supplier, in turn, was also ratcheting up its direct export to China. The meaning of the famous passage in *The Communist Manifesto*, 'The cheap prices of commodities are the heavy artillery with which [the bourgeoisie] batters down all Chinese walls' (Marx & Engels, 1978, p. 476), had taken an unexpected, literal and somewhat ironic turn.[3]

In December 2015, *Coles* took an extraordinary step. It went public. It put signs up on its shelves – next to those limiting the purchases of baby milk powder. It notified its customers that Bellamy had threatened to pull its formula if the grocer did not accept its price rises. It was an unusual strategy of publically embarrassing the supplier by siding with the customer. Increased public pressure had to clear stalled private negotiations. The strategy of naming and shaming was as brazen as it was risky. It could backfire – especially if the offending producer (*Bellamy*, *Arnott's*, others) did not blink and, for example, retaliated by making public the detailed positions of both players in the actual talks. As Steve Allen from *Fusion Strategy* commented, 'It can be shown consistently that *Coles* has refused to shed any margin, as well as requiring all the other fees for stocking that manufactures have to pay ... that their behaviour hasn't been particularly choice for consumers' (Lynch & Low, 2015). Indeed, a good public relations strategy when one is named and shamed, is to objectify. In Hans Paul Bahrdt's words: 'Wenn's peinlich wird, muss man versachlichen'

[When it becomes embarrassing, one must objectify] (Dreitzel, 1983). Such provoked objectification as disclosure and indiscretion could hurt *Coles'* reputation even stronger than a tit-for-tat naming and shaming back.

But how big was the risk for *Coles* from going public in a private conflict? Not much, according to its dominant position. In public, when we pressure those whom we dominate, we also embarrass ourselves. It is reciprocal. The fine difference, however, is that we can afford it. Power entails intolerance toward others (giving them a bad name) and tolerance towards oneself (accepting a bad name). To a degree, we lack sensibility toward the consequences from our actions both for others and us. We do not care. Either way, we will be OK. Dominance allows indifference. To a degree, we accept losses. It is par for the course. It is part of a bigger game. The question is: to what degree?

Bellamy did not respond to *Coles'* upping the ante. It did not, in turn, go public. It had at least two reasons for that. The first was that priorities had changed. Soon after, *Bellamy* started a court battle with a new rival in the baby formula market, *Nutriforme*, which was founded by its former sales manager, Chris Flahey. *Nutriforme* used know-how from *Bellamy*'s organic baby formula, but positioned itself as a budget producer of a non-organic formula, cutting its prices by half. *Bellamy* also fought to purge *Nutriforme* from the baby formula section of *Coles* (Han, 2016). For that, it strategically needed the supermarket on its side.

The second reason was pure common sense. The supplier was in a weaker position to the big retailer. It rightly calculated that it was the one who would lose more from an open stoush. *Bellamy* was one of many – *Coles* not. When you are expendable, you need even more the mutual cover-up of complicit silence. One for all, and all for one. Speaking up against *Coles* would represent one. But the supermarket represents one *and* all. It can afford symbolic politics.

The supplier could not rock or leak the boat. It was not in the position to respond with an opposite strategy. It could not remove the cover and expose 'the way it is', in which it had a vested interest too. This would possibly affect not only *Coles* but also the whole chain. Sacrificing a supplier, however an important *one*, would be the least that *all* can do in the endgame.

Notes

1 This is not unusual for the contemporary society too. In a more specialised context, Aeron Davis has explored the communication strategies of business elites of indirect communication to one another via third parties mostly in the area of financial and investor relations. Publics become, so to speak, the medium and elites the speaker and addressee of the message. It is a game of democracy, in which minorities with real power unmistakably find and influence one another using the 'objectifying' (reifying in many regards) detour of publicity and assigning to audiences with nominal power, respectable but rather supporting (legitimising, pressuring, expectation-building) roles (Davis, 2000, 2003, 2005, 2006).

2 In December 2015, the Australian Competition and Consumer Commission (ACCC) started a procedure against Woolworths, accusing it of unconscionable conduct against suppliers (Lynch & Low, 2015).

3 China's economic slowdown is only the quantitative side of a qualitative change. Its economy is shifting from manufacturing for export to servicing its increasing domestic consumption (Ma, 2015). The export boom of iron ore and other mineral commodities from Australia to China is almost over. Instead, China shows an insatiable appetite for Australian goods and services such as infant milk brands, vitamins (the sensational stock market rise and fall of *Blackmores*) or Tasmanian lavender-scented teddy bears (AFP, 2015). This poses challenges and opportunities to a Western country like Australia, including to the way it communicates with China. To push that statement a bit further, it is about deconstructing deep Western biases, including that of 'whiteness'. The separation of financial from productive capital had in the past underlined the cultural difference between the West (high quality management, clean environment) and China (low quality production, polluted nature). 'Where are those shoes made?' was the question barely hiding the suspicion of the low quality (Chinese origin) of the product. 'They are designed in Australia, with Italian leather and made in China', could be the answer that tries to soften and neutralise the question, which was not a question. With similar prejudice, English customers shunned cheap German imports in the nineteenth century. China, however, is changing its role. It is transforming from major manufacturer for the world into major investor in the world. The Western bias against China is losing not only its material substance but also its rhetorical plausibility.

References

AFP. (2015). *New growth export: Tasmania's lavender bear smells potential of Chinese market*. www.news.com.au. Retrieved 12 June 2017, from www.news.com.au/finance/small-business/new-growth-export-tasmanias-lavender-bear-smells-potential-of-chinese-market/news-story/bda487ee26d546b7a2afef1097fcec67.

Bakhtin, M. M. (1984a). *Problems of Dostoevsky's poetics*. Minneapolis, MN: University of Minnesota Press.

Bakhtin, M. M. (1984b). *Rabelais and his world* (Vol. 341). Bloomington, IN: Indiana University Press.

Baudrillard, J. (1983). *In the shadow of the silent majorities ... or the end of the social and other essays*. New York: Semiotext(e).

Bourdieu, P. (1977). *Outline of a theory of practice* (Vol. 16). Cambridge: Cambridge University Press.

Davis, A. (2000). Public relations, business news and the reproduction of corporate elite power. *Journalism, 1*(3), 282–304.

Davis, A. (2003). Whither mass media and power? Evidence for a critical elite theory alternative. *Media, Culture & Society, 25*, 669–690.

Davis, A. (2005). Media effects and the active elite audience: A study of communications in the London Stock Exchange. *European Journal of Communication, 20*(3), 303–326.

Davis, A. (2006). Media effects and the question of the rational audience: Lessons from the financial markets. *Media, Culture & Society, 28*(4), 603–625.

Dreitzel, H. P. (1983). Peinliche situationen. In M. Baethge, & W. Essbach (Eds.). *Soziologie: Entdeckungen im alltäglichen. Hans Paul Bahrdt. Festschrift zu seinem 65* (pp. 148–173). Frankfurt am Maine: Geburtstag.

Emerson, C. (2000). *The first hundred years of Mikhail Bakhtin*. Princeton: Princeton University Press.

Farmer, F. (2001). *Saying and silence: Listening to composition with Bakhtin*. Logan, UT: Utah State University Press.

Han, E. (2016). Bellamy's bid to purge baby formula market of rival brand Nutriforme. *Sydney Morning Herald*. Retrieved 12 June 2017, from www.smh.com.au/business/consumer-affairs/bellamys-bid-to-purge-baby-formula-market-of-rival-brand-nutriforme-20160519-goyyf5.html.

Lynch, J., & Low, C. (2015, 19–20 December). Coles' new strategy to 'embarrass' suppliers. *Sydney Morning Herald*. Retrieved 12 June 2017, from www.smh.com.au/business/retail/coles-embarrassing-suppliers-in-new-high-risk-strategy-20151217-glqjv9.html.

Ma, W. (2015). *What the Chinese economic slowdown means for Australia*. Retrieved 12 June 2017, from www.news.com.au/finance/executive-lounge/what-the-chinese-economic-slowdown-means-for-australia/news-story/655a8cf4f052e34032ca34d7564c8aa0.

Marx, K., & Engels, F. (1978). The communist manifesto. In R. C. Tucker (Ed.), *The Marx-Engels reader* (2nd edn). New York: W. W. Norton & Company.

Mitchell, S. (2015, 13 August). Coles, Woolworths, IGA to lose market share to Aldi, David Jones, says Moody's. *Sydney Morning Herald*. Retrieved 12 June 2017, from www.smh.com.au/business/retail/coles-woolworths-iga-to-lose-market-share-to-aldi-david-jones-says-moodys-20150813-giy6x0.html.

Scott, J. C. (2008). *Weapons of the weak: Everyday forms of peasant resistance*. New Haven: Yale University Press.

15 Silence as disengagement

Non-engagement and disengagement

Strategic silence may take the forms of both engagement and non-engagement. As it is impossible to define silence without its opposite, non-silence, so it is impossible to think of engagement without its counterpart, non-engagement. Ontologically, like silence in relation to non-silence, non-engagement is neither worse nor better than engagement. Both categories convey meaning to each other in their dialectic contradiction.

I believe public relations rhetoric overuses the category of engagement, especially in the epoch of the Internet. We overdo it as with other categories such as 'voice', 'dialogue' and 'authenticity'. It is partly an ideological reflex, in defence of the profession. We unnecessarily bring in the democratic (misunderstood as symmetric, two-sided, interactive) value of individual and interpersonal communication, although democracy is more meaningful at another, higher and more societal level.

The category of engagement has limits. We engage people and publics when we get them into a genuine conversation. Such conversation is the closest to relations building. But in professional communication, engagement is not the ultimate goal. It is an output, not an outcome. We engage to achieve something else – results, which usually reach beyond talk, communication and even relations (Bundlepost, 2013; Kanter, 2013). We engage our target publics to activate them and change their characteristics, including knowledge, awareness, attitudes and actions.

We also overemphasise engagement against disengagement. Let us start with a simple consideration. Any public relations campaign engages certain stakeholders and, at the same time, does not engage others. This may be just matter of fact or a deliberate choice. Target publics consist of many types, including of those whom we deliberately want to engage or disengage. With publics we do not target we are in de facto relations of disengagement.

Now, we are the target of others too. Others want us to engage with them – or disengage from them. They target both us *and* our strategy that targets (or not) them. We do the same. Mutual inflection of strategies – not only of objectives – takes place. He who targets is targeted. Each strategy is a conceptual how-to for both *having* a target and *being* a target.

There is a difference between non-engagement and disengagement. *Non-engagement* means that one does not engage everyone to achieve an objective. One does not engage publics, for which that objective is irrelevant. Their indifference to it is neither good nor bad. (It could even get worse if we erred and tried to engage them.) *Disengagement* is non-engagement, which is more (pro-)active. It is an intentional, planned and implemented path of non-attachment or detachment. For example, I can refuse to listen to a group and give them a forum – especially when our goals visibly clash and my publics are larger and more influential than their publics. Fending off their advances, I can prevent them from imposing their agenda on my agenda. Otherwise, any trade-off would incur me a loss.

Democracies are crowded with active publics. In policy formation, for example, there are interested and invested third – fourth, fifth, and so on – parties. Strategy is not any longer about how to hit a target but increasingly how to stay or move when others aim at you. There is no one-sided strategy any longer – if there has ever been. It is strategy against strategy – or more precisely, strategy against *strategies* in plural.

We are strategically silent and disengage not only from publics who are not our target but also from those who target us. We are strategically silent when we avoid conversations that would only produce background noise. In this sense, there is no engagement without disengagement. In the communication environment of mutual targeting, where strategies reflect and deflect one another, being heard depends less on raising our voice and more on turning down the noise of others. (The latter is even less under our control than the former. But this is exactly the direction in which our professional skills and strategies develop.) Tailored campaigns engage few but non-engage and disengage many.

Engagement and resistance

I started with the ontological neutrality of engagement and disengagement. I argued that disengagement could also have a positive value. Similarly, engagement could have a negative one. For example, it may take the historic forms of conflict, not collaboration, and of resistance, not acquiescence.

Resistance, for once, is not only opposition and negativity against dominance and power. As discursive practice (and in a Foucauldian sense), it is loaded with positivity, although in an invisible way. It is also 'a critical and ultimately generative reflective process' (Clegg, Courpasson, & Phillips, 2006, p. 727). Leitch and Motion draw on this creative and participative aspect. 'Resistance may be thought as component of engagement – resistance is an attempt to create conversation and communicate' (Leitch & Motion, 2010, p. 108).

I urge my public relations students to treat negative posts and comments on their campaign blogs as signs of engagement. Negativity is an opportunity. Negative is more engaged than indifferent. The transformation from negativity to positivity may be easier than from indifference to engagement.

Resistance may be engagement. Silence can also be resistance. One engages by resisting in silence. But silence can facilitate disengagement too – a vow of silence, a withdrawal from a discourse, taking refuge in silence, conspicuous absence, playing the loser (see Chapter 13).

Resistance may translate into vocal engagement, but it often starts as disengaged (not indifferent) silence. Yet I am not claiming that silence is non-engagement and non-silence engagement. As I discussed above, non-engagement may be vocal – noisy and garrulous, and engagement silent – meditative and profound.

Disengagement as explicit silence

In 2013, the Minister for Health in the Australian Labor government, Tanya Plibersek, mounted a multi-million vaccination campaign. The overall vaccination rate in the country was not bad and not falling. But there were certain postcodes such as Nimbin and Byron Bay in New South Wales and the Sunshine Coast in Queensland, where some parents were more wary of the risks for their kids of vaccinating versus actual contracting of MMR (Measles, Mumps and Rubella). Those geographic areas constantly showed a lower participation rate.

Observers linked the anomaly to particular middle-class demographics. Retirees from Sydney and Melbourne, creative professionals, ageing hippies and New Age intellectuals were overrepresented there. They offered the cultural ground for a small but vocal anti-vaccination movement.[1] A public relation problem for Plibersek was how not to be complacent about the *other* point of view – the perception of risk and concerns of parents (Jones, 2002) – and, at the same time, not to validate the tenuous rhetoric of the anti-vaccination movement (Leask, Chapman, Hawe & Burgess, 2006; Leask & McIntyre, 2003).

The communicators for the Health Minister came up with an overarching strategy, which included various measures of engagement and non-engagement. The main idea was that the campaign engaged with parents indirectly, with the doctors and health experts directly, and did not engage with the anti-vaccination groups at all. The vaccination cause had a strong *value* foundation. A vast majority of the population and all parliamentarian parties supported it. It was not a political issue. Politicians wanted to be in that value space. It is easier to communicate values and harder to communicate policies. The former unites, the latter divides. Communicating the values of vaccination promoted the profile of the Health Minister. But prompting those who have not vaccinated their children to do it was another matter.

For that task, the government found an unlikely Labor ally – the *Daily Telegraph* newspaper. The *News Limited* tabloid with the largest circulation in Australia was also ready to run a campaign on this topic and capitalise on its sheer value consensus. This time the Labor government did not leak to it – something that it had no qualms doing anyway (Dimitrov, 2014). It acted invisibly but in a different manner. The *National Health Performance Authority* was publishing biannual reports about the rates of immunisation in the federation. Plibersek asked them to extend the local section and for the first time add the detailed data for each postcode. Then she pitched the new information internally to the media, expressly to the *Telegraph*.

Indeed, the breakdown of data was newsworthy (NHPA, 2013). The notably lower immunisation rates in some places caught the attention. The *Daily Telegraph* also spotted the marketing niche. Armed with that telling statistics, it launched an aggressive campaign against the objecting parents. What made its language even more unguarded and harsher was the fact that that the sociocultural base of the anti-vaccination movement was outside the traditional readership of the newspaper. Painting the refusers in a radical way, it did the work that the government would rather refrain from.

Minister Plibersek was very visible in promoting the vaccination programme, especially to influencers such as doctors, health specialists and public servant. But she also took the decision not to engage with the anti-vaccination activists, not to address, debate or sanction them in any way. Paul Perry was the Director of Communication for the Minister at that time. He explains her silence:

> So that is part of the decision about who you engage in a debate. If people are pushing an agenda that you don't want to be pushed and they don't have a lot of currency in the media world and are not getting a lot of attention, and if you are a serious player and engage with them, you raise them up. That is a strategic question that doesn't necessarily have to have a moral component to it. What is the effective way of increasing the vaccination rate? Attacking the hard-core of Nimbin/Byron Bay type or prompt parents who forget to vaccinate their kids? It is not at the values level so much. It is about time and physical nature of doing it. No, the *Daily Telegraph* – they were very much into values. It's a great campaign to run if you want to sell papers – to engage readers and create moral outrage. But it's not actually a great campaign to run if you want to increase the vaccination rates. Because the more we go after these guys the more we raise their profile and actually overblow what power they have.
>
> (Personal interview, 3 November 2014)

We see here disengagement as strategy of *explicit and even non-communicative* silence. The Minister refrains from debating a small but active public. Her silence is explicit because some expect her to communicate. Her silence is noticeable by some but it is non-communicative too. She resists speaking to a particular public not because she feels weak but because she feels strong. Her silence says that. It parades the strength of the government's cause.

The Minister's silence is explicit, which also means *discursive*. Non-discursive silence, for example, prevents someone from join a debate or the debate itself. But explicit silence is a strategy, which – along implicit silence – inhabits a discourse. It works in a package of strategies – discursive or not, silent or not. Because silence is not the only way to achieve disengagement. One can disengage also vocally, even loudly, by telling off, warning or threatening someone. But this is the realm of direct, hard power. One does not need public relations strategy there. Indirect, soft power uses strategies of silence. Influence without violence is where the profession is at its best.

Presuppositions in implicit silence

In the campaign, the Health Minister also used *implicit* silence. Its purpose as strategy was not to limit access to the vaccination debate but to *reframe* the whole discourse. In the past, parents who refused to vaccinate their children were called 'conscientious objectors'. Plibersek decided to replace that tag with 'vaccine refusers' in all government documents.

Intellectually more interesting is the change of *presuppositions* behind that substitution of labels. Implicit silence often uses presuppositions – our tacitly assumed and taken for granted knowledge when we speak about other things (Jalbert, 1994; Vallauri & Masia, 2014). Presupposed is what goes without saying. Presuppositions *normalise* knowledge not through deliberative validation but through slipping a presumption under the radar of critical awareness, letting it out of question. Presuppositions include and exclude certain audiences from a discourse by way of 'strategically packaging information' (Chilton, 2004, p. 64). In manufacturing consent, the presupposed content is usually 'accepted without (much) critical attention (whereas the asserted content and evident implicatures are normally subject to some level of explanation)' (Wodak, 2009, p. 49).

Recently, a man in the US, celebrating the vote to repeal Obamacare, learned he was on Obamacare. He hated Obamacare but loved his Affordable Care Act (Kelebohile, 2017). He was shocked when he realised both were the same. The presupposition that Obamacare was bad had lived its own life, unfazed and even buoyed by the facts that refuted it.

One more example: In the sentence, 'She *admitted* (that) she had not vaccinated her child', what is manifestly discussed is whether the mother did it or not. What 'admitted' presupposes, however (watch for similar words and phrases such as *denies, forgotten, regrets, realised,* usually followed by *that*), goes unsaid and unnoticed. 'Admitted' here implies, tacitly attributes guilt – even if the parent in question does not feel that way.

What presuppositions did the Health Minister change, when she replaced 'conscientious objectors' with 'vaccine refusers'? 'Conscientious objectors' presupposes moral decision based on deep conviction. Plibersek did not want people to elevate the anti-vaccination activists to the high grounds, for example, of the pacifists who consciously object to go to war, or even of the parliamentarians who are allowed a 'conscious vote' across the partly lines due to the deeply personal and ethical character of the debated issue (Plibersek, 2015).

The adjective 'conscientious', which modifies 'objectors', is too positive and moral-based. In contrast, 'vaccine', put in front of 'refusers', is a neutral and rather 'physical' modifier. It does not hint at any human value. 'Refusers' also presupposes negation and stubbornness. (And would be an association with the euphemist noun 'refuse' pure coincidence?). 'Refusers' nominalises the verb 'refuse'. The verb petrifies as a noun. It reifies, assigns situational relations as inherent quality to a group. Nominalisation naturalises. And what is natural we cannot change. We take out the motive and even the subject of action. Refusers are nihilists. They reject vaccine – and God knows what else. They always refuse, no matter what. Should we pay attention yet?[2]

Frame as omission

Another communication problem was the introduction of the vaccination for human papilloma virus (HPV) for boys. Before that, only girls were immunised with this vaccine. The reason to extend it to boys was that the HPV formed warts, which can lead to cervical cancer in girls. Yet for a small proportion of men, it can cause similar illness such anal cancers and cancers of the throat. The vaccination of boys essentially benefits the girls because it increases the immunity of the male gender. It prevents the acquisition and transmission of the diseases by boys.

The problem was how *not* to communicate the risks and benefits of the immunisation for boys. How detailed should be the public information in walking the fine line between advantages and disadvantages from the vaccination, necessity for others and self-interest? There were strong and differing opinions in the Health Department about the right strategy. Caroline Turnour worked at that time as political adviser to the Health Minister. She recollects the discussions:

> It was about how much advertising we would do. How to say that it actually has benefits for the boys if they have anal sex in the future because there is a danger of getting HPV. We didn't want to be seen suddenly putting into the mainstream media around genital warts and anal sex. But we also thought the policy was very good and had a beneficial side effect. The debate in the Department was about how much money they would spend for above the line advertising. Or whether we would just let certain details go. Because it was teenage boys who were getting vaccinated before they were sexually mature. Whether we would rather get the process to work – through the school nurses and public health people, for example. Do we pitch the benefits to a small proportion of boys who will potentially go on to practice anal sex? Or can we just promote it as universal because the community is what we are talking about? We decided for the latter – the universal and less talkative message. We went for a short phrase, 'Cancers that boys can get', instead of [expanding] on it. We launched it, Tanya did a press conference, and it got great media. And it was really good. But there were certain parts of the debate we were silent on and we didn't then go into a huge multi-million dollar advertising campaign. We actually used the [public health] systems that are in place just to get it out there so we could just get on with it.
>
> (Personal interview, 4 November 2014)

The national media, including radio and TV, received the minimalist message well. The strategy employed the clinician who developed the original vaccine, Ian Fraser, as an Australian success story. Journalists also liked the story framed as *equity* – finally boys have access to this vaccine. The bulk of work, however, was not with the media. Almost all communication was with the professional stakeholders such as public health scientists, experts and servants. The Department tapped into their good will, practical knowledge and involvement in the process. Meanwhile, the communicators singled out and paid special attention to a few influential health reporters. They regularly conducted with them frank but rarely confidential briefings (see Chapter 18). And the reporters seemed fine about it, and could see what it was.

What the communicators used here was a master frame. They deliberately blowed out and universalised the message. At the same time, they were sparse or silent on details of the impact of the vaccine on boys and girls. Postmodernism has declared such universal narratives, which oversee and delete difference, hegemonic and obsolete (Lyotard, 1984). Foucault has also condemned such manipulation and silencing of the 'local knowledge' (2003). But activist literature also shows that a combination of master and sub frames helps the communicators to focus and strengthen their messages at all levels – international, national, regional and local (Reber & Berger, 2005). In a package of strategies, there is not either/or but and/and. The mastery is in the *combination* of master and subframes.

Notes

1 The movement taped into the arguments published in the journal *Lancet* back in the 1990s (Sabra, Bellanti & Colón, 1998) but retracted by the journal in the same year (Wakefield et al., 1998) about a possible link between MMR and autism.
2 In late 2013, the conservative coalition led by Tony Abbott won the Federal Elections in Australia and replaced Labor in government. Abbott was more amenable to the calls of *Daily Telegraphs* in its 'No Jab, No Play' campaign. In 2015, the government took a harder line and removed family and childcare concessions for parents of unvaccinated children (Gooch, 2015). Oddly enough, it quickly returned to the old vocabulary of 'conscientious objectors', rejecting the 'vaccine refusers' frame of Labor. A reason for that we may find in the ultra-conservative ideology Abbott represents. Yes, 'conscientious objectors' allow for a feel of values, moral and choice. But in Australia, it was historically established and associated not so much with religious beliefs than with left-wing pacifism such as that of the conscription objectors against the war in Vietnam. For *News Limited* and Abbott, that was actually good (bad) enough. In their political ear, 'conscientious objectors' apparently sounded more *leftish* – more damning and demonising than the dubious and untested by ideology 'vaccine refusers'.

References

Bundlepost. (2013, 12 March). Social media is NOT about engagement. Retrieved 12 June 2017, from https://bundlepost.wordpress.com/2013/03/12/social-media-is-not-about-engagement/.

Chilton, P. (2004). *Analysing political discourse*. London: Routledge.

Clegg, S., Courpasson, D. & Phillips, N. (2006). *Power and organisations*. Los Angeles, CA: Sage.

Dimitrov, R. (2014). 'Does this guy ever shut up?' The discourse of the 2013 Australian Election. *Global Media Journal: Australian Edition, 8*(2).

Foucault, M. (2003). *Society must be defended: Lectures at the College de France 1975–76.* London: Penguin.

Gooch, D. (2015, 15 April). Telegraph vaccine campaign forces law change. *NewsMedia-Works*. Retrieved 12 June 2017, from www.newsmediaworks.com.au/telegraph-vaccine-campaign-forces-law-change/.

Jalbert, P. L. (1994). Structures of the 'unsaid'. *Theory, Culture & Society, 11,* 127–160.

Jones, R. (2002). Challenges to the notion of publics in public relations: Implications of the risk society for the discipline. *Public Relations Review, 28,* 49–62.

Kanter, B. (2013, 19 March). *Social media is about engagement with a purpose and how to measure it.* Retrieved 12 June 2017, from www.bethkanter.org/engagement-purpos/.

Kelebohile. (2017, 9 January). *Man celebrating vote to repeal Obamacare learns he is on Obamacare.* Retrieved 12 June 2017, from http://imgur.com/gallery/rWIhcx6.

Leask, J., Chapman, S., Hawe, P., & Burgess, M. (2006). What maintains parental support for vaccination when challenged by anti-vaccination messages? A qualitative study. *Vaccine, 24*(49), 7238–7245.

Leask, J., & McIntyre, P. (2003). Public opponents of vaccination: A case study. *Vaccine, 21*(32), 4700–4703.

Leitch, S., & Motion, J. (2010). Publics and public relations: Effecting change. In R. Heath (Ed.), *The SAGE handbook of public relations.* Thousand Oaks, CA: Sage.

Lyotard, J.-F. (1984). *The postmodern condition: A report on knowledge.* Minneapolis, MN: University of Minnesota.

NHPA. (2013, 11 April). *National Health Performance Authority (NHPA): Health Communities: Immunisation rates for children 2011–2012.* Retrieved 12 June 2017, from Canberra. Retrieved 12 June 2017, from www.myhealthycommunities.gov.au/our-reports/immunisation-rates-for-children/april-2013.

Plibersek, T. (2015, 15 April 2015). Refusing to vaccinate children is not a conscience issue. *Sydney Morning Herald.* Retrieved 12 June 2017, from www.smh.com.au/comment/refusing-to-vaccinate-children-is-not-a-conscience-issue-20150414-1mkke0.html

Reber, B. H., & Berger, B. K. (2005). Framing analysis of activist rhetoric: How the Sierra Club succeeds or fails at creating salient messages. *Public Relations Review, 31,* 185–195.

Sabra, A., Bellanti, J. A. & Colón, A. R. (1998). Ileal-lymphoid-nodular hyperplasia, non-specific colitis, and pervasive developmental disorder in children. *Lancet, 352*(9123), 234–235.

Vallauri, E. L., & Masia, V. (2014). Implicitness impact: Measuring texts. *Journal of Pragmatics, 61,* 161–184.

Wakefield, A. J., Murch, S. H., Anthony, A., Linnell, J., Casson, D., Malik, M., et al. (1998). RETRACTED: Ileal-lymphoid-nodular hyperplasia, non-specific colitis, and pervasive developmental disorder in children. *Lancet, 351*(9103), 637–641.

Wodak, R. (2009). *The discourse of politics in action: Politics as usual.* Basingstoke: Palgrave Macmillan.

16 Strategic ambiguity

Iconicity and ambiguity

The Hon. Antony Albanese is the politician who has possibly issued the shortest ever news release. His statement from 26 February 2015 contains one single word: 'Good' (see Figure 16.1). Its headline, though, is longer: 'Media Statement on News That Sydney Airport Corporation Chairman Max Moore-Wilton Plans To Retire'.

To make sense of the release, one has to be familiar with its context. It suffices to say here that the Australian MP and Labor shadow minister Antony Albanese had a long history of political and personal animosity with the retiring Sydney Airport Corporation chairman. It dates back to when Albanese was transport minister and the resistance of the chairman to a second airport in

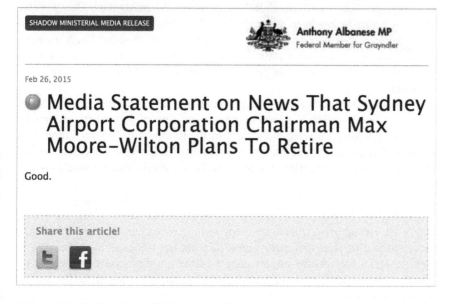

Figure 16.1 Media release of MP Anthony Albanese.

Source: http://anthonyalbanese.com.au/media-statement-on-max-moore-wilton-retirement.

Sydney. The Airport Corporation has the right but also obligation to be the first bidder the government should approach for undertaking such a project.

The message is in the layout. It is not only in the word 'Good', but also in the blank around it. Spatial silence replaces the text body. The shadow minister uses visual *iconicity*. In the *concrete poetry*, for example, the meaning of a word or phrase is not only lexical-semantic but also visual-iconic. In his verse 'Silence', Eugen Gomringer repeats that word many times in five consecutive lines. The verse looks like a wall, the bricks of which are made from the word 'silence'. He leaves an empty space only in the middle of the third line. There, in the hole in the wall, so to speak, silence appears in the blank, as an optical illusion, through its absence (Gomringer, 1954).

In iconicity, not only signs become words but also words become signs. Signs become semiotic. They are linguistic *and* iconic. Images as spatial signs introduce sound imitation and symbolism, multidimensional order and metalanguage (Ephratt, 2005). Gomringer's poetry speaks not about silence but *through* silence (Ephratt, 2008). Like in concrete poetry, the silence of Albanese says not less but more than his word 'Good'. It is not the word that is the figure and the silence the background. The opposite takes place. The silence is the figure and the word the background.

'Good' is also strategically ambiguous. Only silence can carry its equivocal inferences. On the one hand, it looks absentmindedly disinterested. A nod in energy-saving mode, a tick. Being polite to the extent of formulaic. An innocuous, almost irrelevant gesture. On the other hand, Albanese lets pass his ill-concealed satisfaction. He breathes a sigh of relief in a 'let's-get-over-it' fashion. His message, 'Let's not talk about', is purposefully ambiguous. One possible meaning is that he has been above the fray. Now, that it is over, he is cool. It is beneath him to talk about someone who is about to go. Another likely meaning still aims at the former adversary. An unremarkable event. Or the person in the event. He was almost absent in his presence. Why should I make him present in his absence?

As indirect communication, strategic ambiguity takes chances. But it is calculated, too. In his release, Albanese targets an elite of journalists and policy wonks who know, too well, the history of his rivalry with Moore-Wilton. It is rather embarrassing to add anything for them. As a career politician, he has staunch friends and enemies among them. It is unlikely that he would change their opinion.

What he cannot resist, however, is to earn more free media. Through iconicity and ambiguity, he can craft a message that is subtle but 'sticks' (Heath & Heath, 2007). He can surprise and amuse them without reheating an unimpressive and tacky story. Everyone can make sense of what has not been said. Leaving to them to recall (or not) the airport saga, he does not patronise them with petty gloating. At the same time, he allows them to own it as they wish, but also to bring closure to it.

Polyvalence and openness

Strategic ambiguity is an application of silence as discursive strategy (van Dijk, 1997). As a mode of being, silence is ambivalent. Public communication is largely between strangers. 'Silence can render the strange understandable' (Schwartzman, 1987, p. 10). Silence is also *polyvalent* ('polyphone', in Bakhtin's language). Polyvalence is more than duality – double meaning, binary or opposition. It opens up signs and messages to a multitude of interpretations by various publics, each of which is occupying a plurality of positions. In strategic ambiguity, we are silent by not reducing our message to a clear-cut, explicit meaning, which we believe to reflect our or someone else's *only true* perspective. We do not leave the listeners with no choice: 'Take it or leave it'. We invite (though also guide) them to work it out for themselves.

Robert L. Heath introduced the 'co-orientational view' of meaning as an opposite to the 'referential' view of meaning (2001). That view is motivated not purely by the (one) object but also by the realisation of the plurality of inter-subjective angles toward that object. Inter-subjectivity is ambiguous. People learn early to understand external perspectives – those of others. Socialising includes knowing and, to an extent, appreciating how (and why, for advanced learners) others interpret an object differently, from their particular angle (van Ruler, 2005).

People also achieve a second, meta-level of socialisation. They internalise the attitude of inter-subjectivity in an untheoretical, everyday-knowledge way. They accept as 'natural' the paradox that that each subject of interaction deems their position as (the only) 'natural'. This is an aspect that PR adopts from phenomenological sociology and ethnomethodology (Berger & Luckmann, 1966; Garfinkel, 1984; Schutz, 1967). People are capable of a 'co-orientational view' because they are unreflectively 'reconciled' with the fragmented, illogical, inter-subjective nature of the world. They 'naturally' find ambiguity not only bearable but, in a way, expectable.

From a 'socialised' PR perspective, ambiguity can be productive and positive. It all depends on the circumstances, context and purpose of communication. Ambiguous messages carry multiple meanings, which are not quite equal. They allow more than one meaning, but not *any* meaning (Perniola, 2010). Ambiguous meanings are not arbitrary either (see Chapter 16). They are historically motivated and concretely overdetermined (Kress, 1993). There is, so to speak, pragmatic *oneness* in the multitude of limited interpretations, which is grounded in practice. It prevents the relevant meanings from mutual annihilation – from engendering and mirroring one another, from that vicious circle and infinite process of interpretation, which Umberto Eco called 'hermetic semiosis' (1994).

Neither is ambiguity an all-purpose strategy. Its range is not unlimited. There are other, less risky strategies, which are less contingent on the participation of publics. Depending on whether creativity or compliance is sought, there is a range of strategies an organisation can employ, anything between 'discursive closure' and 'discursive openness' (Reed, 1985).

Retail or grand design communication?

For Eric Eisenberg, strategic ambiguity brings multiple and often conflicting goals under one roof. It enables organisational and individual effectiveness. It facilitates 'unified diversity'. There is no abstract strategy. Out of the context of its production, ambiguity – like any other strategy – is a neutral, even empty category. It is neither good nor bad morally. It is neither progressive nor conservative politically. Strategic ambiguity cuts both ways. It facilitates organisational change. But it also amplifies existing attributions and privileged positions (Eisenberg, 1984; Eisenberg, Goodall Jr & Trethewey, 2013).

In other words, the moral and political value of strategic ambiguity hangs on its ends. Effectiveness is only a technical term, a measure of means. Ambiguous content may enable and empower stakeholders. Yet it may also reproduce the 'circuit of power' in an organisation (Clegg, Courpasson & Phillips, 2006).

PR scholars are familiar with Eisenberg's concept of strategic ambiguity, which stems from the field of organisational communication. They have applied it to aspects of both internal and external communication as diverse as delegation of authority, biotechnological innovation and environmental sustainability (Davenport & Leitch, 2005; James, 2015; Leitch & Davenport, 2002, 2007; Leitch & Motion, 2010; Motion & Leitch, 2008).

Critics of the 'positionistas' stress that a brand cannot stand for one thing in the market. Small brands – perhaps. But big brands – from cars to banks, from food chains to supermarkets, from associations to governments – are necessarily ambiguous (Trout & Ries, 1981). They occupy multiple, open to interpretation, positions. Reducing a brand to a single position is simplistic. 'Simplistic marketing is marketing suicide' (Ringer, 2011).

Brands and logos, for example, are strategically silent and ambiguous signs. They are abstract, minimal, laconic, abstract, 'flattened', phatic, almost empty shapes, which buyers 'fill in'. They 'get volume' and materialise only when prospects and buyers insert in them, their, so to speak, 3D living experiences (Lury, 2004).

Eisenberg's concept of strategic ambiguity tackles a common pattern of disambiguation in organisations, to which I will refer to as *aspirational fallacy*. It is the functional, managerial and top-to-bottom notion of clarity. According to this, it is more likely that a clear vision of the roadmap comes from above rather than from below. Managers have to convey the supreme vision to the employees. This involves explicit, linear, standardised explanation down the chain of command. If emotion – aspiration, enthusiasm and devotion – is injected, even better. Every soldier carries a marshal's baton in his pack. The best employee thinks and acts like a top manager. Workers have to replicate rather than interpret the organisational message. The illusionism of the lofty truth: if you are right, your message is contagious. Aspirational fallacy confuses influence with influenza (Dimitrov, 2008a). Eisenberg points out that clarity – as well as ambiguity – is not an attribute of the message but a relational variable. It depends on the combination between sender, message and receiver (Eisenberg, 1984, p. 229).

Aspirational fallacy results from the lack of understanding of the importance of indirect communication when it comes to changing very human and most elaborate things such as beliefs, attitudes and behaviour. It comes down to the managerial preference to communicate to employees all of the good stuff and omit all of the bad stuff. That way, they would focus on what they would like things to be instead of stalling at (and subliminally reinforcing) what they do not like in the organisation. Direct, 'straightforward' communication often gets trapped in the loop of the obvious and trivial; it often becomes tangential. It recycles what is routinely said and rationalised anyway. It circles around things people do not talk about – things invisible because emotional and subconscious. Yet, the reaction of employees to such kind of talk goes like, 'It's all bull'. Instead of overlooking only the bad, they discount the whole, including what may be worth keeping or trying.

After the Global Financial Crisis (GFC), the Head of Client Service and Strategy at *Blaze Advertising* in Sydney, James Wiggins, was contacted by a client organisation, which was concerned about the post-crisis uneasiness of their staff. As in many other organisations, its employees had suffered tougher work environment with pay and promotional freezes, frequent redundancies and bigger workloads. But then, when the economy was recovering, the organisation began to worry that people would start to jump ship. They would do that not so much because they would get a better lot somewhere else but just because – irrationally but humanly – they were fed up with the place where they endured the crisis.

Aspirational fallacy is the organisational variant of 'mansplain'. In this case, for example, the management would directly warn the employees that it was not better anywhere else. It still was a good place to work. There were even those opportunities people had not had in previous years. Yet experience shows that staff grow cynical and 'rubbishes' such messages as condescending and patronising.

Wiggins suggested, and the client accepted, a more indirect and subtle strategy. The company announced an internal online competition. It asked the employees to submit stories about their experiences during the crisis. The communicator had researched and come up with four particular areas of experience, which formed four rubrics in a special web page. Every fortnight, its administrator changed the area to which people had to submit stories. The rubrics were formulated as questions. For example: 'What sort of professional challenges have you experienced in the last couple of years?' Another fortnight: 'What particular experiences have you had with clients or colleagues?' And another: 'What people have given you a buzz?' And: 'What particular situations do you think have opened particular career doors or unexpected career doors for you?'

The employees responded well to the initiative. They keenly wrote and read their candid but also gripping stories about the organisation. It became subliminal:

> Wow, people are actually having these experiences, even during the GFC. So maybe, if my colleagues are actually having these experiences, maybe it's not actually as bad as I thought it was here. It's actually not as good as I think it is out there.

This has a much more powerful impact on their fundamental beliefs and, therefore their actions and decision-making than if the organisation paternalistically asks, 'Trust us'. James Wiggins explains the rationale behind this tactic of strategic ambiguity.

> There is a difference between retail communications and grand positioning communications. Retail communications can typically communicate some information. A retailer will know that communicating a certain price, for example, will drive behaviour, because a lot of people who are already predisposed to act and are just waiting for the right price to come along will be influenced by that communication to make a decision. So if that is your objective, if you are just trying to influence people who are already predisposed to do what you want them to, and are just waiting for a little bit more information, then, if that's your objective, you can take the obvious visible communications route. But if your objective is to try and influence or to change the belief or change the predisposition or to change the awareness of the target audience, you have to choose an invisible route. You have to. There is no other choice. The direct route doesn't work. The indirect one does. Professional communicators should understand both the visible and invisible, so that when they're presented with all the variety of communications objectives, they can make an informed choice about which route they do take.
>
> (Personal interview, 16 September 2011)

This is important. *Retail communication* is direct, vocal and visible. *Grand positioning communication* is indirect, silent and invisible. So is strategic ambiguity. Perhaps the difference between those routes offers another way of distinguishing between public relations and other professional communications such as marketing and advertising.

If public relations is in charge of the grand design of values, dispositions and problem-solving practices – if it taps into the highly emotional drivers of memory, identity, and (self-)awareness, then learning the profession resembles even more climbing the ladder of indirectness toward the most sophisticated strategies of invisibility and silence (see Chapter 20). Strategies that make the speakers listen and the listeners speak. Strategies that let influencers and publics make sense of the message on their own terms and, ideally, take ownership of it. And is that not the ultimate measure for success in public relations?

Ambiguation and disambiguation

Strategic communication is concerned with ambiguity not as a state but rather as a *process*. *Ambiguation* of a discourse is a way to alter the discourse to achieve certain outcome. Ambiguation is not the objective (what), but the strategy (how) of realising it. Ambiguation is the discursive process that sets up the results. We can say the same about its opposite, *disambiguation*. Ambiguation and disambiguation are communicative vehicles, which drive to practical results. In those terms, we can define ambiguation as a move within a discourse from closeness to openness, and disambiguation as the reverse move from openness to closeness.

Cultural anthropology, especially the work of Edmond Leach (1976, 1982), gives ambiguation a border status. People classify the world by bipolar oppositions such as sacred–profane, safe–dangerous and clean–dirty. Yet the reality is more complex than a blend of such dualities. Discrepancies, faults and anomalies emerge as ambiguities – that is as the negative, marked, unusual, dubious, inappropriate and undesirable pols of those oppositions. And what is profane, dangerous and dirty often becomes taboo (Jaworski & Galasiński, 2000).

If a dominant public cannot silence the voice of an emerging one any longer with non-discursive strategies (no access to public forums, inappropriateness of the speaker or act of speaking), then ambiguation is the discursive strategy, which delegitimises that voice within the discourse (as un-natural, oblique, irrational).

Sexism is a contemporary example of how negative ambiguity as silencing works. It is still well and alive, but its forms have changed. It is based on the inequality between men and women. In the past, men did work and women stayed home. Like children, women were to be seen but not heard. Today, ever more women are employed. They enter the labour market from the only possible place – from the bottom, and so push men up. They also take up jobs men do not want. The new inequality is often that women are employees and men their supervisors.

Gender emancipation has changed the way men silence women. Women already have visibility and find their voice. When it is no longer possible to make someone obscure and mute, then there is another way – to make them sound nonsensical or ambiguous (Jaworski, 1993, p. 128). 'Women do not know what they want, but they always achieve it'. This is the relative difference between coercive (physical) and discursive (symbolic) power. Illegible language is illegitimate language. (If there is a link of causation, it is rather the reverse one).

As victims of rape, women often lose their case in court because they cannot prove that they have firmly and unequivocally said 'No'. Men do not have to prove anything. Men interpret silence as subordinance. And voice as confusion. A 'No' may be a 'Yes'. 'And what, if not ambiguous, is the status of a person who is responsible for a crime and is its victim at the same time' (Cameron, 2001, p. 127).

Jaworski and Galasiński use the negative opposition of ambiguation-disambiguation to analyse censorship in communist Poland. The government had used both processes for political silencing. For them, *disambiguation* is the production of a version of reality, which is presented in clear, simple and ideologically correct terms. It does not leave room for interpretation by multiple audiences. It does not accept a plurality of positions. On the contrary, it *de-positions* potential agents, if necessary. That is, it blurs the identities and differences of people, organisations, events and facts. It makes a meaningful discussion about them undesirable or impossible (Jaworski & Galasiński, 2000, p. 189).

A tactic of disambiguation is silencing by *omission*. For example, the rulers compile a catalogue of topics banned from publication. Dissenting voices are not only barred from public venues, but they also cannot be addressed by name. (Public critique of dissidents would only legitimise them, although negatively, as influencers.) One does not mention negative facts from the economic and political reality.

Ambiguation is preferred when omission cannot work. When information cannot be simply cut or, worse still, denied, censorship 'renders uncomfortable situations, people or institutions ambiguous, i.e. not pertaining to any of the clearly defined – and by the same token – *normal* categories' (Jaworski & Galasiński, 2000, p. 198). In the 1970s, one had to refer to North Korea, not recognised (blurred, defocussed) by the West, by the official name 'the Korean People's Democratic Republic'. Yet Poland, like other Soviet Bloc countries, did not recognise Taiwan and South Korea. Silencing those countries by omission in the news was not feasible. At the same time, talking about them as 'states' was not viable. The tool of choice for censors was ambiguation. They made those countries not quite real. They made them disappear as real governments and only re-emerge as geographical locations or vague metaphors such as 'puppet-states' or 'regimes' (p. 194). (In fairness, Western speakers are doing the same in relation to North Korea and Taiwan. One can include other examples such as Iran as a 'rouge state' and the Syrian 'regime of Assad'.)

Sharp analysis often rests on reduced categories. To dissect censorship in Poland, the authors (Jaworski & Galasiński, 2000, p. 197) have undertaken two reductions. First, they suggest 'the censorship practice of silencing by omission is explicit while silencing by ambiguation is implicit'. This is not convincing. They present the strategy of disambiguation only through one discursive tactic, omission, which may be explicit or implicit. Other tactics such as framing, backgrounding and deletion of the subject can also disambiguate and naturalise – that is clarify, simplify and make 'self-evident'. But they are rather implicit. The fault line between disambiguation and ambiguation, in my opinion, does not go along the division between explicit and implicit communication.

Second, Jaworski and Galasiński (2000, p. 198) accept, in the tradition of the cultural anthropology, that 'the opposition of unambiguous-ambiguous can be construed as a positive-negative one'. I believe I get the message. Indeed, it is a cultural, kataphatic thing, that Western societies attribute negative value to ambiguity and positive to clarity. In that respect, aspirational fallacy is, indeed, disambiguation by omission. Yet we should be careful not to extend this bipolar everyday-life opposition as a theoretical model. I believe that disambiguation and ambiguation are useful categories. Their main differences and relations, however, lie outside the opposition between positivity and negativity.

Ambiguation and disambiguation are not two alternatives, which exclude each other. It is not either/or but rather and/and. They may not only tolerate each other. They may also work in tandem to achieve 'unified diversity'. I teach a course in social innovation and engagement. When my students campaign on behalf of a cause, they learn to differentiate between *unity of values* and *unity of purpose*. What to do when the publics and individuals we want to mobilise disagree on the issue we want them to tackle? We employ strategic ambiguity but in *two* different modes.

If, for example, our audiences are divided between different or contradicting values, we remain silent on those values. We do not start cultural wars. We look for pragmatic unity. We become vocal on the situation. We seek for a common understanding of the issue. Often, it is easier to find an agreeable solution first. Solutions look more technical, value-neutral. (They are not.) Then we try to formulate a common definition. Definitions seem to be more difficult, close to the values. (They are.)

There is a medically supervised injecting centre in King Cross, Sydney. Religious and political values pit influential groups against the experiment. (Of course, opportunist politics, 'not-in-my backyard' anxieties and other non-value factors are also in play.) The network that runs the centre consists of a church and a few professional and government organisations (Uniting, 2017). Their communication strategy is to avoid heated debates and only put cool facts on the table. Their argument is experiential – what does work and what does not. Their language is of professional expertise rather than ideological purity. With the help of specialists and volunteers from the centre fewer drug addicts infect themselves with contaminated needles or die. More of them succeed in getting out of the drugs.

I would add a second example of success. In many Western countries, cultural and religious divisions, exacerbated by Middle Eastern terrorism, run deep mainstream and Muslim communities. Clothes and fashion – what is appropriate to wear and where, especially in public places – have become a major field of symbolic integration. In Australia, beach culture is a powerful equaliser. The most significant anti-Muslim riot started after a brawl on a Sydney beach (SBS, 2015).

What is appropriate to wear on a beach? Is the burqa, for example, an acceptable bathing suit? Muslim or Christian, religious or secular, patriarchal dignity or public safety? When advocates and politicians put it as a question of values – 'our' values or 'their' values – something has to give. Then, like in France, municipalities ban the burqa. Police arrest women wearing it on the beach. But when we place the emphasis on practical solutions, the unity of purpose may work better than the diversity of values.

In 2004, a Lebanese-born Australian designer, Aheda Zanetti, established her trademark *Ahiida* (Ahiida, 2017). She created a series of sportswear for Muslim women, among which was the famous *burkini* swimwear – a portmanteau of burqa and bikini. Indeed, other fashion designers followed suit. Burkini has become a generic brand. Today, one can see Muslim women wearing it as swimmers and even lifesavers in many places of the world. It was a marketing and public relations hit. The burkini evolved from a boutique niche to a global movement. It was an example of indirect – skilful, subtle, unobtrusive – handling of multicultural relations (and value differences) through bold (and profitable) innovation in sport and fashion. In both cases – the injecting room and burkini creation – communicators are selectively silent about divisive values and vocal about pragmatic solutions. What we achieve is diversity in values and unity in practice.

This was the first mode. In the second and opposite one, our publics share the same values, but they are rather inactive or their actions are scarce. Here we always start messaging from the values that bring us together. We use the unity of values as a platform from which we discuss possible solutions. The vaccination campaign is an example of that. My students campaign using a website, Facebook page and twitter account. The thing with social media is that most networks grow as digital tribes around hubs such as influencers, forums and hashtags (Gutiérrez-Martín, Palacios-Picos & Torrego-Egido, 2010). Their users already share common values and interests. What our followers need, is to figure out not what is right but rather how to achieve it.

Thus, my instructions: do not preach to the converted; prompt them to act; give them real options; enlist accessible choices; diversify actionable experiences; map up local solutions; shut up; let the next one speak. The attention to your site is not to you. If it rises, 'It's because of three things: names, names, and names' (Heath & Heath, 2007, p. 44). Who is who in the neighbourhood? Who are the local heroes? Which are the resident sources? Where are the closest animal shelters for pet adoption? Where is the nearest place for batteries disposal? Contact hyperlocal sites. Fill the time of small talkback radios. Use the calendar strategically. Study it. Which dates arouse the public attention around your topic? Those days will give your message wings (Dimitrov, 2008b). Use emotional stories. Their language is closest to human action. They are ambiguous but not vague. They open room for various re-enactments.

In that mode, we are vocal about our common values and suggestively let others pick the right solutions. What we achieve here is unity in values and diversity in practice. Strategic silence realises the dovetailing of both processes – ambiguation and disambiguation.

References

Ahiida. (2017). *Ahiida: Freedom, flexibility and confidence.* Retrieved 12 June 2017, from https://ahiida.com.

Berger, P. L., & Luckmann, T. (1966). *The social construction of reality: A treatise in the sociology of knowledge.* New York: Anchor Books.

Cameron, D. (2001). *Working with spoken discourse.* London: Sage.

Clegg, S., Courpasson, D. & Phillips, N. (2006). *Power and organisations.* Los Angeles, CA: Sage.

Davenport, S., & Leitch, S. (2005). Circuits of power in practice: Strategic ambiguity as delegation of authority. *Organization Studies, 26*(11), 1603–1623.

Dimitrov, R. (2008a). Acting strategically: Skilled communication by Australian refugee advocacy groups. *Global Media Journal, 2*(2). Retrieved 12 June 2017, from http://stc.uws.edu.au/gmjau/iss2_2008/Roumen_Dimitrov v2_2 2008.html.

Dimitrov, R. (2008b). The strategic response: An introduction to nonprofit communications. *Third Sector Review. Special Issue: Third Sector and Communication, 14*(2), 9–50.

Eco, U. (1994). *The limits of interpretation* (Vol. 869). Bloomington, IN: Indiana University Press.

Eisenberg, E. (1984). Ambiguity as strategy in organisational communication. *Communication Monographs, 51*, 227–242.

Eisenberg, E. M., Goodall Jr, H. L. & Trethewey, A. (2013). *Organizational communication: Balancing creativity and constraint.* Oxford: Macmillan Higher Education.

Ephratt, M. (2005). Iconicity, Ratosh's lexical innovations, and beyond. *Semiotica, 2005*(157), 83–104.

Ephratt, M. (2008). The functions of silence. *Journal of Pragmatics, 40*(11), 1909–1938.

Garfinkel, H. (1984). *Studies in ethnomethodology.* Cambridge, UK: Polity Press.

Gomringer, E. (1954). *Vom vers zur concrete poesie.* Baden-Baden: Augenblick 2.

Gutiérrez-Martín, A., Palacios-Picos, A. & Torrego-Egido, L. (2010). Digital tribes in the university classrooms. *Revista Comunicar, 17*(34), 173–181.

Heath, C., & Heath, D. (2007). *Made to stick: Why some ideas take hold and others come unstuck.* London: Random House.

Heath, R. L. (2001). A rhetorical enactment rationale for public relations: The good organization communicating well. In R. L. Heath (Ed.), *The handbook of public relations* (pp. 31–50). Thousand Oaks, CA: Sage.

James, M. (2015). Situating a new voice in public relations: The application of positioning theory to research and practice. *Media International Australia, 154*(1): 34–41.

Jaworski, A. (1993). *The power of silence: Social and pragmatic perspectives.* Newbury Park, CA: Sage.

Jaworski, A., & Galasiński, D. (2000). Strategies of silence: Omission and ambiguity in the Black Book of Polish Censorship. *Semiotica, 131*(1–2), 185–200.

Kress, G. (1993). Against arbitrariness: The social production of the sign as a foundational issue in critical discourse analysis. *Discourse & Society, 4*(2), 169–191.

Leach, E. (1976). *Culture and Communication: The logic by which symbols are connected. An introduction to the use of structuralist analysis in social anthropology*: Cambridge: Cambridge University Press.

Leach, E. R. (1982). *Social anthropology.* Oxford: Oxford University Press.

Leitch, S., & Davenport, S. (2002). Strategic ambiguity in communicating public sector change. *Journal of Communication Management, 7*(2), 129–139.

Leitch, S., & Davenport, S. (2007). Strategic ambiguity as a discourse practice: the role of keywords in the discourse on 'sustainable' biotechnology. *Discourse Studies, 9*(1), 43–61.

Leitch, S., & Motion, J. (2010). Publics and public relations: Effecting change. In R. Heath (Ed.), *The SAGE handbook of public relations.* Thousand Oaks, CA: Sage.

Lury, C. (2004). *Brands: The logos of the global economy.* Abingdon; New York: Routledge.

Motion, J., & Leitch, S. L. (2008). The multiple discourses of science-society engagement. *Australian Journal of Communication, 35*(3), 29–40.

Perniola, M. (2010). Silence, the utmost in ambiguity. *CLCWeb: Comparative Literature and Culture, 12*(4), 2.

Reed, M. I. (1985). *Redirections in organizational analysis.* London: Routledge.

Ringer, R. (2011, 18 May). Who is Jack Trout and what's he done for marketing lately? *Narrative Branding Blog.* Retrieved 12 June 2017, from https://narrativebranding. wordpress.com/2011/05/18/who-is-jack-trout-and-whats-he-done-for-marketing-lately/.

SBS. (2015). *Cronulla riots: The day that shocked the nation.* A documentary. Retrieved 12 June 2017, from www.sbs.com.au/cronullariots/

Schutz, A. (1967). *The phenomenology of the social world.* Evanston, IL: Northwestern University Press.

Schwartzman, R. (1987). *The mother of sound: A phenomenology of silence in Wordsworth's poetry.* Paper presented at the Annual Meeting of the Western Speech Communication Association, Salt Lake City, UT, February.

Trout, J., & Ries, A. (1981). *Positioning: The battle for your mind.* New York: Warner Books–McGraw-Hill.

Uniting. (2017). *Medically supervised injecting centre.* Retrieved 12 June 2017, from https://uniting.org/our-services/for-adults/sydney-medically-supervised-injecting-centre.

van Dijk, T. A. (1997). The study of discourse. In T. A. van Dijk (Ed.), *Discourse as structure and process* (pp. 1–34). London: Sage.

van Ruler, B. (2005). Co-creation of meaning theory. In R. L. Heath (Ed.), *Encyclopedia of public relations* (Vol. 1, pp. 135–138). London: Sage.

17 Silence as attention diversion

'Taking out the trash'

There is a bundle of strategies journalists call 'taking out the trash'. The best known of them is the 'Friday news dump'. It refers to the practice of governments and agencies to release bad news and embarrassing documents on Friday afternoons. The creator of *The West Wing*, Aaron Sorkin, has written a whole episode with the title 'Take out the Trash Day' (Season 1, Episode 13). In one of the scenes, Josh tells Donna how it works:

DONNA: What's take out the trash day?
JOSH: Friday.
DONNA: I mean, what is it?
JOSH: Any stories we have to give the press that we're not wild about, we give all in a lump on Friday.
DONNA: Why do you do it in a lump?
JOSH: Instead of one at a time?
DONNA: I'd think you'd spread them out.
JOSH: They've got X column inches to fill, right? They're going to fill them no matter what.
DONNA: Yes.
JOSH: So if we give them one story, that story's X inches.
DONNA: And if we give them five stories....
JOSH: They're a fifth the size.
DONNA: Why do you do it on Friday?
JOSH: Because no one reads the paper on Saturday.
DONNA: You guys are real populists, aren't you?

(Godard, 2012)

There are disclosure standards in government. One has to give certain information. The authority has no choice but to release news, which with non-release would hurt its reputation more than the news itself. It is not whether to do it but how to do it. Strategic silence chooses not the event but its timing. The speaker speaks when the listener does not listen.

On Friday afternoon the government speaks. Officially, it is still work-week. Unofficially, the weekend has already started. At the weekend, citizens want the authority to give them a break (Tanner, 2011, pp. 99–100). They may still listen but they barely hear. Later, on Monday, when they open their ears again, the Friday news is old news. That is, no news.

News decomposes quicker than food. News is for fast consumption. There is no freezer to preserve it. There is no oven to reheat it. On Monday, the Friday news, consumed or not, has already been junk. Weekends are good for dumping bad news. Long weekends are even better. The longer the weekend, the surer the decay.

Josh touts the combination of two factors – time and volume of news release. Time is the first one. Friday afternoon is the default time of release. It is based on the cycle of traditional media, especially newspapers and TV. In the past, newspapers only 'started' the news. Today, they have surrendered this role to the Internet and blogs (Bonk, Griggs & Tynes, 1999; Conrad & Poole, 2002; Holiday, 2012). Volume is the second factor. The larger the bulk of toxic documents dumped on Friday, the smaller the publicity of each separate part. Bad luck if one does not have enough bad stuff.

The Friday news dump is a widespread practice in parliamentary democracies.[1] Bill Clinton's and George W. Bush's administrations were doing it. Clinton's press office looked forward to Friday to regularly offload documents on multiple scandals, including the Whitewater scandal, the Asian fundraising probe and Kenneth Starr's investigation of the Monica Lewinsky case. Bush's nominee to be secretary for homeland security, Bernard Kerik, withdrew his nomination on Friday (he had employed an illegal immigrant as a nanny). The Whitehouse correspondent of NPR, Don Gonyea, recollects how at that time, 'a big city telephone book size pile of documents dealing with the President's [Bush] taxes [and] National Guard's service record that had been the centre of so much controversy came on a Friday the 13th of February 2004' (Norris, 2005; R. D. transcript).

How does this strategy relate to 'best practices'? How ethical is it? And how efficient? Former Clinton press secretary, Joe Lockhart, elaborates:

> Not all days are created equally. There certainly were times when I was in the White House that there'd be some, what we thought was silly Congressional investigation and we were turning over a bunch of documents and we'd wait till Friday night to sort of toss it out to all the reports and then to give it to the Committee.... You have to remember the context for this kind of information. I don't think I ever was less than truthful by way of omission. I think I was always very direct and saying I'm not gonna give you that information right now. That's a completely legitimate answer. But, certainly, the reporters have a right as the proxy for American public to information. They don't have a right to coming to my office and looking at what I am looking at ... I think the public has the ability to go and get the information at they are interested. There are a lot of places. So I don't think

the public is really ill served.... Is it something that should go into the civics textbooks, for every child in this country? Sure, it shouldn't. I mean should we have a better system? Should the media be more responsible? Should the politicians and their minions be more responsible? Absolutely.... It's just not gonna happen. It's part of the game. Much of politics is a game. And if the public is concerned, this will change only if the public is more engaged. Every time the public engages, the standards of the media go up. Every time standards of the media go up, the politicians follow, and sometimes the other way around. So I am not all that concerned about the public.

(Norris, 2005; R. D. transcript)

Torie Clarke was the Pentagon's chief spokesperson in the Bush years until 2003. She takes a different view of how prevalent the practice is and whether silence as timed release helps at all. She has seen Friday news dumping but does think it is a very smart strategy:

Well, sometimes what happens in the news business: it's a long weekend. Sometimes it's not the A-team that's working that weekend. Sometimes it's the B-team. That means, you maybe get the second stringers because it's the long weekend. Not the regulars, not the people who normally cover that particular issue. So the story breaks on the Saturday morning somewhere but you don't have the A-team on. So there you are getting phone calls at home on a weekend and you have to spend twice as much time explaining the issue to them and correcting any bad information they have. It could cost you twice as much work ... I think [Friday news dump] is a holdover from a far simpler time. I think about what the world was like even eight or ten years ago. You did not have the instantaneous, 24/7 global nature of information. Now, they don't have to wait for that newspaper to be flung on the front doorstep in the morning. They could check things at 1 a.m. So I think some of the people who continued to do it, who continued to believe in that are still wrapped up in, still believe in the pattern that's helped people consume the news as it was five, ten, fifteen years ago.

(Norris, 2005; R.D. transcript)[2]

Clarke plays down the strategy as impractical and obsolete. Her first argument is that no communicator wants a B-team calling you at home on the weekend and doubling your work for free. I wonder if the press secretary's boss would agree with that. That phone call, in addition, is routinely off the record. Why would a B-team report it and self-advertise as a B-team? When the A-team is back on Monday, it would know even less about the issue. And who wants to own garbage instead of news?

Clarke's second argument points at the accelerated 24/7 media cycle. Yet the new media have only partly affected the Friday news trash. The time patterns of news writing and news reading are not the same. The work-week–weekend cycle is still shaping the habits of the newsreader. *Quality reading*, for example, requires time and space for reflection. Recent research of 12 of the biggest online and print newspapers in the UK has shown that about 97 per cent of the time readers spent was in reading print, not the online media (Thurman, 2014). Although online reading is more frequent (and also more adjustable, such as during breaks at work), people read print less often but for longer. And the weekend usually offers that slower time for reflection – for a quiet, self-indulgent and undisturbed immersion.

There are also spatial parallels for this temporal mode of silence. The small letters in an advertising blurb disclose but also keep out of sight information about the conditions that apply. Or one can bury publically important but inconvenient information about the organisation deep in its web page. If journalists ask for it, one can always riposte that it has already been there. In other words, the story has been no news.

Firebraking

Taking out the trash is only one in a package of strategies that use *good timing* in the natural oscillation of public attention in weekly and daily cycles. Taking out the garbage uses an attention *low* in the weekly cycle. Other strategies use the *highs*. Such is the *firebraking*.

The Australian population is keenly aware of the literal 'firebraking' – also known as 'backburning' or 'swailing'. On a calm and not so hot day, fire brigades routinely conduct 'controlled burning' of overgrowth to reduce the hazard of it becoming a fuel for a fire disaster. Communicators use the metaphor of 'firebraking' to depict a 'deliberate diversion to take journalists off the scent of an embarrassing story that seems, in the journalist parlance, to have developed "legs"' (Gaber, 2000, p. 512).

On 20 March 2015, the Australian federal government released the Moss Review into the physical and sexual abuse of women and children in Australia's outsourced immigration detention centre on Nauru (Australian Government, 2015). The independent report was damaging for the governing conservative coalition. It found allegations of abuse, which triggered the review, 'credible and convincing'. It also confirmed that detainees were scared to report them (Crikey, 2015).

The review was even more demining because it vindicated the caseworkers of a nonprofit organisation, *Save the Children*, who have previously worked at the detention centre. In October 2014, the government accused ten of them of activist public relations – of coaching detained women and children how to fabricate sexual abuse stories and how to disseminate them to the media and bringing the government policy into disrepute. It sacked them and ordered them off the island. The independent review could not find any evidence to substantiate those claims (Kenny, 2015).

The report was released on a Friday afternoon. Yet it was overshadowed by the concurrent news of the passing of the former Australian Prime Minister,

Malcolm Fraser, which seized the front pages on that and the following days. The death of Fraser, a controversial and towering figure, left few indifferent. Some politicians and journalists accused the government of deliberately delaying the release of the Moss Review report, which was put on the back burner for some time. They blamed it for cynically announcing it on Friday afternoon, together with the news of Fraser's passing. It was a double whammy of 'taking out the trash' and 'firebraking'. The calculation, so the accusers said, was that the outburst of sincere public mourning and ruminations about Fraser's death would take the 'oxygen' – and fire fuel – from the bad news of the Moss Review (Gordon, 2015).

It is secondary if firebraking uses good or bad news to divert the public attention from bad news. Important is not the value of the fired feelings – positive or negative – but their strength. Stronger news trumps weaker news. We call that degree of feeling, *valence* (see Chapter 2). Anger has higher valence than sadness. Passion is stronger than liking. The memory and mourning about Fraser was closer to the hearts of many Australians than the worry for some unnamed detainees offshore.

Stoking the fire

Stoking the fire is another technique, similar to *firebraking* (Gaber, 2000, p. 513). In a way, it is even more strategic, because it keeps a story running. It is using not a one-off event, but a series of occurrences, a running narrative to overshadow embarrassing news. It could be positive news – a string of national wins during Olympic games. Or it could be negative – as the Australian Labor used the saga of embattled conservative politicians, who had misused their parliamentarian entitlements (Snow & Robertson, 2015; Tin, 2017). The advantage of stoking the fire is that it can help a party – in government or opposition – to highjack the political agenda and narrative for a long time.

Valence is critical, but there is not a rule of thumb about what dumped news with what type of event one should match. It is concrete. It is contextual. The choice of strategy and time depends on the flow of events and themes of the calendar. Yet there is a method. A football league, for example, cannot use the day of the cup final to release information about drug allegations against one or more of the players of a finalist club. On the Election Day, a government does not dump self-implicating information.

Events beget events. Attention begets events. On television, for example, it may be the sudden change of programme to broadcast films with an actor who has just passed away. Those films would not enjoy such renewed interest if it were not for the event of the actor's death. Or it may be beating the dust out of an old movie, the remake or sequel of which is about to hit the big screen.

Silence functions in the interaction between speaking and listening, not in the absence of either. The Friday news dump distracts the public from unwanted news by using a habitual low in the tide of attention. The technique is almost fail-safe because it exploits cultural norms – the stable and recurrent patterns of the calendar. The firebraking strategy exploits the differences between the lows of listening and the heights of speaking. It silences bad news by tucking it into the folds of highly emotional events. Stoking the fire keeps the listening high – even when speaking is low. What is the next win of our Olympic heroes? What is the next revelation in the expenses saga?

All those strategies have one thing in common. They do not *avert* the public attention from one thing. They rather *divert* it to another. But as Australians also know, backburning can also backfire. A sudden wind in the wrong direction or an unsteady hand may spark the inferno fire he has to prevent. The arsonist may turn out to be the fireman.

Notes

1 Writing this chapter as one of my first for this book, in early 2015, I looked back at the dates of recent political dismissals in Australia. Soon, it became clear that they have all been on Fridays – from the Federal Prime Minister, Tony Abbott, sacking his whip, Veteran Liberal MP and 'Father of the House', Philip Ruddock (Ulman, Kirk, & Glenday, 2015) to the Queensland premiere, Annastacia Palaszczuk, expelling the Cook MP Billy Gordon from the Labor party and asking him to resign from parliament (Robertson, 2015).
2 The transcripts of Michel Norris' audio-recorded interviews with Don Gonyea, Joe Lockhart and Torie Clarke are mine – R. D.

References

Australian Government. (2015). *Review into recent allegations relating to conditions and circumstances at the Regional Processing Centre in Nauru.* Retrieved 12 June 2017, from www.immi.gov.au/about/dept-info/_files/review-conditions-circumstances-nauru.pdf.

Bonk, K., Griggs, H. & Tynes, E. (1999). *The Jossey-Bass guide to strategic communications for nonprofits.* San Francisco, CA: Jossey-Bass.

Conrad, C., & Poole, M. S. (2002). *Strategic organizational communication in a global economy.* Fort Worth, TX: Harcourt.

Crikey. (2015, 23 March). *'Taking out the trash' on Moss Review reprehensible.* Retrieved 12 June 2017, from www.crikey.com.au/2015/03/23/taking-out-the-trash-on-moss-review-reprehensible/.

Gaber, I. (2000). Government by spin: An analysis of the process. *Media, Culture & Society, 22*(4), 507–518.

Godard, T. (2012). *Friday news dump.* Retrieved 12 June 2017, from http://political dictionary.com/words/friday-news-dump/.

Gordon, M. (2015, 21 March). Someone owes someone an apology. *Sydney Morning Herald.* Retrieved 12 June 2017, from www.smh.com.au/federal-politics/political-opinion/someone-owes-someone-an-apology-20150320-1m49mf.html.

Holiday, R. (2012). *Trust me, I'm lying: The tactics and confessions of a media manipulator.* London: Penguin.

Kenny, M. (2015). Taking out the trash but too clever by half *The Sydney Morning Herald.* Retrieved 12 June 2017, from www.smh.com.au/federal-politics/political-opinion/taking-out-the-trash-but-too-clever-by-half-20150320-1m44fl.html.

Norris, M. (2005, 30 June). Sifting through the Friday news dump (Audiorecord). *NPR*. Retrieved 12 June 2017, from www.npr.org/templates/story/story.php?storyId=47 25120.

Robertson, J. (2015, 30 March). Annastacia Palaszczuk declares: My Labor government still runs Queensland. *Guardian, Australian Edition*. Retrieved 12 June 2017, from www.theguardian.com/australia-news/2015/mar/30/annastacia-palaszczuk-declares-my-labor-government-still-runs-queensland.

Snow, D., & Robertson, J. (2015, 25 July). 'Choppergate' puts politicians' perks under scrutiny. *Sydney Morning Herald*. Retrieved 12 June 2017, from www.smh.com.au/federal-politics/political-news/choppergate-puts-politicians-perks-under-scrutiny-20150724-gijj5o.html.

Tanner, L. (2011). *Sideshow: Dumbing down democracy*. Brunswick, Victoria: Scribe.

Thurman, N. (2014). Newspaper consumption in the digital age: Measuring multi-channel audience attention and brand popularity. *Digital Journalism 2*(2), 156–178.

Tin, J. (2017, 13 January). Ley resigns, Turnbull announces expenses overhaul. *Daily Telegraph*. Retrieved 12 June 2017, from www.dailytelegraph.com.au/news/nsw/ley-resigns-turnbull-announces-expenses-overhaul/news-story/0d89b39f9ffe83b3bdfd035 57a315637.

Ulman, C., Kirk, A., & Glenday, J. (2015, 14 February). Philip Ruddock sacked as chief government whip in wake of spill motion against Tony Abbott. *ABC News*. Retrieved 12 June 2017, from www.abc.net.au/news/2015-02-13/philip-ruddock-sacked-as-chief-government-whip/6093194.

18 Off-the-record communication

On and off the record

Few terms like 'on-the-record' and 'off-the-record' communication are so widely misunderstood. For example, off the record conversation carries the stigma of silence. Contrasted with information for the record, it appears less direct and definite, dodging scrutiny and accountability. Journalists are unforgiving when their professional interest is threatened – the interest of protecting their sources from others if necessary, and not allowing their sources to fall silent to them if not necessary. Indeed, communication off the record is more indirect than communication on the record. As such it rests on discursive silence and a combination of explicit and implicit techniques. Journalists should remain explicitly silent on specific contents or sources or both. Implicitly, however, they can capitalise (and improvise) on the unique access to the information they get, without mentioning it. Off the record briefings are neither less efficient nor less ethical than any other form of source-media communication.

To have security when one goes off the record, one has to know how to go to a certain type of media and a certain type of reporter. Ian Pope, Senior Corporate Communicator at *Edelman*, Australia says:

> Tony Boyd at the *Australian Financial Review* writes the *Chanticleer*, the back page – the most read page in business. He's somebody you can have off-the-record conversations with because he's interested in relationships and building relationships with business. He is somebody who's experienced at doing off-the-record briefings at the highest level. What you're doing when you go to the *Australian Financial Review*, as you do sometimes with *Dow Jones*, [is] you give them stuff off the record with a view that it will make it into the newspaper. It's just you are framing it in a way that it's not attributed to you, and it's just informing their story, providing a different perspective. So, yes, there's a little bit of currency in off the record. It always goes on the record, but does it become attributable to a person or a company? Not if it's properly off the record.
>
> (Personal interview, 18 February 2015)

On-the-record information is not unconditional. When it is 'attributable', reporters can quote and name the source. What is often lost is that they *must* quote and name as strict as they can. The name – of a person or organisation – is the brand. And the quote is the message. Sources are very zealous in that regard. In the reports – in direct or indirect speech, in quotation marks or not – they want to see the message travelling intact, undiluted. But they cannot control that, of course.

On the record can also be 'unattributable'. What is said is reported word for word but not who has said it. Sources speak 'on condition of anonymity' – usually without an explanation of why. The answer seems to go without saying (Carlson, 2011). It is still news. In fact, it is news with added value. The secret news. The anonymity of the revealing source imbues its information with the mystery of a forbidden fruit. It teases curiosity, raises attention. Talkative representatives hide their identity. What is the reason? It is unofficial, perhaps personal. Perhaps the view of the source is at odds with that of the organisation. Does it subvert the official line? Does it smell of a new scandal?

Usually, it does not. Unattributable on-the-record information can just work better than an official statement. An organisation influences its publics without taking responsibility for that. Often, such information is neither informal nor subversive but strategic. For example, the organisation is canvassing the potential acceptance for an already made but unannounced decision. It is checking reactions, cautioning expectations, setting anticipation or testing the message. Anonymous sources, 'not authorised to speak on behalf the organisation', may be just authorised to pass as unauthorised. And when unattributable grabs come from the top, their leakers are unauthorised only in a sense that they authorise themselves.

Power relations do matter. If unattributable information comes from the top of the organisation, it is more likely to be a 'strategic leak'. If it comes from the bottom – and if it is really unauthorised – then it may well be 'subversive'. Whistleblowing is different. The leaker strips their anonymity. They stand up to the organisation in persona. Selfless leaking is subversive *and* attributable (Greenberg & Edwards, 2009).

Off-the-record communication goes a step further. It restricts both naming and quoting of the source. The journalist should remain silent about all new facts and personal views expressed by the source. Even the existence of the meeting should not be reported. Journalists are left with no choice but to use their imagination and figure other, unconventional ways of observing the ban but also benefiting from their temporal competitive advantage – to be privy to something new and even a scoop that no one else knows. As a difficult rhyme, this restriction sometimes becomes a stimulus for creative thinking.

The on-the-record/off-the-record opposition originates from politics, although businesses have also used it for centuries. In the UK, the Chatham House Rule[1] states:

> When a meeting, or part thereof, is held under the *Chatham House Rule*, participants are free to use the information received, but neither the identity

nor the affiliation of the speaker(s), nor that of any other participant, may be revealed.

(Chatham House, 2015)

The rule stipulates the mode of unattributable on-the-record conversation. Similar are the 'lobby terms' for correspondents who have access to the Member's Lobby in the British Parliament. The Lobby journalists are also invited to 10 Downing Street for briefings with the ministers and prime minister's secretary on the same terms (BBC, 2008). The purpose of the non-attribution clause is to allow the participants to speak freely and voice their own opinion even if it is not of the organisation, role or affiliation they formally represent.

In 1996, the US President Bill Clinton and his former press secretary, Mike McCurry, set in place the practice of 'psych-background'. Reporters were not allowed to record ('on tape'), take notes on or directly attribute Clinton's remarks. The next US presidents have keenly adopted it. Its tag has slightly changed to 'deep background'. President Barak Obama had developed it as major communication tool. He regularly invited to the White House a small and personally picked elite of journalists. The briefings, which he transformed into intense conversations, lasted up to three hours each and took place up to three times a month (Byers, 2013a).

There is still confusion about the difference between deep background and off-the-record meetings. In 2013, a White House briefing on revelations about a sensitive Benghazi investigation was conducted on 'deep background', although the existence of the meeting was off the record. An incorrect reference to it as 'off the record' prompted the then White House spokesman Josh Ernest to explain the meaning of deep background. His definition has become sort of standard: 'Deep background means that the info presented by the briefers can be used in reporting but the briefers can't be quoted' (Byers, 2013b).

No comment and off the record

In line with the argumentation in this book, off the record briefings are not a lesser – more restricted, guarded of paranoid – form of communication. It is just more silent – with all particular limitations but also freedoms of manifold mediation. In the same vein, it is not more censored, spun or undemocratic than on-the-record communication. On the contrary, off-the-record briefings represent a central, indispensable and in-depth working communication strategy.

'Off the record' never allows 'on tape'. In Australia, the former Liberal Premier of Victoria, Ted Baillieu, had an off-the-record conversation with the state political editor of the *Sunday Age* paper, Farrah Tomazin, in which he was quite frank and disparaging about colleagues from his own government. The editor secretly recorded his accusations and sent the audio to hundreds of Liberal MPs and party members from a bogus e-mail. Eventually, the recorder came into the custody of the oppositional Labor party, whose operatives later claimed they had destroyed both record and device soon after (*The Age*, 2014). In the heated debate that followed, the editor in chief of *The Age*, Andrew Holden, defended the secret use of 'on tape' in the off-the-record interview as 'a question of intent, in this case to ensure accuracy, just as taking shorthand notes without informing the source that you are doing that to achieve the same end' (ABC, 2014).

Yet from a public relations perspective, this 'small' difference is critical. Confidential talk to journalists should not be captured on audio or video recording. Notes, including shorthand, are interpretations. A tape is a tangible, 'material proof'. The no-tape and unattributed rules guard the speaker from documented slip-ups and gaffs. In the sped-up news cycle, such recordings could cause maximum harm when published as unscripted, self-harming and taken out-of-context howlers, which could later haunt the person for long. President Clinton, for example, experienced that first hand when he dropped on the record that the country was on the 'funk'. There is no coincidence that his slip of tongue occurred only months before he introduced the 'psych background' briefings (Byers, 2013a).

'No comment' is not off the record either. It is a refusal – a declared imposition – to talk. It is not silence either. It is speaking about silence. As I have previously argued, strategic silence works not by talking about silence but when silence speaks. 'No comment' is also a comment. In litigation public relations, for example, it carries the strain between *strict talk*, codified in law, and *loose talk*, the language of public relations. 'No comment' sticks with the strict talk. It is the verbal vow of strict silence.

The rights property belongs to the clients, not to their attorneys or publicists. Yet there is a permanent tension between the representatives of the clients' interests in the courts, the lawyers, and in the court of public opinion, the communicators (Watson, 2002). It terms of strategy, it is also the dilemma of whether to use strict talk or loose talk. Respectively, it is also about the choice between the direct and less informative 'No comment' and other more indirect and richer communications, including off the record. LJ Loch, co-founder and Director of *Republic Consulting*, a reputation positioning consultancy in Sydney, deals with litigation cases on a daily bases.

> We would never use off the record. Anything that happened in terms of pre-litigation briefings and context around the journalists who are likely to be covering the story would be material that was consistent with that that was being presented in court.... Sometimes it can be will against will. It's about holding your ground if you believe that it's in your client's interests to limit the response by not providing a response at that particular time. That can be for a whole range of reasons. That can be because it's material and needs to be disclosed to the stock exchange first. It might be the subject of litigation. It might be commercially sensitive. That is where the person that is being interviewed has to have enough confidence in their own story and their own ability to say, 'That's not the real issue here, the real issue is this', and change the conversation.
>
> (Personal interview, 4 December 2013)

I ask my students why they think people give off-the-record interviews at all. What could they say differently or better than in the usual, on-the-record way? The most common answer I receive is that off-the-record conversation establishes relations of trust and friendship between practitioners and reporters. I do not disagree. Scott Crebbin, public relations consultant in the Sydney Area, shares his take of the strategy:

> It just gives you the ability to give the full information. Some journalists appreciate that stuff. It gets back to trust, you know. And it could be, 'I can't give you comment on that and I have good reason not to give you comment on that'. And off the record you can say, 'this is the reason why....' That's so much about trust. And sometimes they can give it back to you as well, I also think it's not just about the relationship. It's about whatever they are doing. If they're writing a story about such and such and you're just giving them not a hell of a lot of information you could tell them the reasons [for that] and it can nullify the story. Or, they can ring you about something that they've heard and you can nullify the story by giving them the off the record story about it by saying, 'look you're actually going the wrong way with this. Actually you've been given a bit of a bum steer. Off the record this is actually what's going on'. On the record/off the record is bread and butter stuff really.
>
> (Personal interview, 24 February 2012)

Comment is content. Not commenting does not need an explanation when its goal is not to give contact but to keep the contact. In that sense 'No comment' is phatic; it maintains the channel. If the contact, however, is also an important relation, an additional clarification about why the organisation cannot provide the information is useful. Such explanation may not provide much new information either. The off-the-record strategy starts with volunteering this confidential explanation. It may also stop here (explanation but no story) or go one step further and offer an alternative content (explanation and new story).

Trust and affinity

The *relevance theory*, which Dan Sperber and Deirdre Wilson have developed, suggests two types of intent in *overt* communication – that is in conversation that involves mutual manifestedness (Wilson & Sperber, 1988a, p. 30). The *informational* intent aims at changing the communicative environment of the listener – the set of facts manifest to him. Here, we acknowledge that a speaker is telling us (his) facts. The *communicative* intention is to make the listener recognise the informational intent and change his thoughts and actions. Here he appreciates that the speaker 'tells it as it is'.

In public relations literature, the first type of intention roughly corresponds with knowledge and awareness objectives. And the second aligns with motivational and behavioural objectives (Cutlip, Center & Broom, 1999; Wilcox, Cameron, Ault & Agee, 2005). The first intent pursues *cognitive cooperation*, including 'truth recognition'. The second asks for *social cooperation*, including 'trust building' (Sperber & Wilson, 1986). The second enables the first. But the first does not necessarily lead to the second.

Trust is all well and good. And, yes, it is a precious asset in public relations. Yet its obsession with trust is over the top. Is that not telling about the schizophrenic state of the profession that puts 'a fragile human sentiment at the centre of a competitive industry' (Moloney, 2005, p. 551)?

In their *principle of relevance*, Wilson and Sperber posit that trust should not be an essential condition for the intent to inform. For example, a reporter does need to believe in what the politician says. It is sufficient that he is able to adequately reflect it. His report is relevant when it is *faithful* to what the politician has said. Informational relevance reflects the facts of the said, not whether the said reflects facts. In that sense, a representation is adequate when an utterance resembles another one closely enough in a relevant way (Wilson & Sperber, 1988b). It must be faithful to the thoughts expressed (its 'interpretative resemblance'), not to the real state of affairs (its 'descriptive use'). *It does not have to be true to be appropriate* (Tanaka, 1994, p. 18).

Informational relevance is possible without communicative relevance. Faithfull reporting is thinkable without trust between media and source. Thus, the link between trust and off-the-record communication is rather *technical*. Politicians *must* trust reporters that they would not go on the record. 'I trust you', they say, and this expresses a plea or an order or anything else but the fact of trust. The rationale for the selection of the briefed off the record is not to pick those who agree with us and we can trust them in forming a cabal. It is rather to choose those who are the best experts and opinion leaders – even when they hold inconvenient and opposite views.

In off-the-record communication, *affinity* has priority over trust. Trust measures closeness as social relation between people. Affinity measures their closeness in relation to an object. Affinity does not exclude trust. It just asks in addition, 'Trust in relation to what'? And the answer is, 'in relation to an object'. In other words, one can visualise trust as a relation between two people, A. and B. Affinity uses that segment as a side in a triangle, where the angle opposite to that side is the object C. The trust side, A.B., is inter-subjective. The A.C. and B.C. sides delineate subject-object relations. Affinity measures the whole triangle A.B.C. – the closeness between subjects in relation to an object. Trust is inter-personal. Affinity is institutional-professional.

The main function of public relation is not informing but influencing through informing (Berger & Reber, 2006; Turk, 1985). An off-the-record meeting assembles a discursive community, not a circle of confidants. Affinity is at the core of public relations because it reflects the closeness between influencers. In contrast to mass marketing and advertising, where *reach* measures the number of people directly exposed to a message, public relations uses *affinity* to gouge the way of indirect targeting of publics through the mediation of influencers. Using social media analytics, for example, communicators can learn who the followers are and who the following of whom. Then a custom-tailored and cost-effective way is to choosing affinity instead of to reach and influence the influencers whose fellow-ship constitutes the publics we ultimately target (Fine, 2005; Maggi, 2009).

We speak on the record when we directly communicate with large audiences. What we put on record, unattributable or not, is not for the journalist but for the media user. The reporter is transparent, a mailbox. The information is formatted not for a top expert – who the reporter may well be – but for a common audience. When we directly address laypeople, we speak the public language of strangers and laypeople (see Chapter 9). This language is simple and inclusive (Fuchs, Gerhards & Neidhardt, 1992). It has to be relevant to everyone – the lowest common denominator of the citizens' mutual understanding. At the same time, on the record communication can get cluttered. Because it targets mostly amateurs, it is often overloaded with context details. Everyone gets something from it but no one much of it.

In contrast, off-the-record information caters not for the public at large, but for selected reporters. Not for all journalists and not for all media. It involves only proven influencers. Based on affinity, closed and close conversation between influencers is for advanced learners. Its language is highly specialised, more analytical, professionally personalised, and teasing the edges of expertise. No one of the attendants is there by chance. Everyone has reputation to guard. Meetings off the record free both respect and candour. 'With all due respect, …' They resemble more sparing than communion.

The core knowledge of influencers is vast. In conversation behind closed doors, they do understand one another without words. In off the record meetings they go over it as quickly as possible to start working on its expansion – the very the purpose of getting together. They enjoy the luxury of informed silence. For the record, however, they have to spell out to others almost everything they do not talk about off the record. Their silence off the record is larger than what they put on the record. This is the paradox of the off the record conversation: people talk about things on which they will be silent; but they are also silent on things about which they will be talking.

So why is trust still so important, then? Peter Lazar, Founder and President of *Professional Public Relations Asia-Pacific*, recaps:

> And yet it comes back to morals and values and ethics again. If the public relations practitioner has created a good relationship with a journalist and has known the journalist for a period of time, and has never lied to the journalist or hidden things from the journalist, in that situation you can almost always rely on the journalist not to reveal something that is damaging to your client or to yourself. I have to say that in some 50 years in the industry it has worked for me 99% of the time. Okay, there's still that little risk and you can't do it with some journalists and you can't do it with journalists you've just met in the hope that they're going to play the game with you. But I have tended to be more open with journalists rather than the reverse.
>
> (Personal interview, 5 May 2015)

On the record has *exchange* value; off the record has *use* value. In on-the-record interviews, one controls the message but due to the obvious self-interest of the source – attributable or unattributable – its credibility is low. In off-the-record conversation, one cannot control the message, but other and more credible influencers may take ownership of it and increase its impact exponentially (Ries & Ries, 2002).

Chris Savage, Chairman of *Ogilvy Public Relations* in Sydney, summarises it in few words:

> There is a story about a guy who goes to a bar and talks to a girl and says, 'I'm a fabulous lover'. That is advertising and has limited credibility. If a guy walks into a bar and one girl turns to another and says, 'You see that guy – he is a fabulous lover', that is public relations and that's third party endorsement.
>
> (Personal interview, 19 March 2012)

'On the record' is advertising; 'off the record' is public relations.

Off the record has rules

Off-the-record communication presents a problem to the speaker. One cannot control the trajectory of information once it is given to a few. The British Conservative party co-chair, Lord Feldman, contended that he did not refer to party's activists as 'mad, swivel-eyed loons', when he passed by a journalist table in London's *InterContinental* hotel. But someone said it. Or he might have said it off the record, which he thought gave him the right to forget it. But journalists from different, competing media corroborated the phrase, and that was it, with the single off-the-record quote. His identity was leaked because, in the presence of 18 journalists, it was bound to happen (Greenslade, 2013).

The Uber executive, Emil Michael, suggested to a gathering of invited journalists, 'The company should consider hiring a team of opposition researchers to dig up dirt on its critics in the media – specifically to spread details of the personal life of a female journalist who has criticised the company'. A *BuzzFeed* editor brought the story up (Smith, 2014). The first reaction of Michael was to remind the journalists that the meeting had been off the record. The editor, Ben Smith, replied he had never agreed with this stipulation. Then Michael changed his heart and apologised. Then, to make it up with the press, his communication team promised a 'kinder, gentler Uber'. They invited reporters to join them for drinks at a San Francisco bar. The invite explicitly stated, 'The Event is Off-The-Record' (Constine, 2015).

Off-the-record communication is anything but a slip of the tongue. There are rules for it, and the first one is just that. As Michelle Schofield, Manager Corporate Communications, *Communities NSW* states, 'The golden rule is *everything you say is on the record*' (Personal interview, 17 November 2011). The off-the-record strategy is not designed to prevent certain information from publishing.

If you do not want it out there, do not say it. One way or another, it will get out. The purpose of the strategy is to publish it the way the communicator wants. This does not mean that we should as much as possible avoid off-the-record conversations – an advice popular among social media strategists (Phillips, 2012). It is just an imperative that before communicators go off the record, they should set specific rules for the meeting, which should be made clear to all parties.

As there is no off-the-record on tape, off-the-record briefings are not efficient in the presence of many. Lord Feldman had underestimated the power of numbers. So did the former US Attorney General, Eric Holder, when in 2013 he invited top journalists to discuss the guidelines of the *Department of Justice* for dealing with investigations of possible security leaks. He asked them not only as reporters but also as affected by the Department's intervention. The media were angry not only about becoming the story themselves (see Chapter 3) but also about the off-the-record request. Why should they be silent about their silencing? Some boycotted the meeting. Some did not, but found a way to publish its talking points. Holder was 'naïve' to organise a de facto press conference.

> *Alex Jones, Pulitzer Prize winning reporter*: If you are going to invite every news organisation in Washington and tell them it's off the record, I think you are kidding yourself.... This was an off-the-record press conference. Who ever heard of an off-the-record press conference? There was too much interest in it to stay off the record.
> *Tom Rosenstiel, Executive Director of the American Press Institute*: There is a gravitational law.... The more people who are in the room, the less valuable the briefing will be.
>
> (Shister, 2013)

This is the next rule: as does a tape, numbers verify. It takes the validation by two or more to overrule the ban on the shared information. And another rule: communicate off the record with mediators who are influencers, but who do not have a personal interest in the topic. Off the record presents a modern form of secular confession. It requires more than locking a few people in a room. And there is no role for a priest left there. It is not worth trying to simulate it – as the examples with the Uber executive and US Attorney General have shown.

The off-the-record mode protects all participants in a meeting, not only the host. This is not always clear to everyone in the room. During the conversation, reporters offer critical comment and bluntly argue in a way they also would not like to be published. An executive, for example, chases up the feedback of his external critics, which is often more useful than of his subordinate managers. For the off-the-record meeting in the Roosevelt Room at the White House, Obama invited not only his regular favourites[2] but also conservative reporters and respected opponents such as the *Washington Post* columnist Charles Krauthammer and *Wall Street Journal* editor Paul Gigot.

Here is a glimpse of what was going on behind closed doors there:

'It's not an accident who he invites: he reads the people that he thinks matter, and he really likes engaging those people', said one reporter with knowledge of the meetings. 'He reads people carefully – he has a columnist mentality – and he wants to win columnists over', said another.

'For that reason, calling these sessions 'off-the-record meetings' is actually inaccurate', said Ari Fleischer, the former press secretary to President George W. Bush, who held similar meetings.

'It's a misnomer. After these meetings journalists will go on the air and say, "Here's what the White House is thinking on this", Fleischer explained. 'It's smart. Every White House should do it'.

'The facts are off the-record, but the sentiment is not', Chuck Todd, the *NBC News* political director and chief White House correspondent, said of the meetings. 'When you know how the president thinks about something, when you understand the point of view, how do you avoid talking about it?' Todd said. 'It's in your head'.

(Byers, 2013a)

The facts are off the record, but the sentiment is not. Combined with other strategies and applied systematically, off-the-record conversation helps shaping the sentiment – or tone or tenor – of the current discourse. 'It's in your head' works on different levels. A reporter may disagree with the source. His professional instinct, however, will prompt him to adequately reproduce those thoughts as facts in their own right – the facts of how the source is thinking about the reality, not of the reality per se.

In that regard, Obama's selection of reporters was diverse but also rigorous to the extreme. 'Both reporters and journalists believe he prefers talking to people who are thinking about – and willing to be influenced on – grand concepts, rather than those who might pepper him with questions of day-to-day events and processes'.

(Byers, 2013a)

And one more rule: if you go global, you need an intensive course in off-the-record communication. An unintended consequence of globalisation is that international companies have difficulty catching up with the local news. The social media cannot cancel the time zones on the planet. To fill the gap between a potentially significant local event and the official position of the headquarters, branches of global firms are increasingly turning to off-the-record briefings. Today, improved communication culture also gives businesses more confidence in using various degrees of strategic silence. Matthew Gain, General Manager of *Edelman* in Sydney, explains:

We're seeing global alignment across media. So something that's news in Australia for a global brand can – will – make news in in the US, Germany or any other market. We're seeing a global market. So things are speeding up, things don't just happen within national borders now. What that means is that global companies, when faced with something that might originate from Australia, concerned that this could become a global issue, can't make a decision at a local level around how best to respond, because it needs to go to global to get the official statement that will work – because this has got global potential, global PR wants to know about it. The one thing that hasn't changed is we still work in a world that rotates every 24 hours, and so the news might break here in Australia in business hours, but the global PR manager is asleep. So that you have a gap of five, six, seven hours before the company representative is allowed to give any official response. What I'm starting to see now is our clients are doing off-the-record briefings to journalists to give them at least some background on the item. They're not allowed to provide an official comment, and increasingly they recourse to off-the-record briefings.

(Personal interview, 18 February 2015)

There is no coincidence that Obama's White House staff, Westminster's ministers and the company's managers and consultants also attend such briefings. The talk is off the record for journalists, but on the record for the rest. Openness and affinity equalise in this exclusive, inverted mode of publicity. Unequal, including hierarchical roles level as horizontal relations – public relations, that is. In such meetings, organisations sometimes learn more about themselves than reporters do.

Off the record, everyone has willingly participated in the crystallisation of a *unified* message, which in its simple, striking and ready to go form becomes news to both journalists and staff. Then the problem for journalists is how to break it externally without saying it, whereas the problem for organisations is how to absorb it internally without failing to hear it.

As in the eye of a cyclone, there is stillness, so at the core of public relations there is silence.

Notes

1 Introduced at the Royal Institute of International Affairs in 1927, then refined in 1992 and 2002.
2 They included *New York Times* columnists David Brook and Thomas Friedman, Joe Klein of *Time Magazine*, the *Washington Post's* E. J. Dionne, Eugene Robinson, Ezra Klein, Fred Hiatt and David Ignatius, and *Bloomberg View's* Jeffrey Goldberg.

References

ABC. (2014, 4 August). The tape, the journo and the politicians. *Media Watch: Everyone loves it until they're on it*. Retrieved 12 June 2017, from www.abc.net.au/mediawatch/transcripts/s4060720.htm.
BBC. (2008). Lobby correspondents. *BBC News*. Retrieved 12 June 2017, from http://news.bbc.co.uk/2/hi/uk_news/politics/h-l/82525.stm.

Berger, B. K., & Reber, B. H. (2006). *Gaining influence in public relations: The role of resistance in practice*. Mahwah, NJ: Lawrence Erlbaum.

Byers, D. (2013a). President Obama, off the record. *Politico*. Retrieved 12 June 2017, from www.politico.com/story/2013/11/president-obama-off-the-record-99180_Page2.html.

Byers, D. (2013b). White House holds 'deep background' Benghazi briefing. *Politico*. Retrieved 12 June 2017, from www.politico.com/blogs/media/2013/05/white-house-holds-offrecord-benghazi-briefing-163704.html.

Carlson, M. (2011). *On the condition of anonymity: Unnamed sources and the battle for journalism*. Champaign, IL: University of Illinois Press.

Chatham House. (2015). *Chatham House Rule*. Retrieved 12 June 2017, from www.chathamhouse.org/about/chatham-house-rule.

Constine, J. (2015, 12 January). A tarnished Uber tries to woo the press. *TechCrunch*. Retrieved 12 June 2017, from http://techcrunch.com/2015/01/12/but-will-emil-be-there/.

Cutlip, S. M., Center, A. H., & Broom, G. M. (1999). *Effective public relations*. Upper Saddle River, NJ: Prentice Hall International.

Fine, J. (2005, 1 March). How a 'pyromarketing' campaign sold 21 million books. Zondervan Publishing executive details his anti-mass marketing system. *Adage.com*. Retrieved 12 June 2017, from http://adage.com/article/media/a-pyromarketing-campaign-sold-21-million-books/45223/.

Fuchs, D., Gerhards, J. & Neidhardt, F. (1992). Oeffentliche Kommunicationsbereitschaft. Ein Test zentraler Bestandteils der Theorie der Schweidespirale. *Zeitschrift fuer Soziologie, 21*, 284–295.

Greenberg, J., & Edwards, M. S. (2009). *Voice and silence in organizations*. Bingley: Emerald.

Greenslade, R. (2013). *Why speaking to journalists 'off the record' doesn't guarantee anonymity*. Retrieved 12 June 2017, from www.theguardian.com/media/greenslade/2013/may/20/thetimes-dailytelegraph.

Maggi, S. (2009, 25 May). *Influencers: How to find the best ones*. Retrieved 12 June 2017, from www.steblog.net/2009/05/influencers-how-to-find-best-ones.html.

Moloney, K. (2005). Trust and public relations: Center and edge. *Public Relations Review, 31*(4), 550–555.

Phillips, B. (2012, 11 December). 8 reasons why to avoid off-the-record conversations. *Ragan's PR Daily*. Retrieved 12 June 2017, from www.prdaily.com/Main/Articles/8_reasons_to_avoid_offtherecord_conversations_13350.aspx.

Ries, A., & Ries, L. (2002). *The fall of the advertising and the rise of public relations*. New York: Harper Collins.

Shister, G. (2013, 3 June). As journalists become the story, will the rules change? *TVNewser*. Retrieved 12 June 2017, from www.adweek.com/tvnewser/when-journalists-become-the-story-do-the-rules-change/182930.

Smith, B. (2014, 18 November). Uber executive suggests digging up dirt on journalists. *BuzzFeed*. Retrieved 12 June 2017, from www.buzzfeed.com/bensmith/uber-executive-suggests-digging-up-dirt-on-journalists.

Sperber, D., & Wilson, D. (1986). *Relevance: Communication and cognition*. Oxford: Basil Blackwell.

Tanaka, K. (1994). *Advertising language: A pragmatic approach to advertisement in Britain and Japan*. London: Routledge.

The Age. (2014, 29 July). Editorial: Oh, and then they destroyed the recorder. *The Age.* Retrieved 12 June 2017, from www.theage.com.au/comment/the-age-editorial/oh-and-then-they-destroyed-the-recorder-20140728-3cpsv.html.

Turk, J. V. (1985). Information subsidies and influence. *Public Relations Review, 11*(3), 10–25.

Watson, J. C. (2002). Litigation public relations: the lawyers' duty to balance news coverage of their clients. *Communication Law & Policy, 7*(1), 77–103.

Wilcox, D. L., Cameron, G. T., Ault, P. H., & Agee, W. K. (2005). *Public relations: Strategies and tactics* (7th edn). Boston: Pearson Education.

Wilson, D., & Sperber, D. (1988a). Mood and the analysis of non-declarative sentences. In J. Dancy, J. Moravcsik & C. Taylor (Eds.). *Human agency: Language, duty and value* (pp. 77–101). Stanford, CA: Stanford University Press.

Wilson, D., & Sperber, D. (1988b). Representation and relevance. In R. Kempson (Ed.), *Mental representations: The interface between language and reality* (pp. 133–153). Cambridge: Cambridge University Press.

Part VI
Silence beyond strategy

19 Silence as system

System and strategy

Many silences are not strategic, including those which are lasting results from strategic silence. Fixed, prescribed and routine silences, for example, are not strategic. Strategies involve agency, practice of structural change. As strategists, sailors know a headwind is best to pick up speed. Strategic silence uses the flow to progress against the flow.

Professional communicators employ strategic silence to achieve particular objectives in specific situations. People are also strategically silent in their problem-solving practices. If a problem is finally solved, a strategy dies. If no solution comes close, it dies too. Both failure and success are detriment to the longevity of a strategy. But traces solidify in the results. Silence reappears beyond strategy, including as system or as skills.

In public relations, silence as strategy is outwardly directed. It is about quality content (change of themes, discourses and practices) and quality relations (change in positioning, conflict and collaboration). Silence as system and skills is rather inwardly focussed. It is about achieving a higher communicative capacity of the organisation. It is also how it adapts to the constantly changing 24/7 media cycle, which pressure on the public agents is systemic. Professional communication, in that regard, seems to be not only external public relations but also internal consulting such as advising, educating and coaching of the management.

There is a critical difference between PR practitioners and journalists in that regard. To put it bluntly, communicators are not wedded to the media cycle – journalists are. Journalists operate from inside the cycle, communicators from outside. The media primarily structures the audiences. Not the stakeholders. PR practitioners have more choices than journalists. So how to achieve the best outcome for stakeholders by capitalising on the advantage (and the freedom) of being both outside and inside the media cycle? When to include and when to exclude it? Here we need to know more about *systemic* silence – silence as presence and absence in the media cycle.

Silence as strategy is about achieving results that match the objectives. Silence as a system is about filling the communication cycle. Being strategic is situational. Feeding the cycle is systemic. One has to satiate it regularly, methodically and on schedule – systemically, that is. The media cycle does not tolerate vacuum. Silence is no vacuum. It is full. One can starve the cycle by talking. And one can fill it by keeping quiet (see also Chapter 19).

It depends on for whom the communicator works. Small businesses are more privileged. The media often let them off the hook. They are not always worth the attention. Small businesses could get away with just being strategic. Small trades such as mechanical repairs, grocery stores, accounting bureaus and medical practices do not feel the pressure of being constantly scrutinised in public. Many do not need to bring their private relations with clients to a new level of public relations. Big businesses, however, are like government organisations and agencies; they have the status of public institutions. Banks (like the Reserve bank), airlines (private or national) and football clubs (like ministries and sport bodies), for an instance, experience the media cycle as systemic. They cannot *not* be part of its reproduction.

Those are the organisations for which most professional communicators work. They must regularly supply the media with new material. Yet feeding it every day as it comes is not good enough. They have to plan and put out content months in advance. It also has to be sustainable – not just day-to-day news, but background and slow-burn material for multiple uses. Content that influences the issue priorities and frames the questions in the public agenda.

One cannot control the news and bad things happening. Yet a steady and multilayered production of positive content may offset and balance out such bad things. Constant supply also creates positive dependency of the media on that content and its source. Regular content cannot only kill bad news by quick denial (polemic argument). It can also reassert common sense (favourable interpretation). Or it can re-frame the issue as dull by pointing at a more interesting or significant one. The strategic and systemic features do not build a stiff dichotomy. They are categories, which try to capture things in flux. The line between them is moving and fuzzy. They rather work as a whole. They both boil down to the ability of taking into consideration the systemic nature of the media cycle and making the best out of the possibilities inside and outside it.

Theme and opinion

Professional communicators try to influence the tone or sentiment of publications to the advantage of their clients. Usually, this is a no-brainer. They try to decrease the negative and increase the positive publicity about a brand, product, service, etc. I will skip those theories and practices, which contend that there is no negative publicity – all publicity is good publicity. There are cases when increased brand recognition and a single target group are more important than anything else. But such examples cannot lead to a general approach of sentiment-deaf public relations (Holiday, 2012).

The problem with tone is somewhere else. Positive and negative are the values of *verbal judgement*. They constitute the upper and superficial layer of public opinion – the *axiological* one. Opinion polls use dichotomies such as good and bad, likely and unlikely, approval and disapproval to test-market political ideas. Contracted by the resourceful, pollsters seldom ask the people questions people are asking themselves. Such *organically* grown questions are likely to constitute some sort of more authentic public opinion – if there is such. But serving political agendas, pollsters usually ask answers rather than questions. They aggregate the individual responses in their questionnaire and sell them as public opinion. People learn what their opinion is and try to catch up with what the findings tell them they think. This *artificial* product – a result not from collective deliberation but individual summation – then rolls as self-fulfilling prophecy. In that respect, Bourdieu argued that public opinion did not exist (Bourdieu, 1979).

Professional communicators also try to influence a deeper layer of the public opinion – the *issue priorities* of a society. If we could imagine public opinion as an iceberg, the upper *axiological* layer, the *verbal judgements*, is only its tip. Below the surface is the monstrous body, the *cognitive* layer – the *thematic order* in the public sphere. Only few topics make the career from a potential theme to a *social issue* – a publically recognised, interest-based and action-relevant problem – on the cover pages and in the prime time of the media (Hilgartner & Bosk, 1988). What communicators try to influence here are the issue priorities. They arrange themes as important and unimportant, relevant and irrelevant, and interesting and uninteresting.

The hierarchy of issues is the practical, action-based, empirical ground of public opinion. Each theme has its superstructure – the verbal judgements such as 'pros' and 'cons' and 'don't knows' on that topic. In other words, the verbal judgements are secondary and contingent on the theme upon which they are built. The themes are primarily, determining the judgements. Furthermore, verbal judgements are not neutral. A theme often presupposes and tacitly suggests which judgement is unmarked (i.e. common, reasonable) and which marked (i.e. unusual, nonsensical). The fluctuation of issue priorities, not of verbal judgements (which are built and contingent upon each theme) moves the public opinion. Why should I, for example, legitimise a politician, answering a question about whether I trust him or not, while no one asks me whether I do know or want to know him? The dominance of verbal judgements above the surface is visible and vocal. The imbalance of themes beneath it, however, is rather invisible and silent. In that sense, public opinion is not what it seems to be.

The difference between issues as cognitive base, and judgements as axiological superstructures is not new. The agenda-setting scholars, for example, knew it when they said that the main function of the mass media was to tell you what to think *about* rather than what to think (McCombs & Shaw, 1972). It also informs the distinction between issue and crisis management. Even pollsters work with it when it comes to internal party and election polling. To position their candidates, parties have to know what issues have priority for the (undecided in a marginal seat) voters on the one side and for the party ethos (leaders, members and loyal supporters) on the other. The findings inform certain strategic decisions.

For example, the candidates position themselves by being publically silent on issues with high-priority for the party ethos and low priority for voters. At the same time, they may be privately and quietly educating the party on issues that have (gained) high priority for voters but (still) low priority for the 'old guard' (Baines, 1999; Baines, Lewis & Yorke, 1999)

Thematic silence is a tool of influencing issue priorities. Should materials on this particular topic appear on page 1 or page 17? Should the evening bulletin start or finish (if there is still time) with that news? The hierarchy of social issues symbolically reflects the dominant agenda. The map of issue priorities in a society is the real picture of its public opinion. Editors are interested in circulation and web traffic. They pick the bestselling issues first. Communicators work the issues. More precisely, they tamper with their relevance. According to the client's agenda, practitioners do their discursive work. In the public arena, they move topics up or down the ladder of issue priorities. Thematic silence is the art of boosting the boredom of an issue, which does not support the agenda. It feeds the media cycle by noise – not too loud to attract much attention, but also not too hushed to be ignored. One does not fill the cycle with nothing.

Again, the attention span of publics is short. They can focus on only a few issues out of many – and not for long. Communicators use thematic silence to lower the relevance of most of the (actually competing) issues most of the time. It is an orderly work, which often makes up the bulk of what they do.

PR practitioners influence public opinion. But how do we define it? If we see only its surface as verbal judgement and set of attitudes, then we will highlight persuasion – rhetoric, argumentation and deliberation – as the core business of communications. But if we go deeper and add the base of public opinion – the hierarchy of themes and issue priorities in the public sphere – then we should allow for a definition of public relations, which goes beyond communication as persuasion. We should include symbolic relations and discursive practices, which construct the order of relevance – of what people think *about*, instead of only what they think. And this order includes the many more extant themes people do *not* think about. In such a concept, silence, as strategy and, beyond that, as structure and system, will take its important place.

The art of being boring

A deeper understanding of strategic silence may prevent PR theory and practice from a chain of reductionist simplifications. Important as it is, the media cycle constitutes only one of the environments in the stakeholders' ecology. Public relations is more than media management. It is more than 'publicity'. A German substitute for 'public relations', 'Öffentlichkeitsarbeit', points not at 'publicity' but rather 'public sphere work'. The public sphere is a *system* (of communication). The media build only the most indirect channel in its structure. Publicity is just its *product*.

As media management is not all public relations, so creating high news value is not all publicity work. What the textbooks do not say is that the supply of content with *low news value* is equally important and thus widespread. Dull and off-colour content still fills the media cycle. It takes the space and time of other content, which may be more interesting and significant, but is less methodically fed into the system. It is professionally less cultivated – less adequate to the distinctive pulse (and arrhythmia) of all channels. High news value foregrounds. Low news value backgrounds. Boring content sets the agenda by replacing unwanted themes with noise. By dint of quantity, it changes quality.

Now, there is an argument that quality – high news value or pragmatic advice, for example – always beats quantity (steady supply). This is not quite so. Why should organisations as information sources accumulate media capital (Davis, 2002, 2010), if they do not capitalise on it? Governments exploit the 'bureaucratic affinity' of the journalists toward them (Fishman, 1988, p. 143) and regularly supply unimpressive materials to change the topic and calm public opinion. The media publish them, however dreary they read. The value-based content of nonprofit organisations may offset the lower news value – if that is the case – of their information. Even businesses may manipulate their public presence not by spreading exiting stories but by the mediation of expert-influencers who – in grey, specialised and ostensibly disinterested language – can change the priority of an issue. Thus they can indirectly help them move either it the centre of the limelight or outside its spot.

News grabs the attention only once. *No-news* takes hold of it all the time. There is no constant news. There is no one-off no-news. Producing news that is not news can be passive or active. The passive aspect is well known. We neutralise a story either by denying the event (as non-event) or by discrediting it as nothing new (no-story). Journalists do not welcome such answers because it gives away less than the question. Yet we cannot dismiss news in an abstract way. Only a concrete comparison – an apt recollection, for example, which either uncovers old news as *the* (plagiarised) story or, in reverse, dismisses the story as yesterday's news – can passively tone down the media event.

A recent example. It was 1 September 2016, Thursday, early evening in Canberra. In the last seating of the Australian Parliament for the week, the conservative government unexpectedly lost a series of votes in the Lower House despite having a majority of one. It turned out some of its MPs were at that late hour somewhere else in the building or already on the way home, not suspecting a last-minute ambush from the opposition. For the first time in many decades in the history of that country, a majority government lost a vote in the House of the Representatives (Hunter, 2016). The media called the accident a 'stuff up'. The embarrassed PM, Malcolm Turnbull, downplayed it as 'nothing new'. He referred back to a similar event in Parliament half a century ago. A semantic battle set up about the relevance of the gap. Journalists and the opposition insisted, 'I is a precedent'. Turnbull was adamant, 'There have been *precedents*'. The sneaky plural here invokes a sense of repetitiveness. If you are one 'in a raw', you are no one. You lose your face and personality. You become indistinguishable. There is no news in plural.

The pro-active production of no-news requires planning for the future. At first glance, it seems counter-intuitive. Speakers discuss openly what could happen in the future, including the worst-case scenarios. No possibility, as small as it may be, remains uncovered. They do it 'in passing', without ringing the alarm. What can go wrong in the execution of a plan due to factors we cannot fully control? Which are those things we have to watch? What should we know, in order not to be caught off guard? If something really goes awry and makes (bad) news, they can still kill it, if not the story, so at least its 'gotcha'-effect: 'Yes, that could've happened. I'm sorry. And I've told you so'.

Anticipating silence is the active aspect of the art of being boring. It frames an event as no-news by telling it in advance. A told story is no news before it happens. But, if it happens, it is no news because it has already been told. The former Premier of New South Wales, Barry O'Farrell, was famous for disarming journalist accusations of being secretive and not forthcoming with some information by pointing at a page of a government website, where that bit was deeply buried but, indeed, available.[1]

When in February 2007, two of the world-biggest passenger ships, *Queen Mary 2* and *Queen Elizabeth* met in Sydney Harbour for the first time, they caught the NSW road authority off guard. The event caused traffic gridlock and set the social media aflame (ConsumerTravellerForum, 2007; True Believer, 2007). The NSW government and City of Sydney learned from this incident. For the next meeting of those ships in 2011 – and also for *Breakfast on the Bridge*, an annual event when the road over the bridge is blocked and Sydneysiders have a walk and picnic on the bridge road covered with AstroTurf – the state government not only did the necessary preparations and informed the media and populations about the changes but also painstakingly flagged and warned about all possible inconveniences.

Anticipating the unexpected, planning the undesirable? Scott Crebbin, a PR consultant who was involved in the communications for those cases, explains why all possible developments, including the less likely and negative ones advertised.

> My philosophy has always been: tell the media what's going on, tell them all about it. You're going to do all consultation, you're going to have your call centre, you're going to have your website updated, you're going to advertise it if you need to. If the media chooses not to talk about it – after all, a scenario is only a script of a fictitious story – you pretty much nullify 70–80 percent of it by telling them in advance, and they can refer back to, 'Yeah, I knew it was going to be like this', as opposed to, 'What the f... is going on?' Nine times out of ten it completely changes the event. It's strategy that works really well.
>
> (Personal interview, 24 February 2012)

Breakfast on the Bridge closes the bridge over Sydney Harbour for a day. People cannot get across. People have delays, people miss planes, people massively complain. The non-goers to the bridge are more disgruntled than the goers because they feel less interested in the event. In other words, the event is less visible to the less invested. They are more likely to perceive it as an ambush. They are the potentially angry and most difficult public in terms of getting the message. Anticipative silence, however, works well even with them, because it is equally inclusive for the invested and non-invested. Exhaustive representation (see Chapter 4) by comprehensive flagging of all likely misfortunes, even the quite improbable ones, silences the critics. Whatever then happens usually defies the worst fears and hardly turns into bad news. But if it turns, it is also barely news. Its story has already been told when not many were listening.

In that respect, silence is the noise a communicator makes to deafen the effect of grabs, which serve competing agendas. Against interesting, vibrant narrative – boring, stock standard language. Against provocative and colourful TV pictures – grey footage that blunts and sedates. This mix is systemic work: day-by-day, week-by-week and month-by-month. One cannot control the everyday flow of events. But one can shape the discourse over an extended period of time, across the entire national cycle. One can maximise the chances that on any given day, the topics that are of interest to the media are the topics that that one wants the people to talk about. Lachlan Harris offers:

> It's not some crazy Machiavellian evil kind of thing. It's actually how democracy works. You have to get people excited, including the journalists and including their bosses and including their readers, about the issues you think are important and do matter. And that's a combination of using – you can call it *colour* and *blandness*, you know – sound and silence. But it really is not about the non-communication. The silence you are using here is just as important as the communication that you are using there. They are both key elements of it. We spend much more time trying to influence the questions than trying to answer them. And that's when you're influencing question, silence is actually more important than noise, and that's just the reality of how we operate.
>
> (Personal interview, 23 February 2015)

Influence the questions – not the answers. This is perhaps the most important rule in the art of being boring. At first glance, saying things, which people would barely hear and being present without standing out in a debate looks like a waste of time – for everyone. But it may be strategic. It may make a lot of sense when one takes the systemic view of silence. As a theme already suggests a judgement so a question usually implies an answer. Influencing the answers is tactical. There is not much room left. The answer is already framed. And it is not your answer (Lakoff, 2004). Even if you do not answer, it is the wrong answer. Influencing the questions is strategic. The freedom is much greater here. There is no right or wrong question. No one is forced to ask. If you influence a question, you do not have to worry about the answers. Any answer, including no answer, will not be wrong from your perspective.

To repeat myself, people know the answers only of those questions they ask themselves. In the social media, the use of *keywords* is strategic, because they reflect those questions users more frequently ask when they search for content. *High frequency* of search, combined with *low competition* of the word or phrase – that is only few offer it on their digital pages – is a way to match content with demand. Again, the question, not the answer is the key. The passive strategy is to research the questions. The active one is to influence them. For example, *high modality* tactics such as imperative, valence and colour focus the public attention on the few questions that help us stay on course. *Low modality* tactics such as passive voice, blandness and monotony divert it from the many possible questions, which could take the wind out of our sails.[2]

I have discussed the traditional role of PR as a wholesaler. I will replace here 'message' with 'question'. To frame questions in the public debate, the PR practitioner supplies the media with a story. It is up to the editor to decide whether and *where* to retail that story. The imperative of (long-term) issue priorities and (short-term) news value – how good the story would sell – would determine where to publish it – first, in the middle, last, or not at all. Now, because I have replaced 'pitch' and 'message' with 'theme' and 'question', there is a second aspect to this wholesale function. If part of the regular source-media supply strategically churns out sensible but boring stories, the editor will probably publish them nevertheless, although tucked in the last pages or at the end of the programme. The journalist will do it if not just because of the pressure to fill ever more space and time so at least out of loyalty to an authoritative and reliable source. The theme or question is published but also marked as less worthy by dint of its place in the publication. This produces a kind of *reverse earned media* or word of mouth. Silence that makes headlines. Public players also take *reverse ownership*.

Notes

1 From my personal interview with Scott Crebbin, PR consultant:

> You know, Barry O'Farrell said something the other day about somebody [who] criticised him for not having any policies out there and he said, 'well if you just go onto my website there's whole bunch of policies out there'. It's easy to say you've got nothing to say until you've seen something on the 6 o'clock news, but he is probably trying his arse off to try and get stuff out there but the 6 o'clock news isn't running it.

2 The difference between strategy and tactic is important here. For the same strategy of influencing the questions by silence, one can choose and combine different kinds and degrees of modality. For example, one can also attract the attention through *low modality*, as in the example of a real estate picture – a sketchy but curled white-black drawing – in the advertisement of a Victorian terrace-house for sale in Paddington, Sydney. The seller shows the airy and monochrome drawing to a naturalist and a coloured photo to achieve a dreamy, romantic effect of 'a renovator's delight'. The ink evokes historical 'charm'. It selects some architectural features and ignores or suppresses others: peeling plaster, backgrounded tree. Ironwork railing is made to appear as Victorian wrought iron 'lace-work', although in fact it is a cheap substitute (Kress, Leite-Garcia & van Leeuwen, 1997).

References

Baines, P. R. (1999). Voter segmentation and candidate positioning. In B. W. Newman (Ed.), *Handbook of political marketing* (pp. 403–420). Thousand Oaks, CA: Sage.

Baines, P. R., Lewis, B. R., & Yorke, D. A. (1999). *Co-ordinating political campaigns: A marketing planning perspective*. Retrieved 12 June 2017, from London.

Bourdieu, P. (1979). Public opinion does not exist. *Communication and Class Struggle, 1*, 124–130.

ConsumerTravellerForum. (2007, 20 February). Cool! Queen Mary 2 arrives in Sydney. *ConsumerTraveller.com*. Retrieved 12 June 2017, from www.consumertraveler.com/forum/archive/index.php/t-11892.html.

Davis, A. (2002). *Public relations democracy. Public relations, politics and the mass media in Britain*. Manchester: Manchester University Press.

Davis, A. (2010). New media and fat democracy: The paradox of online participation. *New Media & Society, 12*(5), 745–761.

Fishman, M. (1988). *Manufacturing the news*. Austin, TX: University of Texas Press.

Hilgartner, S., & Bosk, C. L. (1988). The rise and fall of social problems: A public arenas model. *American Journal of Sociology, 91*(1), 53–78.

Holiday, R. (2012). *Trust me, I'm lying: the tactics and confessions of a media manipulator*. London: Penguin.

Hunter, F. (2016, 2 September). 'Embarrassed, humiliated, excoriated': Angry Malcolm Turnbull slams ministers. *Sydney Morning Herald*. Retrieved 12 June 2017, from www.smh.com.au/federal-politics/political-news/embarrassed-humiliated-excoriated-angry-malcolm-turnbull-slams-ministers-20160901-gr7235.html.

Kress, G., Leite-Garcia, R. & van Leeuwen, T. (1997). Discourse semiotics. In T. A. van Dijk (Ed.), *Discourse studies: A multidisciplinary introduction* (pp. 257–291). London: Sage.

Lakoff, G. (2004). *Don't think of an elephant! Know your values and frame the debate*. White River Junction, VT: Chelsea Green Publishing.

McCombs, M. E., & Shaw, D. L. (1972). The agenda-setting function of mass media. *Public Opinion Quarterly, 36*(2), 176–187.

True Believer. (2007, 20 February). Two Queens in Sydney. *YesFans.com*. Retrieved 12 June 2017, from www.yesfans.com/showthread.php?35183-Two-Queens-in-Sydney.

20 Silence as skillset

The credibility to say no

Of course, public relations as the choreography of public attention is the art of being both interesting and boring. 'Interesting' may become 'of interest'. 'Boring' may become 'not worth the paper'. News value and high issue priority not only raise the attention to a topic, they also make it more salient. No-news value and low issue priority, in contrast, make a topic not only dull, they also render it less relevant. This is the wholesale, grand design communication PR applies to influences the public agenda.

The challenges of the system reflect in the skillset of the PR practitioners. The art of being interesting is what communicators learn first. The art of being boring is what they learn last.

The first set of skills practitioners learn – whether they work in public relations or run government communications – is to get things into the media. This entry-level of skills has to achieve *more publicity*. One learns, for example, to create soundbites and click-baits, which can increase circulation and traffic. Those basic and media-centric skills especially distinguished the first generation of professionals who had typically come from journalism to public relations. Silence hardly featured in their skillset (see Chapter 2). It mainly had a negative function – to prevent. It had to prevent from pushing publicity at any cost. More publicity should not spill into negative publicity. One had to know when to shut up before things start getting out of hand.

In this primary skillset, silence is already valued as the capability to resist to the pressure and aggression of the media. PR practitioners early learn how to identify, withstand and possibly neutralise a whole arsenal of journalist tricks designed to lure one speak against their best interest. In his book, *Sideshow: Dumbing down democracy*, Lindsay Tanner, a former Australian Labor finance minister, remembers such commonly employed journalist traps:

> A targeted politician is only given the opportunity to respond to damaging accusations close to the publication deadline, to make it as difficult as possible for him or her to refute the claims and thereby kill the story. In this case, I was visiting my brother's place in Melbourne on a Saturday

afternoon, and it was difficult to check facts and figures in a hurry. This technique is commonly used to ambush targets very late on weekdays, too. I was asked around the same time to respond to detailed assertions about spending on government advertising when it was too late in the day for it to be practicable to retrieve and analysed the relevant data.

(Tanner, 2011, p. 27)

Here, silence is still a reactive skill. It is an alert, suspicious silence. It is the instinctive resistance to being rushed. It is the patience and endurance of a speaker to choose when to talk and when to remain silent on their own terms. But silence can also evolve as a proactive skill, a sign of high communicative competence. It is not strategy, which is a product, but close to it. It is rather its personal and professional precondition – the ability to think and act strategically. There is a point in the career of a professional communicator when you are paid for the credibility to say one thing: *No*. You have moved near to perfection, you have become top influencer when you can tell political leaders, ministers or CEOs, 'Do not do anything, do nothing'. And they listen to you, and say, 'Well, I accept that advice. I won't act'.

Peter Lazar, founder and President of *Professional Public Relations Asia-Pacific*, Sydney, tells a story about not making a story from what is not a story:

I got a phone call from then CEO of KFC, Warren Boyd. He was an Australian Olympic swimmer previously. He said, 'Well, would you believe: Kentucky Fried Rabbit?' I said, 'I am coming over'. For no explainable reason, in central New South Wales – in Parkes, Dubbo and Forbes – there was a whisper that the chicken they were serving at KFC was actually rabbit. It was totally illogical. Illogical because at that time rabbits were very hard to find in NSW. They all had been killed by myxomatosis. When once rabbit used to be the cheapest thing an Australian family could have to dinner, it was now among the most expensive items. Boyd was very worrying and also very angry. He wanted to deny this. He wanted to get to the media and say, 'This is nonsense. This is an urban myth for the following reasons....' It took me three days to persuade him to say nothing. Our logic was pretty simple. Maybe 1% of the people in Parkes, Dubbo and Forbes have heard the whisper. It was just that sort of gossip you could not avoid passing on. People were concerned. They were sending the bones from their KFC meal for government analysis.... Three days later everything stopped. I remember thinking a few days later how I'd bill Warren Boyd for telling him to do nothing ... for three days.

(Personal interview, 5 May 2015)

In this case, silence was the answer not to a crisis but to the lack of such. Where there is no credible source verifying a story, a preventive denial of the rumour would only make KFC to that first source, although by negation. KFC would only give oxygen to an urban myth. Lachlan Harris agrees:

> In issue management and crisis communication, 99.9 percent of the time the best thing to do is to do nothing and say nothing and not react. And that's because most things that organisations consider crises are actually not crises. They're the normal, ongoing reality of being an organisation and being subject to accountability. But lots of times they get themselves into trouble when they're a tangential player in a bigger story. For an instance, someone committed crime, and that person is somehow linked to the organisation. In that situation, you'll often see businesses keen to overreact and act proactively thinking that's been defensive and strategic, not understanding that any movement in that situation is going to create more negative outcomes. The unnecessary attempt of kind of avoid scrutiny will actually provoke more negative content in the cycle.
>
> (Personal interview, 23 February 2015)

Political and business leaders tend to exaggerate their capacity to influence positive outcomes in the media cycle. New-born social media strategists also feed on their anxiety about listening more to the media, responding quickly enough to critique and, generally, being all over the place 24/7. Yet silence as an advanced, perfected set of skills leaves the PR practitioner easily unimpressed from any tangential noise. Matthew Gain, General Director for *Edelman* Australia, compares:

> Only 10, 15 years ago I used to have more discussions with clients about the importance of responding to things. I remember having discussions about how you cannot just say nothing. And now I feel like it's the opposite. Now I feel like clients are so influenced by the social media that they want to comment on everything. Yet by even responding to that, it's fuelling speculation, it is rubbish. There's been a bit of flip. And so I feel like 10, 15 years ago I was saying to clients, 'You need to go out and say something, you can't just ignore this, it's not going away'. But now it's like, 'Whoa, it's going to become a bigger issue if you talk about that'.
>
> (Personal interview, 18 February 2015)

A mistake is to believe that professional communicators are there to get more positive results. In fact, they are first there to minimise the negative ones. This is the reality. And this is also the trend.

Sweat equity

The lesson here is not that the more skilled you are as a speaker the less often you talk to the media. On the contrary, professional communicators are in perpetual conversations with publics and mediators if they want to build relations. It is rather speaking with journalists, for example, without giving them a story. But this is not talking for the sake of talking. This silence is not phatic either (Hopkins, 2014; Zegarac, 1998). It is different from formulaic or small talk, which keeps the channel clean by emptying it from content. It is about more spontaneous and relatively regular conversations between practitioners and influencers, journalists included, which are not self-conscious, take place for no obvious reason, and are humanly important for both. Peter Lazar shares his experience:

> I believe the best time to talk to a journalist is when you don't have a story. Now, these days it's getting harder because journalists are so busy – they don't have time to talk to anybody. They're mainly sitting, staring into a screen, and deciding which piece of public relations material will go into the page and which won't. So times have changed. But over the many years the journalists with whom I had a relationship not based on a story were the ones with whom I could subsequently get lots of stories.
>
> (Personal interview, 5 May 2015)

That kind of relationship cultivates both affinity and trust. Then one can freely talk on the record and off the record with such a person, especially in sensitive areas such as public health and safety, when journalists tend to be much more careful than in less risky areas such as entertainment and sport.

Sweat equity is the aptitude to minimise exposure onstage and, and at the same time, build relationships behind the scene. Chris Savage, Chairman of *Ogilvy PR*, Sydney, explains it:

> You are with people, you are doing favours for people, you are building sweat equity with people, but you are giving people limited access to you. I used to do it, not consciously, until I realised that afterwards that what helped build my brand and my influence was that even at the Friday night drinks I was the first guy to leave – and I was there for an hour and everyone else was there for three hours. They missed me when I was gone, but when I was there, they were excited because I was there. So you limit the exposure. When [the late Australian multimillionaire] Kerry Packer said something publically, it got a lot more attention than if he said it every day. You use silence as a power tool so that when you want to communicate something, more attention is given to you.
>
> (Personal interview, 19 March 2012)

Silence as minimalism in communication can increase your power. This is true for leaders as speakers as well as all communicators who build relationships with influencers, employees and publics. Paul Perry, Director of Corporate Affairs for *Avant*, a medical indemnity provider, underlines the difference:

> You can do new grabs saying, 'I don't know'. Only six seconds or seven seconds. That's fine. And say, 'We're looking into this', and you hear the nice little thing on. But to sustain 15 minutes with Alan Jones [an influential conservative talkback radio host in Sydney] is pretty damaging to your career. You may be pleased with saying to the big gun on radio, 'We don't

know'. In hindsight, you can think, 'It was great. I had great visibility and [the hosts] weren't speaking all the time'. You can have that bad interview and then hear the talk guys saying, 'This guy doesn't know what he's talking about', you know? Because you can't fill 15 minutes up on 'We don't know'.

(Personal interview, 3 November 2014)

Being ever present to one's core audience does not necessarily entail continuous presence in the media. Clients and leaders learn to understand the broader strategy rather than to say to communicators, 'I haven't seen you in the media. Why aren't you out there on that?' They know the answer: 'Well, I'm not out there on that because I know I will be asked about this'.

Noise curation

Staying on message means focussing on one thing and, at the same time, not being distracted by many things. And this is becoming increasingly difficult with the social media producing systemic, not episodic noise. Noise curating skills become essential in the effort to stay on message. Actually, those are not two different activities. Both entail actionable listening (Glenn & Ratcliffe, 2011; Kanter, 2010; Macnamara, 2016). One actively stays on message by not producing and, at the same time, filtering, reducing noise. The current media environment is saturated with noise. Everywhere, crowded networks clamour for attention. Influencing questions and getting a message across increasingly depends not on being even noisier but on curating that noise. This requires the skills of silence. Lachlan Harris:

> So how do I not sustain but actually minimise the length of time that a story exists in the media? And then how do I prevent stories of even getting into the media in the first place? It's only once you understand that full spectrum of skillsets that you become a true communications professional. I was the Prime Minister's senior press sec. I worked for a number of large financial institutions, sporting bodies. I did some work for one of the airlines, where the only skillset I offered them was to teach them how to prevent coverage in the media. Silence does not mean cover up. It is not about avoiding accountability. Businesses, as they get more sophisticated and very large, suddenly start to understand that the skillset and the capacity to not appear in the media in an unnecessary, negative, non-productive cycle is very, very important for them. And large organisations now have people, and pay people like me for that kind of outcome. It's about accepting that we're not a media company. We do it because it's a particular positive outcome. And you don't just do it for the hell of it. Most businesses still have an infrastructure and a skillset around noise. The really sophisticated ones now have an infrastructure and a skillset around silence.

(Personal interview, 23 February 2015)

Professional communicators have the relative freedom to be inside *and* outside the media system. As Harris says, the skillset around silence is 'about accepting that we're not a media company'. For the PR practitioner who works on behalf of non-media organisations, the media are neither the only nor the main stakeholders. That is why they can reduce noise at two levels – the level of the individual noise, of its source, and also of the system, of the media. The tool is a double-switch. This is luxury. The media does not have it. Accountability to the stakeholders is not necessarily noisy. It follows a different, often opposite logic to that of attempting constant media ruckus to turn the eyeballs of people who are bored.

Another tool of noise curation is the ability to turn down speculative questions as *'hypotheticals'*. A speaker refuses to speculate about what would happen, especially when decisions have not been made yet. Business people and politicians are familiar with the 'gotcha' game that will ensue if they are not careful. Any extracted prediction or promise is news. Then the media can double down with bigger stories about leaders who do deceive the public and do not keep their word. It is the journalist discourse against the political discourse. On the one side it is: 'As our representatives, politicians are accountable both for their deeds and words'. On the other: 'Do not take responsibility for events out of your control, for which you could be made liable for the sake of making news'. It is maximisation of news against minimisation of noise.

Noise curation restores priorities. It involves selective listening – not only talking. Organisational listening should focus on *core* stakeholders. They may be more silent than other publics. But they are the most invested of all publics. Their voice, even when they do not speak, counts most. You start listening and talking to the media when *they* – not the media – expect you to.

Ian Pope, from *Edelman*, Sydney, did work for a large property group, ASX 50. They own shopping centres all over Australia. A big shopping centre in Canberra was discovered, or rumoured, to have asbestos in it. More critically, some feared that an asbestos leak was going through the air conditioning system and could have been there for some of time. Remediation efforts were going on. The *Canberra Times*, the local newspaper of the *Fairfax* network, broke the story. The question that the company posed to *Edelman* was what they should do. Do we go out with something? Do we deal with it in the press? Or do we stay quiet and only deal with the people that matter?

To decide whether to respond and what kind of response to give, Pope's team analysed tens of factors. Who's going to be really important? Is it national news? Is it everybody walking around? Where are the questions from the organisation coming from? Are the sales teams getting questions? Are they coming from the company in Canberra, or from the Western Australian branch or Darwin office, who have only heard about Canberra?

Filtering of all information confirmed the decision to remain silent. There were no direct questions from affected employees, but only indirect inquiries from other branches about what was going on in Canberra. As expected, the publication in the *Canberra Times* did not reverberate in other, bigger media centres of the country. The first concerns were not even of a communicative nature. Business calculation, for once, came before media dexterity.

> What clients are really buying from a consultant is not necessarily the ideas we come up for them, but our experience around their industry and with people we've worked with in the past. So the first questions a crisis manager will ask, if there's asbestos leaking in its assets, is what's the internal rate of return (IRR) on this asset? From that you start factoring out where it ranks in terms of its material assets. That gives me an equation. What's the probability of somebody from *Patterson's* or *RBS Morgans* [former *ABN AMRO Morgans*], for example, making a call and asking questions about that asset, as it could affect potential knock on earnings over the last year? Is that asset in Canberra? It's the capital city, but it's a small population. So what are the chances of that [issue] getting out of Canberra? Because it's amazing how much news breaks in Canberra that doesn't get out of Canberra, outside the political field. The only three metro centres that really matter to Australians on the eastern seaboard, is Sydney, Brisbane and Melbourne. That's where the propensity of news, the day-to-day news flow, comes from. Similarly in WA – a lot of news doesn't get out of Perth. When you read the *West Australian*, 80% of that paper is made up of stuff that never hits the eastern seaboard. So our stock standard response [was] to say to the client, the company: 'Forget that. Who do we need to get to and make sure that we're correcting it? The people that matter are staff, you know, business partners, people you've got key contracts with, people you are about to sign key contracts with. Don't engage with something that just blows up and doesn't have foundation. Go to the people who might be reading it, and go direct.
>
> (Personal interview, 18 February 2015)

The core stakeholders of ASX 50 were staff, partners and clients. Employees usually are the key link to other publics. They listen to partners and clients the way the organisation should listen to them. Staff's feedback is perhaps the best barometer of whether the silence still absorbs the unnecessary noise.

Today, the Internet is the most powerful producer and amplifier of noise. The bulk of content curation deals with filtering digital noise. One of the problems is polarisation of information. Bloggers and online editors crank up the valence of the stories, because they sell best when they are extremely positive or negative (Holiday, 2012). Exaggeration and violence is the new normal (see Chapter 2). The effect of *flaming* is palpable. One is sharper and shriller with people online than when one faces them offline (Alonzo & Aiken, 2004). It leads not only to incidents of bigotry and abusive behaviour but also to innerved idle chatter – perhaps the biggest source of noise pollution. Opinionated texting passes as engagement. Matthew Gain sees here another reason for people to think twice before they open their mouth.

What you are starting to see is the traditional and mainstream media are splitting their stories into either hyper positive stories or hyper negative stories. And you [have to be] very wary of a media environment where there is potential for something to be seen as negative. The media will be working very hard to try and push the story as far down in the negativity end as possible, because that's what engages and that's what shares and that's what works the most today. People who are talking have lost that ability to have control and provide deeper rationale for why they might be saying something. And so now, today, when you're practically advising companies and realise that something you say could be filtered into 30 different platforms, you sometimes think it's better to say nothing. Because whatever you do say will end up in a soundbite of no more than 24 words. It's 24 words. The average human being says three words a second, and the average human being can consume information in eight seconds. In 24 words, incredibly – that's not a great deal of information for a company to be heard. So usually now, it's sometimes better to say nothing until you get the opportunity to be heard on something which you have the time to focus on being understood.

(Personal interview, 18 February 2015)

Politicians, for example, tend to overreact to what both the tabloids and the social media say – although for different reasons. Their hope is that they can use the tabloids to politicise the indifferent and Twitter to activate the converted. The former Labor Prime Minister, Kevin Rudd, was famous with constantly leaking to the *Daily Telegraph*, which is a *News Limited* newspaper with the largest circulation in Australia. He not only wanted to move blue-collar workers and 'tradies' away from the conservative (more apolitical, in a sense) lager. He also expected back loyalty from Murdoch in the fashion Tony Blair in the UK used to have it (for a while). In that gambit, the *News Limited* chairman emerged as the better player. He did not blink when he eagerly assisted Rudd's demise in the Australian 2013 elections (Dimitrov, 2014b).

It is similar with politicians who live in the bubble of the blogosphere. Chatter often does not transform into action. What is more, it often prevents from action. Caroline Turnour, shares her experience from working for a centrist-left government:

Twitter is really just trying to get as many of our members to agree, to see that we are saying and doing stuff, so it's really just getting it out there. I mean it can be skewed though because if all you do is listen to [opinion leaders], trolls and other people on social media, then you would get a skewed idea of what the public actually believes. Because, it's only a small minority of people who are engaging in that commentary, whereas the vast majority of people may have a different point of view. So you have to be very careful if you are monitoring and listening to what's going on in the social media to actually recognise that there might be a silent majority who are not speaking.

(Personal interview, 4 November, 2014)

This is the babble of *auto-noise*. Listening to the social media has become standard procedure. The problem, however, is that digital analytics cannot replace the research and conversation with clients, constituencies, voters and all other publics, which emerge and grow not along the lines of single-media audiences. Political leaders fixated on the social media may end up with another bubble on the hill – with obsessively watching and reading only those who watch and read them and not the many – among them their potential supporters, upset loyalists and undecided voters – who do not watch and read them.

Attribution and accreditation

Public relations is *ideal work* in terms of not being self-sufficient. Taken separately, it does not make sense. No one can measure it exactly. Strategic silence is perhaps its most immaterial form. PR work is ideal because it is truly cooperative and symbolic. There are multiple folds and turns before an ideal strategy materialises as implemented tactics. The final outcomes often become visible and measurable only at the endpoint of a chain of symbolic interactions – as *numbers* of sales, of managed cases, of recruited members, or of phone calls to a contact centre, for example.

Paul Matthews, Communication Strategy Manager of *Sydney Water*, explains the paradox nature and cooperative character of ideal work:

> We are trying to be strategic about what we are doing. We are not actually doing a lot of the doing. We're getting others to do it. Yes, it does make it harder because we're involved in everything so ideally … I work across nine different divisions. So if we were involved in any reward and recognition, they'd start to think we are just freeloaders. It's hard to articulate the value you've added because a lot of communications is not measurable. I'm up against scientists. I'm up against engineers. They're very evidence driven. They are focussed on qualifications and accreditations so they build stuff and they measure stuff all the time – that's much harder therefore for us to demonstrate success within a goal.
>
> (Personal interview, 25 November, 2011)

The ideal feature of their work makes PR practitioners rather invisible. As discursive *technologists* in a Foucauldian sense (Leitch & Motion, 2007; Motion & Leitch, 2007), they are directly responsible for the means, and only indirectly for the ends of the communications. Their invisibility serves to increase the visibility of those who have hired them and represent the whole lot – an organisation, a community, an idea. Their silence is the conduit of the collective voice.

In other words, the visibility of the communicator should not become an obstacle to the visibility of those for whom he works. One can instantly detect communications rookies who love to be seen near their bosses in front of the cameras. Professional communicators do not represent themselves. Ideally, they are transparent. They help others represent – even themselves, what publicists do. *Ideal representation is not real representation.*

How visible should the communicator who works for a leader be? Paul Matthews:

> I spoke at a conference about five or six months ago and I was asked by the Chairman just beforehand, 'What would be your ultimate success?' And my instant remark was, I would like to empower our leaders in communications so that they wouldn't need a comms team'. It's almost like, and lots of people do it here: they defer to us to communicate. It's actually a leadership function. We're here to advise and coach and mentor. We're now here to speak for people. You become invisible because you defer the visibility to the leaders. I see that as the first point of engagement. People won't follow communication; they will follow a leader. People won't buy into an empty message, e-mail or campaign. Unless it's got some person carrying a torch.
>
> (Personal interview, 25 November 2011)

The communicator is usually an *attributed* source. The leader – CEO or politician or any other representative – is an *accredited* source. The responsibility of the attributed source is delegated and limited. The accredited source – the authorised and accountable one – assigns duty to the attributed one. This, of course, may go awry. We see that happening in real life. The leader may abdicate from his responsibility and saddle the communicator with tasks that may exceed his job description and specific duties. Such 'do me it' culture (Dimitrov, 2014a) may innocuously start with, 'Knock it into shape for me, will you?' But it then ends with hints or shots at the inability of the PR practitioner, department or director. Public relations workers are invisible when they succeed; they only become visible when they fail. It is hardly a surprise that of all executive jobs in the world, public relations is one of the most stressful.[1]

The invisibility of the communicator or consultant is not unqualified. In the US presidency, for example, the Press Secretary is officiated as the speaker on behalf of the president – on and off the record. In this political tradition, the extended visibility of the attributed source, the Press Secretary, does not necessarily decrease the visibility of the accredited source, the President. The former rather protects the latter by taking over the risks of slip-ups and incorrect representations – inevitable in the business of running commentary. If after a gaff of the Press Secretary, he corrects himself or the President corrects him, this will hardly hurt the authority of the President. Such division of more visibility for the Press Secretary and less for the President makes sense only in political systems of strong administration, in which the head, the President, is directly elected. The President does not speak either when the event is not so important (tactical silence) or when his quietness is the right response (strategic silence). In the Westminster model of Parliamentary democracy, however, where the Prime Minister is (indirectly) elected by the Parliament, the Press Secretary cannot take away much from the already reduced clout of the Head of State.

Part of the ideal work of the PR practitioners is the production of others. This work is full with dilemmas. Should the communicator steer entirely from the limelight and defer visibility to those who are more accountable? What is his accountability? When should he speak on behalf of others and when on his behalf? When should he, as an accredited source, withdraw from public conversation and tacitly help – coach, script and publish – others, the accredited ones, to become better speakers? In other words, is it not the destiny of public relations to disappear for good when it finally succeeds?

Note

1 A recent study ranked the public relations executive as one of the most stressful jobs (Perman, 2014). He (still more often than *she*) is under the pressure of modern rather than postmodern expectations (Holtzhausen, 2014). His publicity role, for example, is to get positive media coverage about a company or product or to prevent the negative one. The expectations are that he succeeds in both. When he succeeds, it is the company's success, not his. Ideal work. No congratulations, that is what he is hired for. When he does not, it is his fault. No matter that the casual link between him and publicity is often as strong as between rainmaker and clouds. The 'public relations disaster' is a cliché, which reflects this unequal (and inadequate) distribution of expectations and credits. The jobs of PR practitioners and executives are the first to cut when the economy is in bad shape – for reasons usually unrelated to their performance.

References

Alonzo, M., & Aiken, M. (2004). Flaming in electronic communication. *Decision Support Systems, 36*(3), 205–213.

Dimitrov, R. (2014a). Bringing communication up to agency: UNESCO reforms its visibility. *Public Relations Inquiry, 3*(3), 293–318.

Dimitrov, R. (2014b). 'Does this guy ever shut up?' The discourse of the 2013 Australian Election. *Global Media Journal: Australian Edition, 8*(2).

Glenn, C., & Ratcliffe, K. (Eds.). (2011). *Silence and listening as rhetorical acts.* Carbondale, IL: Southern Illinois University.

Holiday, R. (2012). *Trust me, I'm lying: the tactics and confessions of a media manipulator.* London: Penguin.

Holtzhausen, D. R. (2014). *Public relations as activism: Postmodern approaches to theory and practice.* New York: Routledge.

Hopkins, K. (2014). The phatic nature of the online social sphere: Implications for public relations. *PRism, 11*(2).

Kanter, B. (2010). *The networked nonprofit: Connecting with social media to drive change.* San Francisco, CA: Jossey-Bass.

Leitch, S., & Motion, J. (2007). Retooling the corporate brand: A Foucauldian perspective on normalisation and differentiation. *Journal of Brand Management, 15*(1), 71–80.

Macnamara, J. (2016). *Organizational listening: The missing essential in public communication.* New York: Peter Lang.

Motion, J., & Leitch, S. (2007). A toolbox for public relations: The oeuvre of Michel Foucault. *Public Relations Review, 33*(3), 263–268.

Perman, C. (2014, 7 January). The most stressful jobs for 2014. *Yahoo Finance*. Retrieved 12 June 2017, from http://finance.yahoo.com/news/the-most-stressful-jobs-for-2014-163028892.html.

Tanner, L. (2011). *Sideshow: Dumbing down democracy*. Brunswick, Victoria: Scribe.

Zegarac, V. (1998). What is phatic communication? In V. Rouchota & A. H. Jucker (Eds.), *Current issues in relevance theory* (pp. 327–361). Amsterdam; Philadelphia: John Benjamins Publishing Company.

Part VII
Conclusions

Conclusions

I have to admit that, when I started writing this book, I thought I was just going to add another volume in the long shelves of the public relations library. I hoped that, in the best case, I would be able to shed some light on an obscure and, for reasons I discuss in the second part of the book, neglected topic in public relations theory. I felt encouraged from my interviews with PR practitioners and consultants. The professional communicators turned out to be aware of the significance of silence as strategy and tactic in their daily work. All practitioners agreed that it was easier to learn how to speak than how to remain silent – including while one keeps talking!

The interviewed communicators came up with their own ad-hoc theories, some fragments of which I found to be nuggets of gold. The gap between theoretical and practical knowledge about strategic silence did not bother me much, especially at the beginning. On the contrary. I thought the bigger the gap, the more interesting the exploration. I knew I was after something, and the rest would take care of itself.

Still, the gap bothered me. It was odd and not quite explicable. The language of the interviewed consultants was that of frolic practical wisdom. Everything one needed was there, but flattened and sealed in a professional, functional jargon. We talk of sociocultural and postmodern and other turns in PR theory, and how they have already become mainstream. I see nothing like that in PR practice. Professional communicators speak the vernacular of their organisational environment. It is still the decades-old modernist, input-output, managerial language. Period.

This poses problems of decoding. They grow even bigger when it comes to the concept of silence. There are disciplines in communication studies, which have advanced further than public relations in that aspect. They all have applied advanced, post-positivist approaches to silence, including feminist studies, functional linguistics, pragmatics, constructivism, discourse analysis and semiotics. So when I use them as keys as well, am I decoding the PR practitioners correctly? Am I thinking what they are thinking? Am I closing the gap or jumping around it?

But there is another dimension to that deficit. Although there have been dozens of approaches to silence in communication studies, very few focus specifically on *strategic* silence. I did not brood about that too much at first. Even better, I was glad the niche I have discovered was even more obscure. The gap was even deeper. I admit I was not fully aware of what I was in for.

But was it a gap? I use here a metaphor, which conveys a metaphysical notion of knowledge (as ballast). We fill with knowledge what we still do not know. But how about the historical construction of knowledge? Perhaps I write about strategic silence *now* because the time has just come. Perhaps the current trend of ever more complex and mediated communications is prompting PR theorists *now* to re-evaluate and elevate strategic silence as the power to influence and build relationships. Perhaps silence as strategy *and* skillset – as *communicative capacity* – has rather slowly and only recently transformed from a peripheral to a core issue of public relations strategy.

Professional communicators can hear silence and speak in silence better today. This is their response to the increasingly mediated, ever more indirectly inflected communications environment. This change in practice beckons change in theory. It is not about how to figure the gap – how to verify the knowledge of lack of knowledge. It is about how we help it show itself – how we articulate that gap. I later discovered that I was not filling a gap but rather trying to start a discussion in the PR and promotional communications field about things that did not feel like an empty space. I felt the book was becoming a question mark, not about missing bits of theory but about present assumptions taken for granted.

One does not 'add' or 'fill' knowledge. It turned out that, to 'accommodate' strategic silence, I had to problematise 'safe' concepts in public relations such as those of silent, indirect and strategic communication. In many respects, this was mission impossible. It is a daunting task, far beyond the endeavour of a book or an academic. I have written down a few generative rather than systematic ideas. They invite for re-thinking the hasty, defensive and moral dismissal of silence as inherently bad avoidance of communication that honest PR people do or should not use.

I would like to highlight three of the main conclusions. First, if public relations is choreography of public attention, strategic silence strikes a balance between *attracting* and *diverting* the attention. Today, everyone is a publisher and everyone is a public. Public relations theory has taken some time to move form a one-sided and asymmetric model of (active) organisations and (passive) publics to a two-sided and interactive (but still asymmetric if strategic) under-standing of relations between more or less organised agents. Theory has only caught up with practice.

In public relations research, for example, it is no longer enough to study audi-ences of interest so that we can come up with objectives and strategies that make them our target. Today it is more likely that those (and other) publics, including their influencers, are already researching and targeting us at the same moment. As in a game of cards, targeting is mutual. Laying one's cards on the table is the exception; keeping them close to one's chest is the rule. Our strategies are part of the research of our competitors. So their strategies must be part of our research. Researching their strategies should come before forming our strategy.

Should we talk or not? Should we engage or disengage? Should we hold ground or reposition? *Silence becomes essential when strategy meets strategy.*

Second, public relations increasingly employs silence as *noise reduction*. Sounds, signals and voices cancel one another in the cacophony of framing and message competition. They waste one another; they conjointly decompose into noise. Overflow of information becomes refuse. Today, the new media environment is saturated with noise. Unfortunately, news degrades quickly into noise, but noise degrades slowly as waste. It is difficult to get rid of it in general and curate it in particular. In that regard, silence as *communicative capacity* has become an even more precious and scarce resource.

As such, silence is the strategy and skillset to increase or reduce your noise and to choose communication environments with less foreign noise. In crowded policy networks, for example, actors clamour for the attention of decision-makers (Birkland, 2007). Is it a good strategy to fight the noise by raising the voice? Or would 'venue shopping' – changing the place (forum, channel, influencer) with a quieter one where more people would pay attention – be a better strategy (Baumgartner & Jones, 1993)? When to frame a discourse (conversation, debate) and when to stay away from it? How to influence the hierarchy of public tropes? How not to overreact to tangential issues? Which media are overrated? When PR is the media, and when it is not? How not to be distracted from serving the patron?

Silence as strategy and skills can be learned and taught. Only few decades ago, consultants coached CEOs and clients how to speak. Today, they teach them how to remain silent. Novices in the profession are judged against their ability to speak eloquently. Top communicators, however, are highly valued for their sweat equity and credibility to say 'No'.

Third, I believe strategic silence provides a strong argument for conceptualising public relations as the *art and science of indirect, strategic communication*. Strategic communication creates *public* relations. I put here the emphasis on 'public'. In Habermas' sense, relations that are public are inclusive, not exclusive. They are not private relations – not between friends, relatives or specialists, not within 'tribes'. They are not 'strong ties' in terms of online networking. Those relations are rather between strangers and laypeople, between diverse communities and publics. They are rather networks of networks, 'weak ties' in the same Internet terms. Thus, relations between publics, including their representatives, are predominantly *indirect* – so are the communications that build them (Krebs & Holley, 2006). In 2008, Obama's presidential campaign raised over half a billion dollars online, using the same indirect strategy of mobilising 'weak links' politically through the apolitical 'strong links' of friends, families and their primary influencers (Vargas, 2008).

Strategy is indirect; tactics are direct. Strategy keeps in mind; tactics are close to reason. When surprising strategy succeeds, tactics fail. Strategic communication is always indirect. Strategic silence extends indirectness toward its most radical forms. It that sense, 'more silent' is also 'more strategic'. Yet I would not substitute 'more indirect' with 'extreme' or 'peripheral'. Public relations as the practice of indirect communication takes place not at the fringes of the pluralist and democratic society. Far from this, it replicates its central mode of communication. The more complex, diverse and fragmented the society is the more indirect its communications become. In that sense, PR has become *mainstream* communication. That is why I believe *public relations is the most strategic of all communications professions* today. Neither marketing nor advertising, for once, can make use of many of its strategies, especially the highly indirect ones such as explicit and implicit silence. Both communications remain more direct, closer to PR tactics rather than strategies.

Working with strategic silence places on PR ethical and political demands. When what is said but not meant must be deconstructed? When what is meant but not said must be articulated? Each type of strategic silence may work either way – or both ways concurrently. Strategic ambiguity, for example, may be used either to silence those who have become vocal as unintelligible voices or to open up contents for the interpretation of those, who do not have the power to define a situation. And those opposite communications may target different publics and take place at the same time, semantically supporting each other in a bigger, main narrative.

What I am not doing, including in the example above, is that I am not pointing at good or bad, ethical or unethical silences. There is nothing good or bad in direct or indirect communication. There is nothing ethical or unethical in overt or covert communication. For example, I have analysed how silence can function both overtly and covertly in on-the-record and off-the-record communication. Attempts to classify communication along some inherent (metaphysical) qualities such as 'overt–covert' and 'ethical–unethical' – for example 'denying oxygen' as 'overt unethical' and planting 'soft questions' as 'covert unethical' (Hobbs, 2015) – are futile. One should not confuse theoretical with empirical knowledge and strategic silence with its applications.

Strategic silence is *transformative*. It is not innocent; it changes the world for good or bad. Its effects depend on the circumstances and context of the intervention. Who is silent to whom, how and for what? Whose relations are transforming in that fashion? The role of the PR practitioner as a strategist is heavily loaded with ethical and political questions. Communicators carry *responsibility* for the transformative and critical possibilities in the reality they help to transform (Medina, 2004). And here comes the significance of their critical self-consciousness as professionals and citizens. What is not said may be as important or more important than what is (Lentz, 1991). We have to constantly ask questions such as, 'What (that could be said) has not been said here'? (Neubauer & Shapiro, 1985) Our critical role is to deconstruct noise, where no silence is hearable. In other words, critical minds articulate silence making it audible, recognisable and relevant – subject of public inquiry and scrutiny. 'We create silence by creating relevance' (Bilmes, 1994, p. 82).

The lesson for PR theory is that one cannot analyse discourse using the functionalist paradigm of 'co-creation' and 'sharing of meaning'. As Neubauer and Shapiro argue, such an approach would only 'suppress a history of struggle'.

Conceiving discourse as a practice helps us to think a political question which can be posed to any discourse: why this practice rather than another, why these statements rather than others?.... As *practices* they have the effect of administering silences.

(Neubauer & Shapiro, 1985)

Public relations needs a critical theory that *reconstitutes* the silences that can be heard. If no one can hear them, they do not exist. In Bilmes and Hall's words, the PR academics and practitioners should be able to create relevance and articulate silences. That is they should have the capacity and skillsets to give the silences meaning, which is not directly available to the participants themselves (Bilmes, 1994, p. 85). Their role as PR activists will be both *critical* (to make people aware of the silent and invisible forces that affect them) and *emancipatory* (to help them reshape their experiences into practical tools).

The critique and articulation of the silences of others – and our own silences for that matter – is a powerful way of learning. But it is not the only transformative approach. 'Heroic' rhetoric and suspicious minds also have their limits. Critique should not neglect the practical, extra-linguistic and semiotic (multi-modal) dimensions of silence. It should also keep open the treasure trove of PR expertise, often locked in positivist language. Critical approaches in public relations often do not – and cannot – inform practice about the (counter-)use of strategic silence. In that regard, post-structuralist and postmodernist approaches offer a more positive (but not positivist), pluralist and flexible notion of silence. In this book, I have tried to combine those approaches of both epistemological critique and appreciation.

I do not see a dramatic difference between theory and practice of strategic silence in public relations. We can use the same research methodology to explore 'their' and 'our' silence. How do we know we hear silence? How do we recognise the unsaid as a possibility of saying? What are the technical, symbolic and human mediums of silence? How do we see its equivalents in extra-linguistic modes such as image, music and gesture? How does a research method preserve (or distort) the perception of silence or lack of such? What are the ethical and political implications of creating and responding to strategies of silence? How can we observe and capture silence without translating it into something, which it is not?

And lastly, how do we embed public relations in silence? When its strategic use conserves and when it transforms those relations? The study of *what* is said and not said is a vital one. It informs PR objectives. But equally important is the exploration of *how*. And it informs PR strategy. How is something present *and* (at the same time) absent? How is it silent *and* (at the same time) vocal? How is it unsaid *and* (at the same time) heard? How do people decide what makes sense and what does not? How do they know who the appropriate speaker is and who not? Who tells them and how?

What do we do about it?

References

Bamgartner, F., & Jones, B. (1993). *Agendas and instability in American politics.* Chicago: Chicago University Press.

Bilmes, J. (1994). Constituting silence: Life in the world of total meaning. *Semiotica, 98*(1–2), 73–88.

Birkland, T. A. (2007). Agenda setting in a public policy. In F. J. Fischer, A. Miller & M. S. Sidney (Eds.), *Handbook of public policy analysis* (pp. 63–78). Boca Raton: CRC Press.

Hobbs, M. (2015). The sociology of spin: An investigation into the uses, practices and consequences of political communication. *Journal of Sociology, 52*(2), 371–386.

Krebs, V., & Holley, J. (2006). Building smark communities through network wearing. *Appalachian Center for Economic Networks.* Retrived 26 July 2017, from www. acenetwroks.org.

Lentz, R. (1991). The search for strategic silence: Discovering what journalism leaves out. *American Journalism, 8*(1), 10–26.

Medina, J. (2004). The meanings of silence: Wittgensteinian contextualism and polyphony. *Inquiry, 47*(6), 562–579.

Neubauer, D., & Shapiro, M. (1985). *The new politics of mediation: Disclosing silences.* Paper presented to the XIIIth World Congress of the International Political Science Association, Paris, France.

Vargas, J. A. (2008, 20 November). Obama raised half a billion online. *Washington Post.* Retrieved 12 March 2016, from: http://voices.washingtonpost.com/the-trail/2008/11/20/obama_raised_half_a_billion.html.

Personal interviews

Grant Butler, Managing Director, *Editor Group*, 9 April, 2013.
Scott Crebbin, Public Relations Consultant, 24 February 2012.
Matthew Gain, General Manager, *Edelman*, Australia, 18 February 2015.
Lachlan Harris, co-founder of *One Big Switch*, former Press Secretary for the Australian Prime Minister, Kevin Rudd, 23 February 2015.
Peter Lazar, Founder and President, *Professional Public Relations Asia-Pacific*, Australia, 5 May 2015.
Richard Lazar, Managing Director and CEO, *Professional Public Relations Asia-Pacific*, Australia, 16 May 2013.
L.J. Loch, co-founder and Director of *Republic Consulting*, 4 December 2013.
Paul Matthews, Communication Strategy Manager, *Sydney Water*, 25 November 2011.
Jim Macnamara, Professor, *University of Technology*, Sydney, 14 February 2014.
Paul Perry, Public Affairs Consultant, former Director of Communication for the Australian Health Minister, Tanya Plibersek, 3 November 2014.
Eileen Pittaway, *UNSW Centre for Refugee Research*, 10 November 2007.
Ian Pope, Senior Corporate Communicator, *Edelman*, Australia, 18 February 2015.
Steve Riethoff, Managing Director, *Reservoir Network*, 30 April 2012.
Chris Savage, Chairman, *Ogilvy Public Relations*, Australia, 19 March 2012.
Michelle Schofield, Manager Corporate Communications, *Communities NSW*, 17 November 2011; 7 March 2012.
Caroline Turnour, Head of Corporate Affairs, *Avant*, Sydney, 4 November 2014.
James Wiggins, Head of Client Service and Strategy, *Blaze Advertising*, 16 September 2011.

Index

Page numbers in **bold** denote figures.